Canan Valley Wild Pido Rel .... 3 —

Dolly Sods Birds
      8/15 - 10/15
Red Creek camp ground
    parking area & street

Contact

Dear Readers:

Every effort was made to make this the most accurate, informative, and easy-to-use guidebook on the planet. Any comments, suggestions, and corrections regarding this guide are welcome and should be sent to:

> The Globe Pequot Press
> c/o Editorial Dept.
> P.O. Box 480
> Guilford, CT 06437
> editorial@globe-pequot.com
> www.falcon.com

We'd love to hear from you so we can make future editions and future guides even better.

Thanks and happy trails!

A FALCON GUIDE®

Hiking
WEST VIRGINIA

Steven Carroll and Mark Miller

FALCON®

GUILFORD, CONNECTICUT
HELENA, MONTANA

AN IMPRINT OF THE GLOBE PEQUOT PRESS

Falcon and FalconGuide are registered trademarks of The
Globe Pequot Press.

Photo credits: All photos by Steven Carroll and Mark Miller
unless otherwise noted.

Maps created by Tony Moore © The Globe Pequot Press

ISBN 0-7627-1173-6

Manufactured in the United States of America
First Edition/First Printing

Mark would like to dedicate this book to Cindy and to his children.
Steven would like to dedicate this guide to Gina.

Thank you for all of your support.

Hike Locator Map

EASTERN GATEWAY

11 12
13
14

To Winchester, VA

GEORGE WASHINGTON
AND JEFFERSON
NATIONAL FORESTS

50
69
70

Romney

POTOMAC
HIGHLANDS

21 22

19

To Harrisonburg, VA

59
60
67
66
33

MONONGAHELA
NATIONAL
FOREST

Kingwood
16
5
68
61
63 64
65
62

To Covington, VA

MOUNTAINEER
COUNTRY

6
7 8

Grafton
9

Elkins

23
24 25
26
27 28
57 58
56
17 18
15
37

38

To Pittsburgh, PA

79

NORTHERN
PANHANDLE

3

4
2
1

10

Weston

20

32

29

Richwood

64

MOUNTAIN
LAKES
REGION

53 54

31 30

Glenville

33

MID-OHIO
VALLEY

55

50

33 34

39 40

35
41

77

To Wytheville, VA

19

Charleston

36

Macarthur
42 43

48 49
47

NEW RIVER/
GREENBRIER
VALLEY

To Cambridge, OH

77

52

51

64

Huntington
44

METRO
VALLEY

45

To Lancaster, OH

To Jackson, OH

50

46

To Ashland, KY

N

Kilometers
100

Miles
100

0

Contents

Map Legend

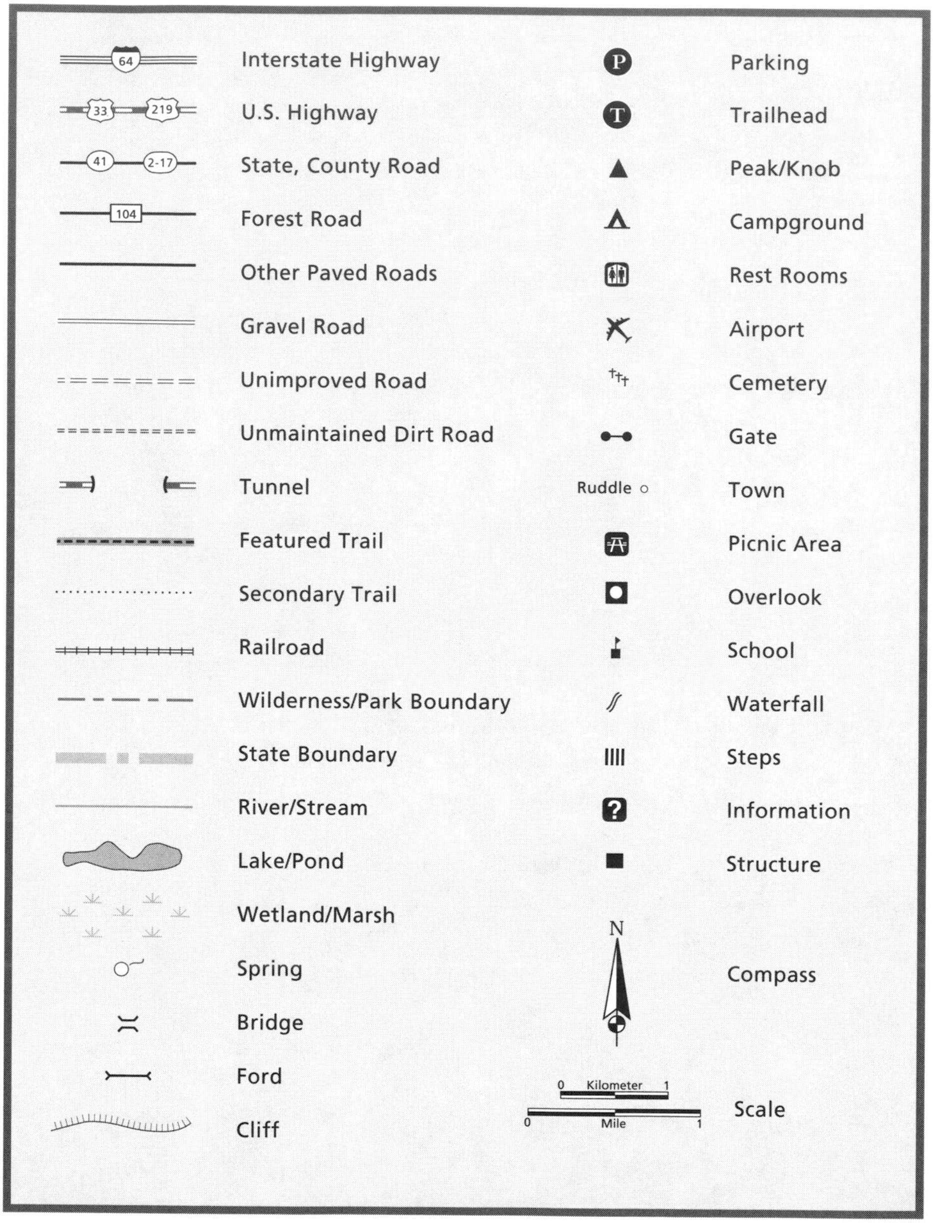

64	Interstate Highway	Ⓟ	Parking
33 219	U.S. Highway	Ⓣ	Trailhead
41 2-17	State, County Road	▲	Peak/Knob
104	Forest Road	Δ	Campground
─	Other Paved Roads	🚻	Rest Rooms
═	Gravel Road	✈	Airport
═ ═ ═	Unimproved Road	†††	Cemetery
- - - -	Unmaintained Dirt Road	•─•	Gate
⊐ ⊏	Tunnel	Ruddle ○	Town
▬ ▬ ▬	Featured Trail	⊼	Picnic Area
⋯⋯	Secondary Trail	◙	Overlook
┼┼┼┼	Railroad	⚑	School
— - — -	Wilderness/Park Boundary	∫	Waterfall
▬ ▪ ▬	State Boundary	‖‖	Steps
─	River/Stream	?	Information
⬬	Lake/Pond	■	Structure
⩛	Wetland/Marsh	N ↑	Compass
○~	Spring	0 Kilometer 1 0 Mile 1	Scale
≍	Bridge		
⊢⊣	Ford		
⌇⌇⌇	Cliff		

Acknowledgments

Firrst, we would like to thank Jeff Serena, Shelley Wolf, and the staff at The Globe Pequot Press for putting their time and effort into readying this guide for publication. We give our thanks to the various city and state park, State Forest, National Forest Service, and National Park Service personnel for their maintenance of West Virginia's trails, for their guidance, and for their expert review of trail descriptions. Also invaluable for his review of trail data was Roger Hardway. Thanks to Charlie Dundas, Chris Kyle, and Ron Wiley for their assistance on the Kanawha Trace Trail. We would also like to thank the Potomac Appalachian Trail Club for the hard work maintaining the AT and the Tuscarora Trail. And a final thanks to Madelyn Miller for first-line review for errors and corrections.

Introduction

This guide is an invitation to experience the natural beauty of West Virginia. Hiking West Virginia will lead you throughout the state from the misty mornings on the Appalachian Trail near Harper's Ferry to sunny afternoons on the banks of the Greenbriar River, from the town-hopping Americana experience that is the North Bend Rail Trail to a hike in secluded Dolly Sods Wilderness, from the deep New River Gorge to the state's highest peak of Spruce Knob. This book attempts to guide you through a proud state rich in natural wonder.

The rugged terrain is a source of state pride in West Virginia. The state nickname is the Mountain State. The state motto is Montani Semper Liberi, Mountaineers Are Always Free. The Division of Tourism sells the state as "Wild and Wonderful." Even the opening lines of the official state song, "The West Virginia Hills," show how the natural environment is revered in the great state of West Virginia: "Oh, the West Virginia hills! How majestic and how grand." Those hills are a part of life. The land has molded and has been incorporated into the culture of the state.

West Virginia has preserved much of its natural heritage through the State Parks system. The West Virginia Division of Natural Resources manages thirty-five state parks, nine state forests, and two trails. State parks preserve more than 80,000 acres in West Virginia. Parks offer various facilities, including fair-weather day-use-only parks, year-round lodge parks, picnic tables, fine-dining restaurants, golf courses, and horseback riding. There are nine state forests, eight of which are managed by the Division of Forestry. State forest lands conserve another 80,000 acres, which are used for wildlife management, industrial purposes, and recreational activities, such as hiking, biking, and horseback riding.

West Virginia natural areas are also conserved as Wildlife Management Areas (WMAs). There are forty-eight WMAs in the state, totaling a whopping 1.3 million acres! The land is managed by the state and by the federal National Forest Service. Land in WMAs is primarily managed for game habitat.

Probably the most well known of the natural areas in West Virginia are the national forests. The National Forest Service oversees the Monongahela National Forest and the George Washington National Forest, a portion of which lies in West Virginia. The Monongahela covers more than 900,000 acres in eastern West Virginia; the George Washington totals approximately 18,500 acres. The Monongahela contains five wilderness areas and one National Recreation Area, Spruce Knob–Seneca Rocks. With more than 500 miles of hiking trails to explore, this forest is a hiker's paradise.

The National Park Service is also in charge of land in West Virginia. The New River Gorge National River and associated lands cover more than 70,000 acres of roaring rapids, steep ridges, and sandstone cliffs. At 4,200 acres, the Bluestone National Scenic River is small in comparison. The pristine Bluestone Gorge, however, is perfectly situated between Bluestone and Pipestem State Parks. The lazy Bluestone Turnpike Trail connects the two parks as it travels the banks of the river. Both the Bluestone and the New River Gorge provide a multitude of outdoor activities. Water sports like white-water rafting, kayaking, canoeing, and fishing are by far the most popular. There are miles of hiking trails near steep cliffs, powerful white water, or babbling trout streams. The steep cliffs bring climbers to the premier climbing destination in the east, the New River Gorge.

Finally, the U.S. Fish and Wildlife Service manages two National Wildlife Refuges in West Virginia: Canaan Valley NWR and Ohio River Islands NWR. National Wildlife Refuges are created to protect the nation's native wildlife by preserving and, when necessary, restoring natural habitats. The Ohio River Islands NWR protects island habitat on 362 miles of the Ohio River. Canaan Valley NWR, which protects the southernmost range of traditionally northern species, is projected to comprise 24,000 acres as land acquisitions continue.

The outdoor resources in West Virginia are virtually boundless. Nearly 80 percent of the state's 15.5 million acres is covered by forests. The protected or managed lands mentioned above total nearly 2.5 million acres. This is approximately 16 percent of the total landmass of West Virginia. Trails cross the land, and hikers take to the hills. The proud state built on a rugged land has seen fit to preserve its natural heritage. But is it enough? Only the individual can decide that. Every day some of our "protected" lands are lost to the economic uses of mining and logging, and management of land is reevaluated. What is protected today may be gone tomorrow. If knowledge is power then experience is omnipotence. To know West Virginia's lands, it is necessary to experience them. Luckily, this is an enjoyable necessity. Appreciate the natural beauty of West Virginia by hiking the trails. With all the acres to explore, the choices seem endless. We hope that Hiking West Virginia can help narrow those choices and guide you to all corners of the Mountain State.

Geology

The West Virginia Geological and Economic Survey breaks the state into two basic geologic areas: The western two-thirds of the state is mostly flat and contains minable coal; the eastern one-third of the state is folded and contains no minable coal. This is a rather simplistic economic view, but quite correct nonetheless. Processes that occurred millions of years ago set the "groundwork" for the beautiful topography and mineral development that we observe today.

The economic value in the flat, minable two-thirds of West Virginia was created relatively early in state's geologic history. The vast resources of coal in West Virginia are the result of sedimentation and deposition. Approximately 500 million years ago, an inland sea covered much of the land that would become West Virginia. Sedimentation and marine deposition occurred, creating much of West Virginia's limestones. By 300 million years ago the sea had retreated and the area was covered by swampland. Approximately 50 million years of growth and decay of plant matter deposited shales and the rich organic coal seams. Sedimentation and deposition during this time produced a wealth of resources for the state. West Virginia has produced oil, gas, and high quality coal. Mines in the state extract limestone, sandstone, sand, gravel, salt, and iron.

The aesthetic value of West Virginia's beautiful landscape has been created and re-created throughout the state's geologic history. Shortly after the sediments were deposited, the process that lifted the eastern one-third of West Virginia began. Approximately 250 million years ago, the Appalachian Mountains were created as eastern West Virginia was folded and the high plateau was thrust upward. Today's landscape is a result of 250 million years of erosion. The New River and others cut gorges up to 1,000 feet deep into the high plain. Rains washed away softer rocks from the ridges, leaving the harder, more resistant sandstones, such as the "fin" of Seneca Rocks.

The everyday result of West Virginia's geologic history is a state rich in landscape and minerals. The "flat" western two-thirds of the state actually rolls in the extreme west and builds as it becomes deep gorges and tall eastern ridges. Hikers can enjoy various terrains in a single weekend, and often in a single day.

Zero Impact Outdoor Ethics

Zero Impact is a philosophy of outdoor use that has become the standard for responsibly enjoying the outdoors. The idea is to minimize human impact on the land and the natural flora and fauna. There are seven basic principles of zero and low impact camping. By following these guidelines as closely as you can, you will help others to also have an enjoyable outdoor experience.

Plan and prepare ahead of time. Planning ahead and being prepared keeps you safe and will help limit impact to the environment. Hikers go out every weekend knowing very little about the area, the terrain, or the trail they're hiking. Hikers leave the trailhead without a map and without ever hearing a local weather report. To prepare, read hiking guides, park trail guides, and Web sites. Call the area contact to get current local conditions and area regulations, and look at the contour lines on a map of the region.

Once you know about the area and conditions, you can plan your hike. Can you do that 20-mile loop or will 2,000 vertical feet in 2 miles slow you down a little? The dawn-to-dusk summer hike will take you until after dark in the winter. Knowing where you'll be at the end of the day will help you plan for a campsite and will keep you on the trail and away from bushwhacks. And remember, should something happen to you, mountain rescue involves a lot of manpower and a lot of time. Impact to the environment will take a back seat to saving human life. Make sure accidents are truly accidents and not a result of being unprepared.

Hike on trails, camp at campsites. The use of West Virginia's outdoor resources is increasing every year. Hiking on established trails and camping at established campsites concentrates impact to certain areas and minimizes impact to the whole. Trails generally travel to the most interesting landmarks, and most trails are dotted with campsites. When hiking a trail, do not cut switchbacks. This causes serious erosion problems, and saving a few steps out of several miles will not be noticeable.

Backcountry campsites are located throughout the wild lands, generally along streams, near vistas, and almost always near the trail. Camping in these previously used campsites benefits the hiker and the wilderness. These areas are usually the best spots around for camping: The ground is level, a stream is nearby, and there is room for a tent and a place to cook. Using established sites keeps impact from getting dispersed throughout the wilderness. If a site looks unused and is attempting to recover, don't camp in it. If you must camp in a new area, make sure the ecosystem is durable enough to recover. Pitch the tent on hard ground at least 200 feet away from streams. If camping in a meadow, move your tent every other day.

Use stoves whenever possible and limit use of fires. In today's low-impact camping world, the era of the campfire is nearly over. Campfire rings scar the land, are slow to decay, and are eyesores to other hikers. Camp stoves, on the other hand, pack up clean and leave no evidence of their use. They also burn with higher, more controllable temperatures. Campers generally build campfires for aesthetics and not for cooking. Admittedly, the campfire has its place in the hearts of camping romantics. The light from a campfire, though, has a tendency to create a tiny "room" of light, effectively shutting you off from anything that lies outside that room. Spending an evening at camp without a fire allows one's eyes to adjust to the darkness, allows the creatures of the night to become alive, and allows the camper to be part of the environment. Finally, and most obviously, fires can be dangerous to both humans and the wilderness. It takes years for a forest to recover from the damage of one forest fire. During dry times of the year, fires are often banned altogether. If a fire must be built, place it in an established campfire ring at an established campsite. Use only dead sticks on the ground for wood, and make sure there is a water source nearby for dousing the fire when you're done.

Dispose of wastes properly. Pack out everything you pack in. The goal is fairly simple: Leave nothing behind. Before leaving, inspect your campsite to make sure you've gathered everything you brought in, including all trash and leftover food. There are entire books written on the subject of proper disposal of human waste. The basic idea is to dig a hole far from any water source. No backpacker, hiker, or any type of outdoor enthusiast should be without a small shovel. After doing your "business," stir it up and cover it. If it's not buried 6 to 8 inches, it's not properly disposed of. Some minimum-impact campers subscribe to the idea of packing out human waste too. In some ecosystems, decay occurs at an extremely slow rate, making this philosophy appropriate. Although packing out human waste is a lower-impact way of camping, in most cases burying waste is acceptable.

Leave the area undisturbed. Part of the definition of *wilderness* contained in the Wilderness Act describes an area where "man himself is a visitor who does not remain." Think of yourself as a visitor to the outdoors. Leave the stones unturned and the flowers on the stems. Their beauty lies within the brief moment you experience them on the trail. Your goal is to slip in and out without the environment ever noticing.

Respect wildlife. This means to respect that they are wild and to respect their right to be wild. Do not feed the wildlife; it alters the animals' behavior and often makes them dependent on man's presence. Make sure all leftover food at your campsite is packed out. Do not approach wild animals; view them from a distance.

Respect other visitors. By respecting other visitors' rights to have an enjoyable outdoor experience we ensure the same for ourselves. Be courteous and treat others as you would like to be treated. Camp away from where others are camped. Keep noises and voices low. Yield to others on trails, especially to horses or other pack animals.

By keeping these seven principles in mind when you head out on a trip, you greatly increase the quality of your outdoor experience while minimizing the effect you have on the environment. These ethics are not a high mark to strive for, but rather a minimum of care that must be adhered to. With the use of outdoor resources ever increasing, it is everyone's responsibility to care for West Virginia's natural beauty.

Preparedness and Safety

Hiking is a sport, and it requires the athlete participating to be responsible for his or her own preparedness and safety. There are no hikers' licenses and no hikers' safety courses you must pass. Safety is directly related to preparedness; the two go hand in hand. A hiker who is prepared will avoid many of the problems an unprepared hiker will face. Unprepared and unsafe hikers put themselves and others at risk. To prepare for the sport of hiking, one must have the right equipment, one must practice, and one must have a knowledge of the sport.

As with any sport, you first need the right equipment. Too often hikers go into the woods without proper boots or clothing, or without enough food or water. A "short list" of essentials for all hikes includes:

- food and water
- a map and compass
- a first-aid kit, including insect repellent and sunscreen
- rain gear
- matches (preferably waterproof)
- a flashlight with fully charged batteries
- a knife
- a whistle

Second, a hiker must practice. Hiking is a physical activity. We have all heard of the desk jockey turned weekend warrior who hobbles into work Monday morning after being hurt in Saturday's softball game. Practice for hiking by exercising regularly and staying in good shape. Stay fit during the week by doing other aerobic activities like walking, running, biking, swimming, or weight lifting.

Third, knowledge of the sport is required. The participant must know the rules and the risks. Prepare for the hike by reading up on the rules and regulations that pertain to the area you will visit. Know what risks are involved, such as extreme weather conditions, dangerous cliff areas, or poisonous plants or animals. The following sections list outdoor issues particular to West Virginia. Please remember that this list is not all-inclusive. Hiking is a sport, but the playing field is constantly changing.

Weather. There is one uncompromising truth: If we're going to be outside we're going to be in the weather. Weather is part of the joy of the outdoors, part of the experience. Weather in West Virginia ranges from hot in the summer to frigidly cold in the winter. Sunny days can change to downpours in minutes. Knowing what weather to expect on a hike is a first step. Being prepared for changes in weather and knowing how to react to weather emergencies will keep a hiker safe and confident.

Hot and humid summer weather can be dangerous if the hiker is not aware of the risks of dehydration, which occurs when water intake does not keep pace with fluids expired as the body tries to cool itself. While hiking, body temperature rises and fluid is lost as perspiration. The evaporation of perspiration cools the body. If more fluids are lost than are ingested, the result is dehydration. The simple solution to this problem is to drink plenty of water. Drink before the hike and drink while on the trail. Strenuous exercise often requires a liter or more of water per hour. With this type of intake, you will probably need several "refueling" stations. Before beginning a hike, determine where water will be available on the trail. Pack water according to the availability of filterable water sources on the trail. For example, a creek hike provides ample water; you may have to carry just a one-liter bottle. A ridgeline hike, however, may travel for 10 miles before reaching a water source, thus requiring you to carry a bladder pack of 100 ounces or more.

Heat exhaustion and heatstroke are potentially life-threatening situations and are serious hazards of hiking in warm weather. Both ailments result when the body is not cooled properly. Heat exhaustion occurs first; if not treated, it can develop into the serious and sometimes fatal heatstroke. If extensive hiking is planned during warm weather, consult a first-aid guide on the symptoms and treatment of heat exhaustion and heatstroke.

Cold weather brings its own risks and dangers. Two cold-weather emergencies to be concerned about are hypothermia and frostbite. Hypothermia results when the body temperature drops below the normal temperature. If hypothermia is not treated it can lead to death. As hypothermia worsens, it can cause disorientation and cause the hiker to make poor decisions, thus compounding an already bad situation.

Frostbite occurs when skin is exposed to cold, causing ice crystals to form in the body. Extremities such as fingers, toes, hands, and feet are at the greatest risk for frostbite. If hiking when the possibility of cold weather exists, consult a first-aid guide for the symptoms and treatment of frostbite and hypothermia.

Although not a guarantee of safety, both hypothermia and frostbite can be avoided by wearing proper clothing. This does not necessarily mean wearing more clothing. It is important to dress in layers that will keep you warm and wick away sweat and moisture. Clothing that becomes wet with sweat will rob the body of heat. As the hike becomes strenuous, remove layers to avoid becoming too hot. Add layers while resting to avoid becoming chilled. Always pack extra clothing for the worst-case scenario. Consider what you would need to be wearing to survive the night outside.

Wind chill and wet weather can play a big role in both frostbite and hypothermia. Blowing wind and rain rob the body of heat. Frostbite and hypothermia can occur quickly when the wind or wetness is a factor. It is good idea to carry windproof and waterproof clothing while hiking, especially in areas with exposed ridges.

Storms are another weather risk of which to be aware. Especially in the higher elevations, storms can develop suddenly and become severe. During a thunderstorm, temperatures can drop 20 degrees and wind speed can increase by 20 miles per hour in less than an hour. Severe thunderstorms can bring with them driving rain, lightning, and hail. Any one of these conditions could be life threatening. If severe weather presents itself, find shelter from the storm. Move off of exposed ridges and rock outcrops. Travel to the base of rocks and look for overhangs to provide shelter. Do not take shelter under trees, especially on ridge tops. Be aware that heavy rains can cause flash flooding in narrow gorges.

On bright days, sunburn can be a problem in both summer and winter. Sunburn can be painful and can also significantly increase one's risk of developing skin cancer. The risk of sunburn exists even on partly sunny days. While hiking, wear a hat to protect the face, and a shirt to protect the back and arms. Shirts are not completely effective at blocking the sun's rays, especially when wet. Sunblock lotions above SPF 15 are also effective in preventing sunburn.

Plants. Several potentially harmful plants are found in West Virginia. Learning to identify such plants is the most effective way to avoid them. The most common of these is poison ivy, a climbing plant found along many trails. It grows best in sunny, open areas such as old clearings and trails. This plant has compound leaves of three leaflets. When touched, the plant leaves a residue that causes a skin rash, characterized by itchy redness and blistering. Treatment usually involves applying lotions to the affected areas to keep them dry and reduce the sensation of itching. In severe cases a doctor may need to be consulted. The best way to avoid the plant is to know what it looks like.

Stinging nettle is another type of plant that can be an annoyance while hiking. This plant stands about 24 inches high, with toothed leaves that grow in pairs opposite each other on the stem. The leaves have bristles that contain a watery juice. The juice can produce an intense but short-term itch. The best way to avoid problems with nettles is to wear long pants or gaiters while hiking.

There are many other plants in West Virginia that may cause allergic or toxic reactions. These include poison sumac and various species of mushrooms. Consult a field guide to educate yourself on their characteristics. Knowing the local flora is a pleasant way to enjoy the outdoors and the best way to keep safe.

Animals. It is important to remember the forest is the home of many animals and that we are visitors. Although most animals in the forest are small, even the smallest animal will defend itself when threatened. The best way to avoid unwanted problems with animals is to leave them alone. The rule of thumb is simple: Enjoy wildlife from a distance.

Animals like food and spend most of their time acquiring it. Over the years, many animals have learned that hikers represent a supply of food. To avoid problems with animals while on an overnight trip, place a rope over a high limb and suspend your food pack above the ground. By placing the pack in the air, animals will be unable to reach it and therefore not eat the food or destroy the pack. The mental image of a bear clawing through a tent wall to get to a pack should be enough to convince you to hang your food bag.

There are two types of poisonous snakes in West Virginia: rattlesnakes and copperheads. Both snakes will bite when threatened. Know what the snakes look like and where they are most likely to live. Both snakes prefer wooded hillsides, rock outcrops, and streams, ponds, and flooded areas (that is, everywhere a trail might go in West Virginia). If a copperhead or rattlesnake is encountered, stay away from it. If bitten by a snake, stay calm and seek medical help quickly. While hiking solo, it is advisable to carry a snakebite kit. Having a first-aid guide and knowing the procedure for dealing with snakebites is a must.

Insects can be a problem in the forest. The most notorious insect is the mosquito. In wet areas, these insects thrive and can make life miserable. When bitten by a mosquito, the area will swell slightly and itch. Try not to scratch the affected area. To avoid bug bites, wear extra layers of light clothing. Several brands of insect repellent are available. Ticks are also a concern. Inspect your skin for them periodically. If you find one, remove it with tweezers, taking care to pinch the head and not the body. Follow accepted first-aid procedures to minimize the risk of disease caused by a tick bite.

Heights. West Virginia is known for its sandstone cliffs. The eroded ridge tops are often lined with ever repeating outcrops. Care should be taken to avoid injury in rocky environments. Be aware of high cliff areas and be especially vigilant with children and pets. Night hiking in cliff areas can be extremely dangerous.

Self-protection. This is a broad category and yet a very important one. There are many general precautions to take that will make a hike safer and more enjoyable. Let someone know where you will be hiking and when you expect to return. Know your travel route, its length, and the level of difficulty. Assess your ability to hike the trail.

Always carry a map and a compass. Before entering the wilderness, learn methods of outdoor orienteering. If you become lost, you will have the skills necessary to find your way out of the woods and back to your vehicle.

Clothing is another important consideration. Good boots are essential, protecting against turned ankles, wet feet, and a host of other minor problems that can make a hike miserable. As good as boots are, they are only as good as the socks worn inside them. Wool socks are good for hiking because they stay warm even when wet. There are also excellent brands of synthetic socks. Summer and winter versions of socks suit various thermal needs. A hat is important too. A hat protects the head and face from sunburn, keeps the head dry when it's raining, and prevents blowing winds from cooling the body. A lightweight windbreaker should be carried in case of severe wind; a waterproof one can double for protection against the rain. During the cooler months, hikers need to take extra precautions. Carry extra clothing, even on mild days. Many a day that began as clear morning has ended with a snowstorm. Dress in layers so that you can regulate your temperature by adding or removing a layer. Perspiration that soaks clothing will chill a hiker when he stops to rest. Gloves and a hat protect the extremities.

The woods in West Virginia are open to hunting most of the year. Because the timing of hunting seasons varies from year to year, it is necessary to obtain a schedule from the Division of Natural Resources (304–558–2771; www.dnr.state.wv.us) and plan a hike accordingly. Deer and turkey seasons are probably the most dangerous, but be aware of any type of hunting activity. It is best to stay out of the woods during the general firearms season. If planning to hike during hunting season, wear blaze orange and bypass bushwhacks if possible. Blaze orange may not be much of a fashion statement, but it will reduce the chance of being involved in a hunting accident.

West Virginia's State Parks and State Forests are very popular among hunters. If you plan overnight trips to a park or forest during hunting seasons, advanced reservations are recommended. Many parks and forests cater to the needs of hunters and adjust their schedules of operation accordingly. For example, many camping areas are open until the end of the deer rifle season, which typically ends on the first Saturday in December. If there are any questions regarding the availability of park or forest facilities during hunting seasons, please call the management offices for the area in question. (See Appendix B at the end of this book.) Remember, planning for your trip will ensure that it is both safe and enjoyable.

How to Use This Book

This guide is meant to provide accurate and concise information on some of the best hiking in West Virginia. Our goal is to answer the question, "Where should I go hiking this weekend?" The Hike Locator Map plots hiking destinations in relation to geographic regions and major roads.

The guide groups hikes into the following ten geographic regions: Northern Panhandle, Mountaineer Country, Eastern Gateway, Potomac Highlands, Mountain Lakes Region, New River/Greenbrier Valley, Metro Valley, Mid-Ohio Valley, Monongahela National Forest, and George Washington and Jefferson National Forests. Hikes within a region are similar in ecology, habitat, flora, fauna, and geology.

Use the map to decide on a hike in the part of the state you would like to visit, then read the appropriate hike descriptions to begin more detailed planning of your trip.

Each hike description contains the following information:

Overview. This section contains information for each area the hike is contained in (e.g. a particular state park or wilderness area). The information may include history, highlights of the area, flora and fauna, and basic trail information.

General description. This section provides a very brief description of the hike.

General location. The distance in miles to a nearby city or town is listed here.

Length. The distance in miles that the hike travels is listed here.

Difficulty. A subjective opinion made by the authors of the difficulty of the hike. Hikes are classified as easy, moderate, or difficult.

Special attractions. Interesting aspects of the hike are described in this section.

Maps. This section provides a listing of maps particular to the hike. Maps listed will include park maps and USGS 1:24,000 quad maps. (A detailed map is provided for each hike, showing trailheads, parking, trails, peaks, and other landmarks. These maps are not, however, meant for orienteering or compass work.)

Camping. Information regarding campgrounds and camping rules are provided in this section.

Season. This section tells when the trail is open to the public.

For information. The address and phone number for acquiring up-to-date local information is included here.

Elevation profile. A small graphic depicts the hike in cross-section to give a general idea of the ruggedness of terrain. Be careful to examine altitude changes versus the distance of the hike. Hikes with an elevation change of less than 200 feet do not have an accompanying elevation.

Finding the trailhead. Directions to the trailhead are provided. Often, two or more sets of directions are listed to get you to different trailheads or to guide you from different starting points. This information should be used in conjunction with the maps in this guide, USGS maps, and state road maps. Abbreviations used in this section include:

- I – interstate
- US – US highway
- WV – West Virginia state route
- CR – county route
- VA – Virginia state route

The hike. Generally, the hike described is the most interesting or most scenic hike in the park or area. Alternate routes or suggestions for other nearby hikes may also be included here.

Northern PANHANDLE

The geographically obvious Northern Panhandle lies in the extreme north portion of West Virginia. Tucked in against the Ohio River, the Northern Panhandle occupies a narrow sliver of land between Pennsylvania and Ohio. Barely 5 miles wide in some places, this region is characterized by lazy rivers, rolling hills, and shallow stream-cut valleys.

Hiking in the Northern Panhandle is more of a pleasurable jaunt than an expedition. Trails here tend to be well manicured and easy to follow. Because there are no national forests in the area, hikes travel state parks, municipal parks, and even city streets. After the hiking is done, parks provide other curiosities, such as museums, zoos, and golf courses. Overnight stays are equally indulging. Camping can be found in campgrounds rather than backcountry campsites; because the car will carry the load, you have the luxury of taking anything and everything you might desire.

If campgrounds aren't suitable, many fine hotels can be found in Wheeling, the picturesque metro center of the Northern Panhandle and a city steeped in history. In 1862 the city's Independence Hall witnessed the birth of the state when West Virginia split from Virginia. The city's Victorian heritage is evident in the beautiful architecture throughout the town. River culture abounds along the Ohio River, where towns made their living on the currents of the water.

Overlook Trail
Grand Vue Park

Overview: *Grand Vue Park has something for everyone. This small municipal park sits high on a bluff overlooking the Ohio River. In addition to hiking and mountain biking, the park offers cross-country skiing, golf, a par three golf course, and tennis.*

General description: This short trail wraps around a high bluff along the Ohio River. The trail passes through mature stands of hardwoods and green grassy meadows.
General location: Moundsville
Length: 2.4 miles
Difficulty: Easy
Special attractions: The Overlook Trail traverses the high bluff overlooking the Ohio River, offering several glimpses of the river and the state of Ohio.

Maps: Grand Vue Park map; USGS quad: Moundsville
Camping: Tent camping is not available, but the park does rent cabins.
Seasons: The hiking trail is open year-round.
For information: Marshall County Parks and Recreation, Road #4 Box 16A, Moundsville, WV 26041; (304) 845–9810

Finding the trailhead: At the intersection of US 2 and US 250 in Moundsville, turn south on US 250. Proceed 0.8 mile to a stoplight and turn left on First Street. Continue 0.2 mile and turn left on Forstoria. Continue 0.8 mile and take the right fork at the Y. This is Ivy Avenue. Proceed 1.2 miles, turn left into a parking area, and park in front of the red barn. The trailhead is located behind the barn.

The hike: Walk down the hill to the meadow located behind the red barn. The trail begins on a grassy road that enters the woods. Just below the ridge crest, the road bends left and then right. In the right bend, about 0.3 mile from the trailhead, the Overlook Trail exits the road to the left and enters the woods. Watch closely for the turn, as it is easy to miss.

After entering the woods, the trail begins a short descent down a finger ridge. About 50 yards from the road, the trail makes a right turn and begins contouring just below the ridge crest again. The trail passes through a forest of small hardwoods. The footpath is easy to follow but is marked sparingly with red arrows. At the steep escarpment, the trail bends left and continues to contour just below the ridge.

Approximately 0.75 mile from the trailhead, there is a trail fork. For a shorter hike, take the left fork, climb back to the road, and walk back to the

Overlook Trail

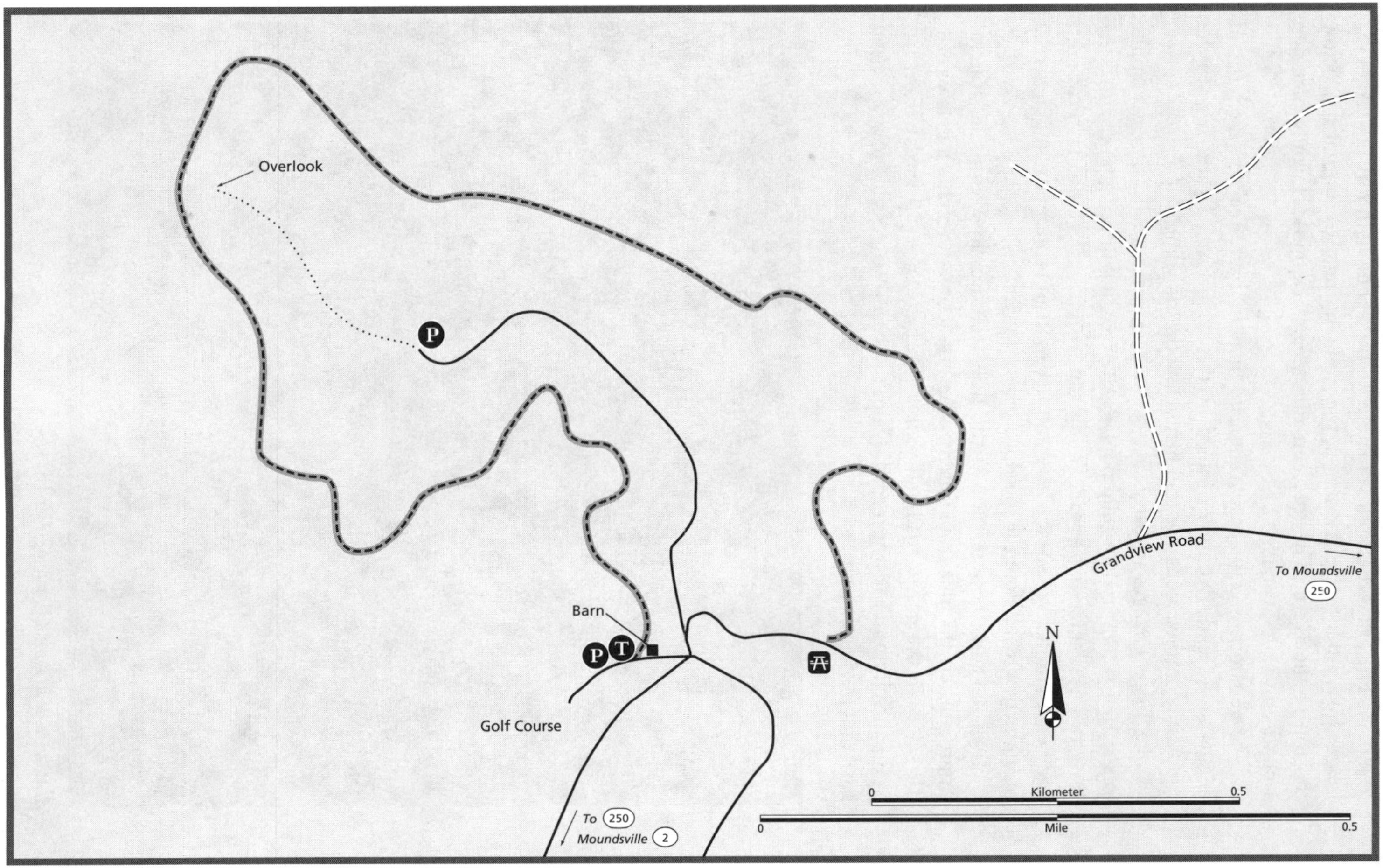

Grandview Road

To Moundsville 250

N

Overlook

P

Barn

Golf Course

P T

To 250
Moundsville 2

Kilometer
Mile

0   0.5

0   0.5

red barn. The distance is approximately 1.0 mile. The right fork continues the longer hike. After the trail junction, the trail continues to contour just below the top of the ridge. The forest in this area is composed mainly of older, second-growth hardwoods.

The next fork is confusing. It appears that the trail breaks to the left and begins to descend. Do not be fooled by this well-traveled path. Bear to the right and continue along the trail just below the ridgeline.

The forest changes to early-succession hardwoods such as thorny apple, locust, and young straight tulip poplar. After passing under a power line, the Overlook Trail intersects a road. Follow this road to a trail crossing, turn right, and begin a moderate ascent. Cross another road and continue climbing to the trail junction just before the meadow.

Turn right on the footpath. At the next trail crossing, continue straight. Approximately 0.2 mile from this crossing, the footpath reaches a grassy road. Turn left on the grassy road and walk a short distance (50 yards). Turn left again and climb to the paved road. From the road it is possible to see the red barn and the parking lot.

Early summer on Overlook Trail.

2

A. B. Brooks Discovery Trail
System / *Oglebay Resort*

Overview: *Oglebay Park is a 1,650-acre resort near Wheeling. The park has a mansion museum, an environmental learning center, and a zoo.*

General description: The A. B. Brooks Discovery Trail System is 3.5 miles of self-guided trails that wind through butterfly gardens and rich deciduous forests.
General location: Wheeling
Length: 3.5 miles
Difficulty: Easy
Special attractions: Both trail spurs lead to a small picturesque waterfall.

Maps: Oglebay Resort map; USGS quad: Wheeling
Camping: Camping is not available. The lodge and cabins offer guests an overnight stay.
Seasons: The park is open for hiking year-round.
For information: Oglebay, Wheeling, WV 26003; (800) 624–6988

Finding the trailhead: Take I–70 to exit 2A and turn north on WV 88. Travel 0.7 mile and turn left at the light to remain on WV 88. Continue 3.1 miles to the big, yellow brick buildings on the right; turn right at the sign for the Schrader Environmental Education Center. Proceed 0.7 mile and turn left at the Environmental Nature Center sign. The parking area is on the left. The A.B. Brooks Discovery Trail System begins at the stairway.

The hike: From the parking area, walk down the steps and turn left on the Habitat Discovery Trail, a short (0.3 mile) self-guided nature trail. After a short distance, the trail bends right and descends to the intersection with the Hardwood Ridge Trail.

The Hardwood Ridge Trail is marked with green blazes and exits to the left. Approximately 2.5 miles long, this out-and-back trail is wide and easy to follow. The path begins with a short, easy climb to the junction with the Falls Vista Trail, which exits to the left and descends. Bear right to remain on the Hardwood Ridge Trail. About 0.2 mile past the junction, there is an overlook in a stand of hemlock on the left. Just beyond the overlook, there is a small amphitheater on the right.

As the trail bends right, wooden steps on the left lead to another overlook. The Hardwood Ridge Trail continues around the bend to another trail junction, marked by wooden steps on the left. Continue straight along the wide path. A sign marks the halfway point.

A. B. Brooks Discovery Trail System

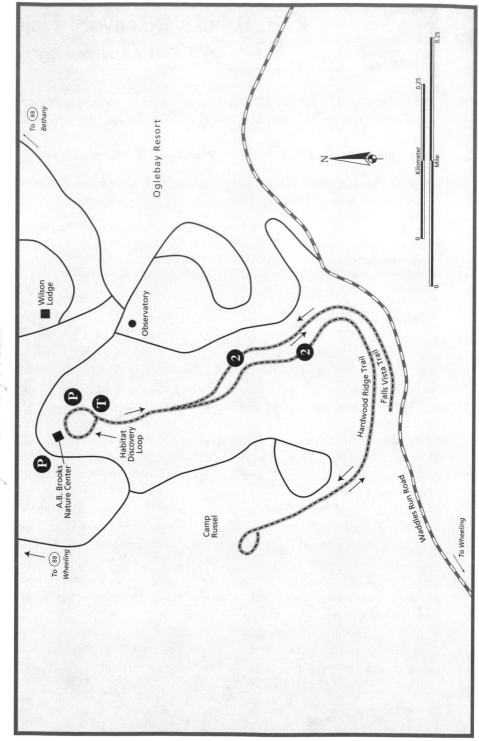

After the trail enters a narrow creek drainage, an arrow points downhill. Turn left at the arrow and descend to a wooden overlook in a small hemlock grove. There is a view of a small waterfall from the platform. Climb the stairs up the hill back to the path. Turn right on the path and return to the junction of the Falls Vista Trail.

The Falls Vista Trail, marked with blue blazes, descends to the left off the Hardwood Ridge Trail. A small creek is on the left. Wooden steps lead through a lush, green, narrow, steep-walled ravine. Small shelf waterfalls can be seen from the steps.

Where the stairs end, the Falls Vista Trail becomes a narrow path. When the weather is wet, sections of the trail can be muddy. Just before the road, a raised wooden platform provides a view of a 5-foot waterfall. Turn around and retrace your route to the junction of the Hardwood Ridge Trail. Turn right to return to your starting point.

The reward for hiking the Falls Vista Trail.

3 Laurel to White Oak Trail Loop
Tomlinson Run State Park

Overview: *Tomlinson Run State Park is a 1,398-acre park located in the extreme northern portion of the West Virginia panhandle. The park is named for the slow-moving creek that runs almost the entire length of the park. In addition to the trails described here, the park offers another 5.5 miles of trails, as well as swimming, picnicking, and paddleboat rentals.*

General description: All the trails of Tomlinson Run State Park are marked by easy climbs through hills covered with tall, second-growth hardwood.

General location: 10 miles north of Weirton

Length: 7.5 miles

Difficulty: Moderate

Special attractions: The Laurel Trail travels through an undeveloped section of the park, skirting the edge of a bluff that overlooks the Tomlinson Run. The White Oak Trail drops down to the Tomlinson Run and parallels this picturesque creek.

Maps: Tomlinson Run State Park trail map; USGS quad: East Liverpool South

Camping: The park has a fifty-four-site campground that is open from mid-April to October. Fees are $13 and $17.

Seasons: The park is open year-round for hiking.

For information: : Tomlinson Run State Park, P. O. Box 97, New Manchester, WV 26056; (304) 564–3651

Finding the trailhead: At the intersection of US 2 and WV 8, head north on WV 8. Take an immediate left and proceed 4.1 miles to the park entrance. Turn left into the park and continue 1.6 miles to a small parking area on the left. This is the trailhead for the Beech Trail. To reach the trailhead for the Laurel Trail, continue another 2.3 miles to a T intersection. Turn right and proceed 0.1 mile to a small parking area on the right. The signed trailhead is on the left side of the road.

The hike: The Laurel Trail, marked with blue blazes, begins with an easy climb through a stand of second-growth hardwoods. Near the top of the rise, the trail begins to meander along the edge of a steep bluff that overlooks Tomlinson Run. The Laurel Trail parallels the bluff and descends gradually to an old road approximately 0.2 mile from the trailhead.

This old road is the beginning of the loop trail. There is a large flat rock at the junction. *Remember the rock*, because it is easy to miss this junction at the end of the loop. Turn right on the old road. The trail climbs briefly, providing scenic views while hugging the bluff overlooking the river. At the intersection near the 1.0 mile mark, the Laurel Trail bends left; turn right on the White Oak Trail.

The White Oak Trail follows an old road and is marked with white blazes.

8

Laurel to White Oak Trail Loop

Late fall colors paint the White Oak Trail.

The trail descends gradually to Tomlinson Run, with large beech and maple trees lining the trail. Rock walls that were built years ago shore up the left side of this old road. About 0.6 mile from the junction with the Laurel Trail, the White Oak Trail reaches Tomlinson Run.

At the creek, the trail begins to hug the left bank. Large flat rocks occupy the bed of the shallow, slow moving creek. Towering hemlock and cove hardwoods dominate the canopy. Small cliffs line the side of the creek. At a creek junction, the trail bends right and begins following another small creek upstream. Not far from this creek junction, the White Oak Trail ends abruptly at a small bridge abutment. A sign painted on a tree states THE END OF THE TRAIL. Turn around and follow the White Oak Trail back to the Laurel Trail.

Turn right on the Laurel Trail, which makes a moderate descent to the Tomlinson Run. The rock face of the bluff is on the right. Near the creek there is an old bridge abutment with a wonderful view upstream. After this abutment, the trail becomes a rugged path, passing through a narrow, steep-walled canyon. Rhododendron thickets crowd the trail, which hugs the left side of the canyon wall for approximately 0.3 mile. There is a small waterfall cascading off the canyon wall on the opposite bank.

Shortly after passing through this rough section, the trail again follows an old road and the hike becomes much easier. There is some trail confusion in this area. At a fork in the trail, one trail exits to the left and begins to climb. Take the trail that exits right and continues to parallel the creek. Just before reaching the creek, there is a left switchback and an easy climb. Be on the lookout for the flat rock that marks the end of the loop, approximately 0.1 mile from the switchback. Turn right and backtrack to the parking area.

Beech Trail Option: The Beech Trail, marked with yellow blazes, begins with a short, steep descent to the Tomlinson Run. The trail is wide, gravelly, and easy to follow. About 0.1 mile from the trailhead, the Beech Trail crosses the run, passes through a small stand of hemlock, then bends right and begins an easy climb to CR 3 (Washington Road). The trail follows an old road during the climb. The distance from the trailhead to the road is approximately 1.1 miles. The Beech Trail ends.

Just before reaching CR 3, there is a left switchback. To return to the parking area, turn left and continue the easy climb. About 0.1 mile from the switchback, the old road passes three small brick buildings. Just beyond the buildings, a small trail exits the road to the left. Watch carefully for this little path. There are no blazes marking this junction.

The path descends at a moderate rate for about 0.25 mile through a stand of second-growth hardwood. The trail terminates at the park road; turn left and walk 0.3 mile back to the parking area.

4 Ohio River Trail

Wheeling Heritage Trails

Overview: *The Wheeling Heritage Trails consist of two sections: the north-south section, which runs along the Ohio River, and the east-west section, which leaves the north-south section in the downtown area and heads east into the neighborhood of Elm Grove. The north-south trail is complete, and fully open for public use. The east-west section is 75 percent complete, and the completed sections are open to the public. The portion of the trail from Rock Creek Road to Washington Avenue should be finished by Fall 2003; the last mile of trail has no scheduled date for completion.*

General description: A flat, paved trail along the Ohio River.

General location: Wheeling

Length: 8.5 miles

Difficulty: Easy

Special attractions: This trail passes through an urban area with the Ohio River as a backdrop.

Maps: Wheeling Heritage Trail map; USGS quads: Wheeling, Tiltonsville

Camping: The Heritage Trails are day-use only.

Seasons: The trails are open to the public year-round from dawn to dusk.

For information: Heritage Trail Partners, Department of Development, 1500 Chapline Street, Room 305, Wheeling, WV 26003; (304) 234–3701

Finding the trailhead: To reach trailheads for the Ohio River Trail, take I–70 to exit 1A. Turn right (north) onto WV 2. Drive 3.4 miles to Ninth Street, turn left, and continue 2 blocks to the parking area. The Pike Island Lock parking area is 2.7 miles farther north and is on the left.

To reach the southern trailhead, turn left (south) on WV 2 and proceed 3.2 miles to the parking area on 48th Street.

The East-West Trail trailhead is at the Wheeling Civic Center on 14th Street.

The hike: This description begins at the Pike Island Lock and milepost 8.5. The locks are on the right and WV 2 is on the left. The grade is easy along the paved trail. At milepost 8.0 the road is left behind as the trail enters a warehouse section. Small row houses line the left side of the trail near milepost 7.5 in the town of Warwood. Near the 7.0-mile mark, cross a small stream and enter another industrial zone. There is a small park on the left down by the river.

Just past milepost 6.5 is the Ninth Street parking lot. The Warwood Lions Club has placed several benches along the trail. Near the 5.5-mile mark, there is a good view of the river and the hills of Ohio. Pass the Centre Foundry and Machine Company on the left, and make a short climb back to WV 2. Parallel the highway for about 0.75 mile, exercising caution along this stretch, as there are several industrial entrances.

Ohio River Trail

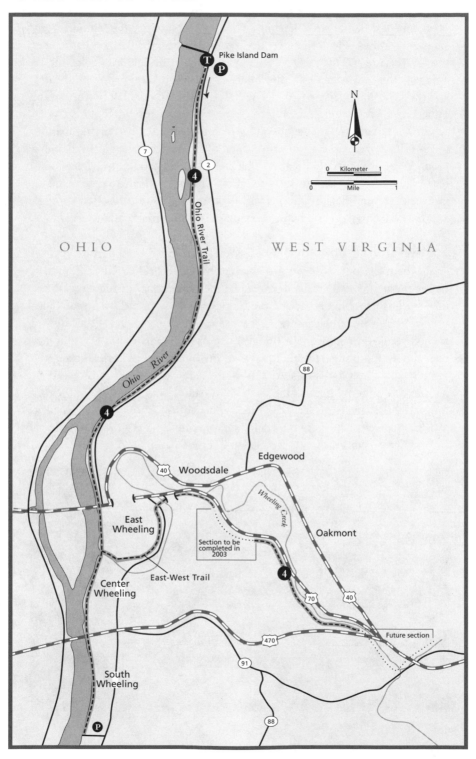

Pike Island Dam

T P

7

2

4

Ohio River Trail

N

0   Kilometer   1

0   Mile   1

OHIO

WEST VIRGINIA

88

Ohio River

4

Edgewood

40   Woodsdale

Wheeling Creek

Oakmont

East
Wheeling

Section to be
completed in
2003

4

East-West Trail

Center
Wheeling

70   40

Future section

470

91

South
Wheeling

88

P

At 4.5 miles the trail drops away from the road back to the railroad grade. Near milepost 3.5, enter Wheeling. There is a church on the left and many small row houses. The trail enters the downtown area at 3.0 miles. Pass under the I–70 bridge and the 1849 Wheeling Suspension Bridge. In the downtown area pass the War Memorial, the children's park, the Veterans Amphitheater, and the Wheeling Heritage Port. The East-West Trail exits left in front of the Wheeling Civic Center at the intersection of Water Street and 14th Street.

Cross a bridge and enter a grassy area. At milepost 1.0, the trail passes under the I–470 bridge. Make a right turn, then a left turn, and begin paralleling a road. At the athletic field for the Wheeling Middle School, turn right. Many barges line the riverbank in this area. Pass through a residential area and an industrial section. Belair, Ohio, is visible on the opposite bank. Pass through another residential section before reaching the 48th Street parking area.

East-West Trail Option: The East-West Trail leaves the Ohio River Trail along the riverfront in downtown adjacent to the Wheeling Civic Center. It passes through commercial and residential neighborhoods of the original city of Wheeling, then jumps back on the former rail corridor at 17th Street. Continuing west, the trail passes through more residential sections of the city and then crosses over (via two new bridges) new WV 2 and an old rail bed. Once over the second bridge, the trail passes through a tunnel. Before entering the tunnel, out of view and up a steep trail to the right, is where the historic Wetzel's cave is located. After passing through the tunnel and traveling another 0.5 miles, the trail temporarily ends. Turn right and follow Rock Point Road to Washington Avenue, where the trail resumes. The East-West Trail continues to Elm Grove along a slightly wooded and serene path.

Traveling the banks of the Ohio River.

Mountaineer
COUNTRY

Mountaineer Country occupies seven counties between the northern and eastern panhandles in the rugged foothills of West Virginia's mountain region. Early settlers worked hard and lived off the land mining coal, timbering forests, and building railroads to carry goods across America. Development of the region was far from total, however, and many natural wonders exist throughout.

Hikes in this region are contained in some of the state's most beautiful state parks and forests. Trails for all ability levels can be found here. Cathedral State Park has many short scenic trails that shouldn't be missed. Camping is found in campgrounds only, and many area parks are day-use only.

Amenities can be found in Morganton, the largest city in the region. Located right on the Pennsylvania border, Morganton is a college town and then some. Bustling with students and commerce alike, the city is alive with activity. When the day's hike is done, take a trip into town and enjoy the college nightlife. One word of warning: Be aware of crowds on Saturdays in the fall. Football at WVU is very important, and it seems as though the entire state of West Virginia converges on the city on game days. If you plan to visit the city in the fall, check a schedule and plan for crowds if the Mountaineers are playing at home.

5 Cathedral to Giant Hemlock Trail Loop / *Cathedral State Park*

Overview: *Cathedral State Park is one of the smallest state parks in West Virginia. However, what the park lacks in size (133 acres) is more than made up for by its biodiversity. The park has approximately 3.5 miles of trail. These trails pass under towering hemlock and cove hardwoods. The largest hemlock in the state is located within the park boundaries.*

The park possesses the only stand of mixed virgin timber in the state. It is a testimony to the value of the preservation of old-growth stands and the diversity such stands support. Some of the trees climb to a height of 90 feet, and circumferences of more than 20 feet. More than 170 types of vascular plants, 30 tree species, and more than 50 species of wildflowers have been identified within the park boundary.

General description: An easy, short loop trail travels under towering virgin hemlocks.

General location: 1.1 miles east of Aurora

Length: 1.7 miles

Difficulty: Easy

Special attractions: A quiet and serene walk under towering hemlock trees. The canopy high overhead creates the impression of a vaulted cathedral of trees.

Maps: Cathedral State Park map and trail guide; USGS quad: Aurora

Camping: The park is a day-use-only area.

Seasons: The park is open year-round.

Special considerations: Open-air fires are prohibited in Cathedral State Park.

For information: Cathedral State Park, Route 1 Box 370, Aurora, WV 26705; (304) 735–3771

Finding the trailhead: Take US 50 1.1 miles east of Aurora. The park entrance is on the left. After entering the park, turn left and continue 150 feet to the parking area. The stairway at the parking area is the beginning of the hike.

The hike: The Cathedral Trail is a short, easy loop trail that begins with a walk down the steps at the parking area. The red-blazed trail crosses Rhine Creek and passes a historical plaque and picnic shelter. Once on the trail, the sheer immensity of the trees seems to dwarf the visitor. Past the shelter, the Cathedral Trail splits; take the left fork. Just past this junction, turn left on the Wood Thrush Trail, which almost immediately crosses US 50. Be careful of traffic when crossing the road. The trail climbs gradually and then begins an easy descent among massive trees. The crowns towering high overhead give the distinct impression of being in a cathedral. The Wood Thrush Trail crosses a small spring creek and begins to parallel US 50 a short distance. After crossing US 50 again, the Wood Thrush Trail intersects the Cathedral Trail.

16

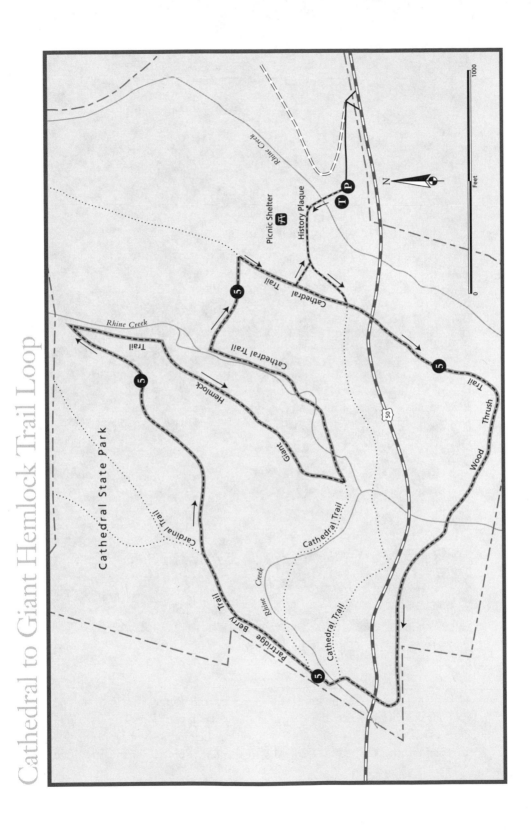

Cathedral to Giant Hemlock Trail Loop

Rare West Virginia old-growth forest.

Turn left on the Cathedral Trail and cross the Rhine Creek. Soon the Cathedral Trail intersects the Partridge Berry Trail; turn left. The Partridge Berry Trail is an easy stroll through towering hemlocks. Not far from this intersection, the Cathedral Trail exits to the left. Remain on the Partridge

Berry Trail and make an easy descent to a clearing near the park boundary, where the trail turns right and begins to parallel the Rhine Creek.

Just before a creek crossing, turn right on the Giant Hemlock Trail. The white blazed trail climbs gradually and begins to meander along a low bluff parallel to Rhine Creek. After passing a large hemlock lying across the trail, there is a short descent to the intersection with the Cathedral Trail.

Turn left on the Cathedral Trail. The trail stays very close to the creek, crossing it three times. Rhododendron crowds the trail. At the junction with the Partridge Berry Trail, turn right to remain on the Cathedral Trail. The trail leaves the creek and reaches a T intersection. Turn right, continue 25 yards, and turn left to complete the loop.

Cross Country Ski to Scott Run Trail Loop / *Coopers Rock State Forest*

Overview: *The Coopers Rock State Forest is a 12,713-acre region in north-central West Virginia. There are nearly 50 miles of trail located within the forest boundaries, ranging from easy leg-stretchers to long, difficult day hikes. Many of the trails are also suitable for cross-country skiing in winter. Picnic facilities are located in several areas throughout the forest.*

General description: This long hike travels through the heart of the State Forest.
General location: 10 miles east of Morgantown
Length: 7 miles
Difficulty: Difficult
Special attractions: The historic Henry Clay Furnace and an easy walk along Scott Run.
Maps: Coopers Rock State Forest map and trail guide; USGS quads: Bruceton Mills, Masontown, Lake Lynn

Camping: April 1 through deer rifle season. There are twenty-five campsites with electric hookups. The cost for camping is $17 per night. There is no backpack camping allowed within the forest boundaries.
Seasons: The forest is open year-round.
For information: Cooper Rock State Forest, Route 1 Box 270, Bruceton Mills, WV 26525; (304) 594–1561

Finding the trailhead: Take I–68 to exit 15 and turn south on the State Forest Road. Proceed 0.2 mile to a parking area on the right.

The hike: The intermediate Cross Country Ski Trail begins near the privy at the end of the parking lot. After crossing a small bridge, there is an easy climb to an old road. The trail is now flat and easy to follow. At 0.25 mile the trail

Cross Country Ski to Scott Run Trail Loop, Raven Rock Trail,
Virgin Hemlock to Tyrone Trail Loop

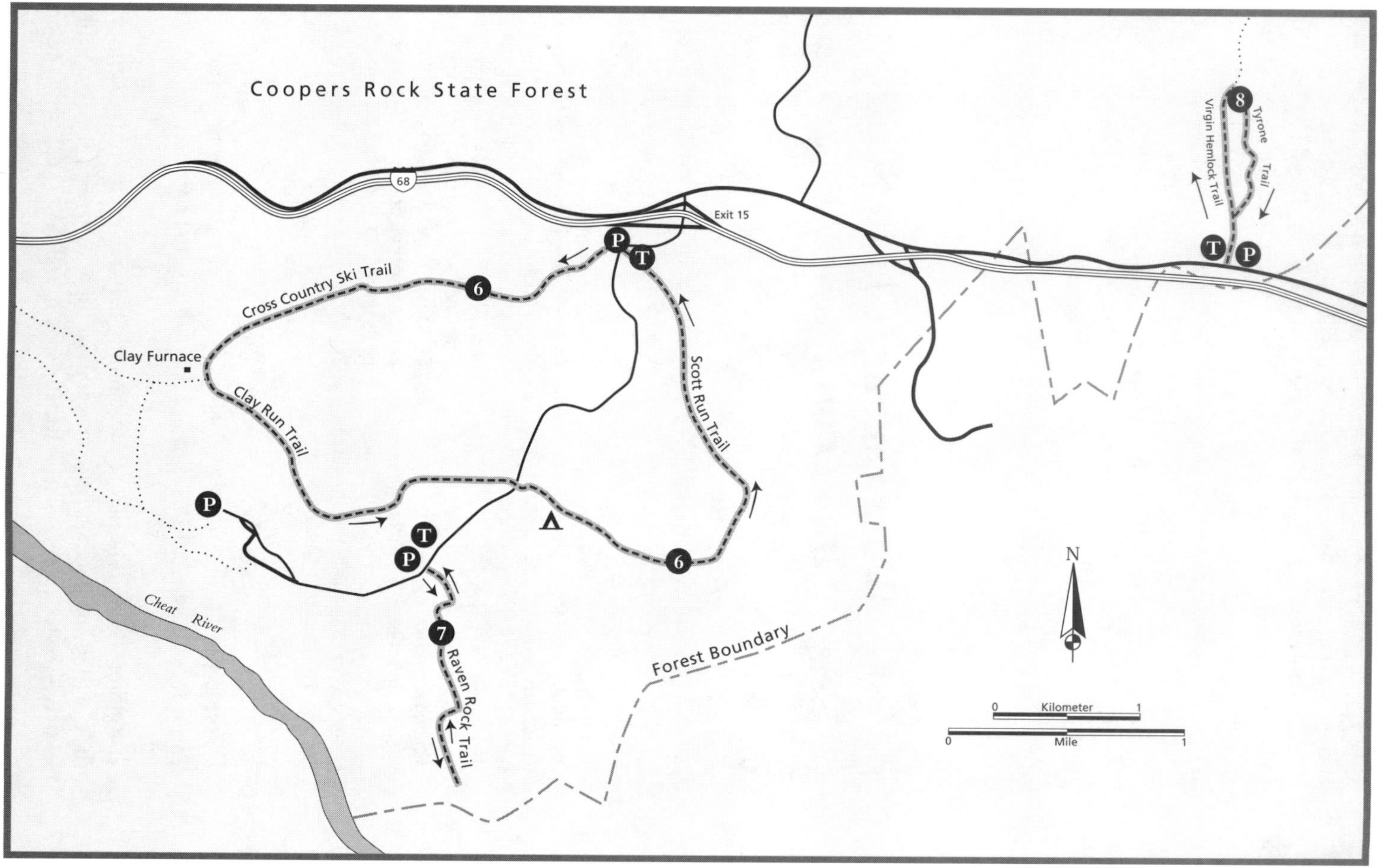

Coopers Rock State Forest

N

Kilometer
Mile

Exit 15

68

Clay Furnace

Cheat River

Forest Boundary

Scott Run Trail

Cross Country Ski Trail

Clay Run Trail

Raven Rock Trail

Tyrone   Trail

Virgin Hemlock Trail

Wet days can be magical days to hike.

enters a small clearing and then crosses a paved road. There is a sign on the opposite side of the road for the ski trail.

The grade is now a gradual descent. After a short distance, a side trail exits to the left at a sign for the Henry Clay Iron Furnace. Continue straight at this junction. The blazes along this section of the trail, which are few and far between, are white, sometimes with a picture of a blue cross-country skier. The gradual descent continues. After a broad, sweeping right bend, another trail junction is reached; continue straight, passing another trail that exits to the left. The mountainside here is peppered with many large boulders. The trail crosses a small feeder creek at approximately 1.25 miles.

After a left bend, the trail enters a narrow hollow at the upper reaches of the Right Fork. The beginning of this small stream can be heard farther below. After passing under a power line, the trail makes a short climb before descending to the creek. The trail is straight as an arrow during this descent.

At the creek, there is a small clearing and an old iron furnace, built between 1834 and 1836, that was used for smelting pig iron. The distance to the iron furnace is 2.0 miles; the elevation is approximately 1,640 feet.

In the clearing there are two bridges; one crosses the Right Fork, and then the other crosses Clay Run. After crossing Clay Run, there is a trail junction. Blue blazes mark Clay Run Trail, which exits to the left. A sign here says MCCOLLUM CAMPGROUND, 2 MILES.

The Clay Run Trail begins with a gradual climb, crossing Clay Run again after 0.1 mile. Cross the creek once more and begin a moderate climb to an old logging road; turn left. The climb is now more gradual again as the trail leaves the creek bed and enters a beautiful hollow. Climb to a broad flat saddle and cross a small creek. A road exits to the right at a sign for the camping area; continue straight. The trail crosses a small earthen dam and follows a gravel road to the park road. Turn left on the park road to continue the loop. The elevation in this area is 2,150 feet.

Turn right onto the McCollum Campground entrance road and continue to a silver gate on the left, which marks the beginning of the Scott Run Trail. The best time to hike this trail is late June when the rhododendrons are in bloom. Initially, the trail is marked with white blazes, and begins with a moderate descent along a rocky old road. Large boulders dot the landscape. The blazes soon change to yellow. After approximately 0.5 mile, the trail crosses a little creek and begins a gradual climb through a broad left bend. Mountain laurel grows thick in the understory. The trail begins to descend to Scott Run, reaching it approximately 1.0 mile from the campground road.

At the creek the trail turns left and becomes a narrow footpath. There is a sign at this junction that reads FOREST ENTRANCE ROAD. The Scott Run now parallels the trail on the right. The trail wanders away from the creek and back again several times before entering a broad, flat region. Beautiful ferns cover the forest floor. The trail crosses the run several times on small wooden bridges. Near the 2.25 mile mark, Scott Run Trail crosses a small feeder stream and turns left. There is a sign for the Forest Road and entrance. Here the trail leaves the run behind and climbs gradually to the entrance road. The parking lot is across the road.

7

Raven Rock Trail
Coopers Rock State Forest

Overview: *The masterpiece of Coopers Rock State Forest is the Cheat River Canyon and the spectacular rock bluffs located high above the river. Rock climbing and mountain biking are other favorite activities allowed in the forest. The best time to hike this trail is late September to early October when the fall colors are at their peak. The host of colors on the opposite escarpment at the end of the trail is truly a sight to behold.*

General description: This trail descends gradually to a rock escarpment overlooking the Cheat River.
General location: 10 miles east of Morgantown
Length: 4 miles round-trip
Difficulty: Moderate
Special attractions: A great rock outcrop overlooking the Cheat River.
Maps: Coopers Rock State Forest map and trail guide; USGS quads: Bruceton Mills, Masontown, Lake Lynn

Camping: April 1 through deer rifle season. There are twenty-five campsites with electric hookups. The cost for camping is $17 per night. There is no backpack camping allowed within the forest boundaries.
Seasons: The forest is open year-round.
For information: Cooper Rock State Forest, Route 1 Box 270, Bruceton Mills, WV 26525; (304) 594–1561

See map on page 20.

Finding the trailhead: Take I–68 to exit 15 and turn south on the State Forest Road. Proceed 2.1 miles to the trailhead. Parking is on the right.

The hike: The Raven Rock Trail begins at the gate across the road from the parking area. Red blazes mark the trail, and the elevation is 2,180 feet. The trail follows a wide road for 100 feet, to a sign for Raven Rock. Turn right and follow a narrower dirt road, which descends gradually through a forest of small second-growth hardwoods. Striped maple is well represented in the understory. After approximately 0.25 mile there is a trail junction; continue straight.

The trail is dotted with huge boulders on the upper slope of the mountain. A road exits to the left; continue straight. After a mile of easy descent, the trail climbs a short distance then descends again. After a right bend, there is a short, moderate climb to the ridge crest. The trail passes under a power line and terminates at the end of a large rock outcrop (elevation 2,000 feet). The view of the Cheat River 1,100 feet below is awesome.

8 Virgin Hemlock to Tyrone Trail
Loop / *Coopers Rock State Forest*

Overview: *Coopers Rock State Forest in managed jointly by the West Virginia Division of Forestry and West Virginia University. One of the primary purposes of the West Virginia State Forest system is to demonstrate forestry practices. Forest management practices are developed and tested. The State Forest system is a working and growing laboratory. Management practices attempt to increase the vertical layering of the forest to ensure multiple habitat systems. Approximately 21 percent of the entire state forest system has been designated to become old growth or mature forest to ensure another layer of habitat diversity.*

General description: This short hike follows the lazy Laurel Run.
General location: 10 miles east of Morgantown
Length: 2.5 miles
Difficulty: Easy
Special attractions: A creek crowded by rhododendrons and covered by towering hemlocks.
Maps: Coopers Rock State Forest map and trail guide; USGS quads: Bruceton Mills, Masontown, Lake Lynn

Camping: April 1 through deer rifle season. There are twenty-five campsites with electric hookups. The cost for camping is $17 per night. There is no backpack camping allowed within the forest boundaries.
Seasons: The forest is open year-round.
For information: Cooper Rock State Forest, Route 1 Box 270, Bruceton Mills, WV 26525; (304) 594–1561

See map on page 20.

Finding the trailhead: Take I–68 to exit 15 and turn north at the end of the ramp. Turn right at the stop sign and proceed 2.6 miles to the trailhead. There is parking on both sides of the road.

The hike: The Virgin Hemlock to Tyrone Trail Loop begins on the north side of the road. A sign marks the trailhead. The white blazed trail begins with a short descent through a mixed hardwood forest. Rhododendron thrives in the understory. The trail is easy to follow as it weaves through the boulders that dot the landscape. After 0.2 mile, the trail drops down to and crosses Lick Run on a rickety bridge, then bends left and parallels Laurel Run. This the where the return trail crosses Laurel Run to complete the loop.

The creek on the right is a series of small shelf riffles and low falls. This scenic area is quiet except for the sound of the creek tumbling over rocks. A 300-year-old hemlock grove dominates the canopy above the creek. The trail follows an old railroad grade, with some old cross ties still remaining. After crossing a second small feeder via a bridge, the Virgin Hemlock Trail reaches a T intersection at a pipeline road.

The trail on the opposite side of the road is the Ken Run's Trail. Turn right on the road and descend to Laurel Run. Cross the run, which can be difficult when the water is high, and begin a short easy climb. There is a short descent and then a second short climb. Watch for a narrow trail that enters the woods on the right, about 150 yards from the creek. This is the Tyrone Trail.

The trail descends gradually, but it is rocky and footing can be difficult. About 0.25 mile from the creek, enter a stand of tall straight hardwoods, and begin a short moderate descent. The area along the creek is flat. Parallel the creek a short distance, then cross it under a canopy of large hemlocks. Turn left on the Virgin Hemlock Trail, cross the rickety bridge, and walk back to the trailhead to close the loop.

Rocky to Rhododendron Trail
Loop / *Valley Falls State Park*

Overview: *The 1,145-acre Valley Falls State Park lies in a narrow valley dominated by the Tygart River. Valley Falls is a 12- to 18-foot waterfall over which this wide river tumbles. The park offers several miles of hiking and biking trails. Picnic shelters are also available.*

General description: This loop passes through tall stands of sheltered cove hardwoods and makes several ascents and descents of varying degrees of difficulty. The loop can be shortened by utilizing other trails within the Valley Falls State Park Trail system.
General location: 10 miles southeast of Fairmont
Length: 6.5 miles
Difficulty: Moderate

Special attractions: Upland hardwoods and streamside views of the Tygart River and Valley Falls.
Maps: Valley Falls State Park hiking and trail map; USGS quad: Fairmont East
Camping: Valley Falls State Park is day-use only.
Seasons: The park is open for hiking year-round.
For information: Valley Falls State Park, Route 6 Box 244, Fairmont, WV 26554; (304) 367–2719

Finding the trailhead: Take I–79 to exit 137 and head south on WV 310. Travel 8.0 miles to CR 31/14 (Valley Falls Road). There is a sign for the state park. Turn left and at the next two forks bear left. Pass the park office and trailheads for the Red Fox Trail, Wild Turkey Trail, and Dogwood Trail at 1.7 miles. To reach the trailheads for the Rocky Trail and Rhododendron Trail, continue on the park road 1.2 miles to the parking area on the left.

Rocky to Rhododendron Trail Loop

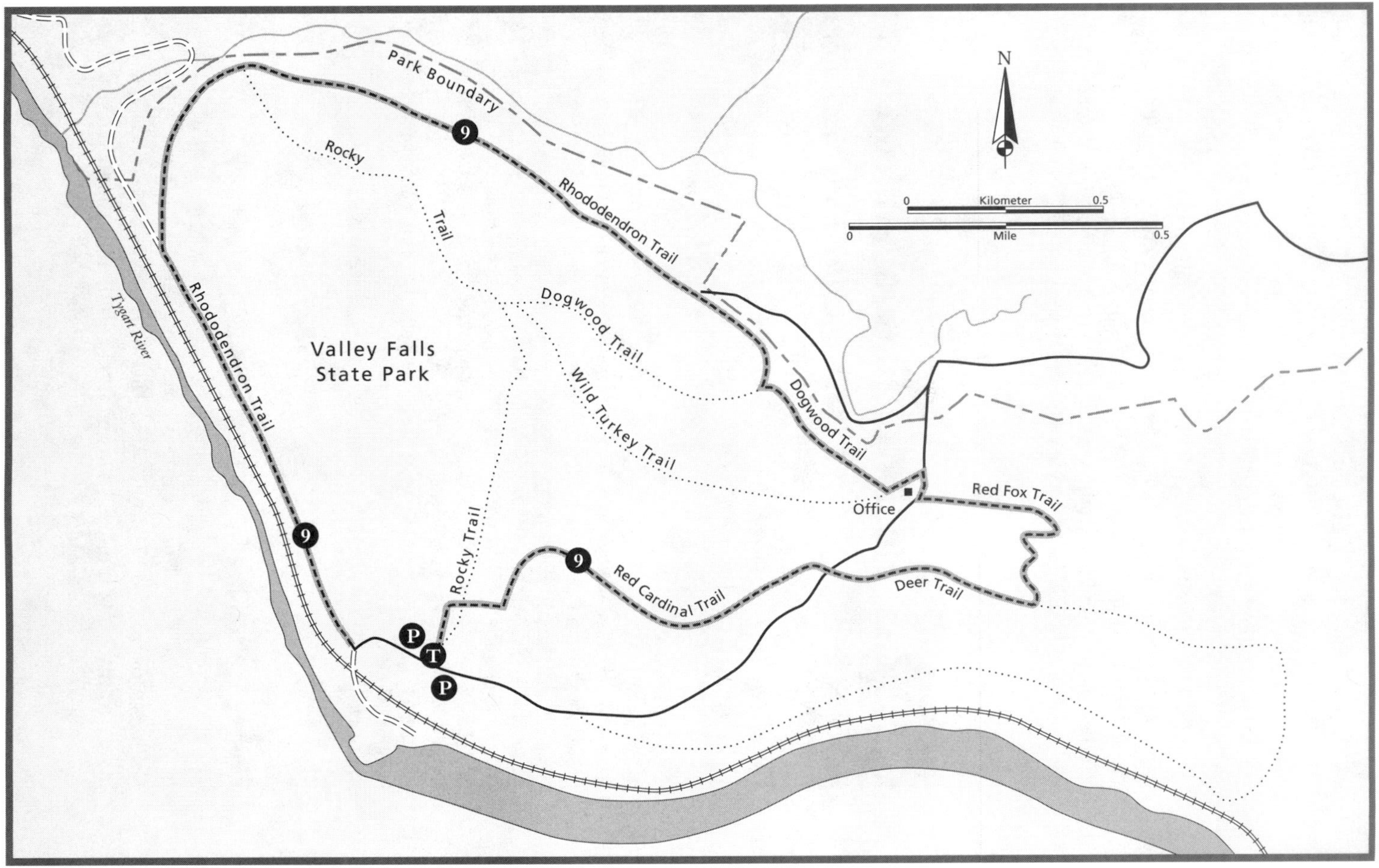

N

Kilometer
0   0.5
0   0.5
Mile

Red Fox Trail

Deer Trail

Office

Dogwood Trail

Rhododendron Trail

Park Boundary

Dogwood Trail

Wild Turkey Trail

Red Cardinal Trail

Rocky   Trail

Rocky Trail

Valley Falls
State Park

P T P

Rhododendron Trail

Tygart River

The hike: To begin this loop, drive down to the lower parking area. The signed trailhead for the Rocky Trail is located near the stairs on the east portion of the parking lot. The trail is yellow blazed and is marked by a series of stones laid along the path. After approximately 0.1 mile of moderate grade, the Rocky Trail intersects the Red Cardinal Trail. Turn right on the Red Cardinal Trail and follow the red blazes. For a shorter hike, continue straight on the Rocky Trail and climb the ridge to the intersection with the Dogwood Trail and the Wild Turkey Trail, then descend to join the Rhododendron Trail.

The Red Cardinal Trail passes through a forest of second-growth hardwoods. At 0.25 mile there is a left bend and the trail begins a short, steep climb. The trail enters a narrow hollow and bends to the right around a big red oak. It drops down through the hollow and climbs up the opposite side. The grade now becomes easy. The Red Cardinal Trail contours along the ridge for about 1.0 mile and then descends gradually to the park road. The distance to the road is 2.1 miles and the elevation is 1,300 feet.

Cross the road to the trailhead for the Deer Trail, marked with white blazes. The Deer Trail follows an old road and descends gradually. There is a holly tree not too far into the woods. About 0.25 mile from the road, the Deer Trail intersects the Red Fox Trail. To hike a shorter loop (5.5 miles), stay on the Deer Trail and follow it back to the parking area

Turn left on the Red Fox Trail and begin a short, steep climb up the ridge. After two switchbacks, the trail makes a hard push up the finger ridge. On the crest there is a left switchback and the grade becomes somewhat easier. There is a small clearing just before the trail reaches the park road. Turn right on the park road and walk past the office. The trailhead for the Wild Turkey Trail and the Dogwood Trail is located on the left side of the road just past the park office. The distance to the park office is 2.9 miles and the elevation is 1,450 feet.

Turn left off the park road and make a short descent, followed by a short, steep climb. At the top of the climb, the Wild Turkey and Dogwood Trails diverge. Take the right fork and follow the Dogwood Trail, marked with orange blazes. The trail follows a wide old road into the woods on an easy grade. After 0.5 mile, the trail bends left. Tall, straight cove hardwoods give the forest a parklike feel. The trail then makes a short, moderate descent to a small meadow. In the meadow, signs point to the Dogwood Trail and the Wild Turkey Trail. Continue straight. About 75 feet past these signs is a sign for the Rhododendron Trail. The elevation is 1,400 feet.

Turn left and begin a moderate descent. The Rhododendron Trail, marked with yellow blazes, follows an old rocky road that soon gives way to a rocky footpath. Near the beginning of the footpath, the grade becomes easier. The trail then descends gradually to a Y, about 1.0 mile after leaving the Dogwood Trail. Tall beech trees are located in this area. Take the uphill fork. At the next

The Tygart River tumbles over Valley Falls.

fork, continue straight along a small creek. There is a long, flat stretch and then a short descent through a rhododendron tunnel.

The trail makes a left bend away from the creek and intersects the Rocky Trail 5.0 miles into the hike. The Rocky Trail exits to the left and climbs the mountain. Remain on the Rhododendron Trail, which begins to parallel the Tygart River about 0.3 mile past the intersection with the Rocky Trail. There is a sign for the Rhododendron Trail at the next fork; continue straight. The trail now follows a wide gravel road. On the right there is a rock outcrop and a great view of the river. The trail continues its easy descent to the parking lot.

10 Dogwood to White Oak Trail
Loop / *Watters Smith Memorial State Park*

Overview: *The 532-acre historical park has many buildings built during the 1800s. Burr Smith willed the park's land to the state in honor of his great-great-grandfather, who bought the land in 1792. The park offers horseback riding, swimming, and picnicking.*

General description: The loop trail makes a steep climb to the highest point in the park and then descends into an area with a small stand of virgin timber before passing through an open meadow near the trailhead.

General location: 15 miles south of Clarksburg

Length: 3.3 miles

Difficulty: Moderate

Special attractions: A beautiful stretch of trail along a ridge crest and tall old-growth hardwoods in a sheltered cove.

Maps: Watters Smith Memorial State Park map and trail guide; USGS quad: West Milford

Note: The park is incorrectly shown on the USGS quad. The actual location of the park is a little northeast.

Camping: The park is a day-use-only area.

Seasons: The park is open from April 15 to October 15.

For information: Watters Smith Memorial State Park, P. O. Box 296, Lost Creek, WV 26385; (304) 745–3081

Finding the trailhead: Take I–79 to exit 110 and head west on Route 270. Travel 4.2 miles and turn left on Duck Creek Road (CR 25/6). Continue 2.5 miles to the Park Office Road. Turn left and travel 0.3 mile to the parking area.

The hike: The signed trailhead for the Dogwood Trail is located just uphill from the park office. The trail begins with an easy descent to the end of a small bowl, where it makes a right bend and crosses a small feeder stream. This is followed by a gradual climb to the junction with the Racheal Hershey Trail. The distance from the park office to this junction is 0.5 mile. The Racheal Hershey Trail, marked with orange diamonds, exits to the left and begins an easy climb through a forest of small black cherry. After a left bend, the trail enters a strip run, then crosses a small feeder stream before making a moderate climb to a flat, open strip run and the junction with the White Oak Trail. To make a shorter loop, turn left on the Racheal Hershey Trail and follow it 0.9 mile back to the park office.

The loop continues on the narrow White Oak Trail, which crosses the strip run and begins to climb the ridge. There are strip runs on both the left and right. After 0.1 mile, the trail flattens out for a short breather space. The crest and trail are rocky. A second steep climb sends the trail to the crest of the ridge.

Dogwood to White Oak Trail Loop

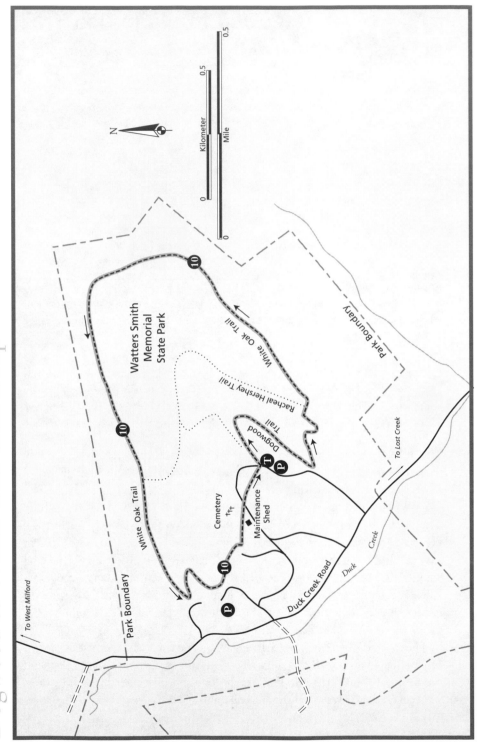

The trail contours just below the crest and the going is easy. At 0.4 mile, there is a grassy area that has been planted in autumn olive, a small tree that is a food source for animals.

The trail reenters the woods and follows a wide road. The grade continues to be easy. At 0.6 mile the road begins to descend. The trail exits to the right and begins an easy climb back to the crest. The narrow footpath crests a small knoll; at 1,484 feet, it is the highest point in the park. The summit is about the halfway point of the hike. After a short descent to a flat stretch, the trail makes a steep descent back to the strip run.

Continue straight as the Racheal Hershey Trail turns left. At a large white oak, the trail turns right. There is a sign with an arrow. The trail gradually descends as it follows an old road. Pass some large red oaks on the right and then parallel a pasture and fence line. There is a good view to the west, then the trail drops off the finger ridge and makes a short descent to the Oak Ridge Shelter.

In the picnic area, walk to the end of the parking lot. An unnamed trail leads into the woods and heads up an easy grade in a narrow hollow. There are many large old-growth trees in the sheltered cove. The trail crosses a small feeder stream, passes through a downed oak tree, and bends around a couple of large standing oaks before wrapping around the end to the hollow. The trail climbs out of the woods and into a grassy area.

Cross under the power line and head back into the woods. Follow the trail a short distance through the woods to the next meadow, and pass behind the maintenance shed. The loop continues by dropping down the hill and crossing a small creek. Finish by making a short climb back to the parking area.

Eastern
GATEWAY

The Eastern Gateway covers the three counties of Morgan, Berkely, and Jefferson in the extreme northeast portion of West Virginia. The Eastern Gateway is bordered to the south and southeast by Virginia, and to the east and north by Maryland. Very rural and characterized by wide valleys and tall, flat ridges, the region is a symbolic gateway linking West Virginia to the metropolitan areas of the east.

The hikes here are often a small part of a much larger whole. The Eastern Gateway is home to the famed Appalachian Trail, which travels more than 2,100 miles on its course from Georgia to Maine. From Harpers Ferry, it is possible to hike the path nearly 1,000 miles in either direction. Also passing through the Eastern Gateway is the Tuscarora Trail, a side trail of the AT that was originally built in case the Appalachian Trail had to be rerouted around development in northern Virginia. The Tuscarora travels from Shenandoah National Park in Virginia, through West Virginia, Maryland, and Pennsylvania, and rejoins the AT 252 miles later. From West Virginia, the Tuscarora Trail travels roughly 125 miles to both the north and the south.

Harpers Ferry National Historic Park is a must-see in the Eastern Gateway. Home to the Appalachian Trail and its governing body, the Appalachian Trail Conference, Harpers Ferry is also an important part of American history. The fuel that ignited the Civil War was fanned at Harpers Ferry in 1859 when abolitionist John Brown overtook the U.S. arsenal there. John Brown eventually lost his battle, and his life, but not before imaginary lines had been drawn between North and South. The geographic location of Harpers Ferry made it a frequent battleground during the heat of the Civil War. The town was alternately controlled by Confederate and Union troops throughout the war. Today the town is operated by the Park Service as a reminder of life as it used to be. The entire town is a working museum that highlights a difficult time in our nation's history.

Laurel Trail
Cacapon Resort State Park

Overview: *Nestled at the base of Cacapon Mountain is Cacapon Resort State Park. At 2,300 feet, Cacapon Mountain is the tallest peak in the Eastern Gateway region. Hikers can scale the ridges of Cacapon Mountain on the park's 17.25 miles of trails. If you need a day off from hiking, the "resort" state park offers swimming and fishing in the park lakes, horseback riding, and an eighteen-hole golf course.*

General description: This hike is an easy loop to a small mountain meadow and back.
General location: 10 miles south of Berkeley Springs
Length: 2.0 miles
Difficulty: Easy
Special Attractions: Blueberry-filled forests, mountain meadow.
Maps: Cacapon Resort State Park map and trail guide; USGS quads: Great Cacapon, Ridge

Camping: There is no camping at Cacapon Resort State Park, but a forty-seven-room lodge and twenty-five rental cabins provide a less primitive way to relax.
Seasons: Open year-round.
For information: Cacapon Resort State Park, Route 1 Box 304, Berkeley Springs, WV 25411; (304) 258–1022

Finding the trailhead: From I–81 in Virginia, take US 522 north 27 miles to the park entrance on the left side of the road. From I–70 in Maryland, take US 522 south 16 miles. The park entrance is on the right, just after the town of Omps. From central West Virginia, take US 50 or US 220 to the small town of Junction. Follow US 50 east out of Junction past Gore, VA. Five miles east of Gore, turn left onto VA 600. Follow VA 600 to US 522. Take US 522 north to the park entrance on the left side of the road. Once in the park, follow the main park road to the lodge parking lot.

The hike: Although Laurel Trail passes by several trail intersections, it is well marked and easy to follow. The hike begins at the lodge parking lot. Walk back to the main park road, cross a small bridge, and walk to the cabin area. The signed trailhead for Laurel Trail is near Cabin 24. The trail is marked by green blazes.

From the trailhead, follow the green blazed trail past the white blazed Cabin Loop Trail. Laurel Trail travels uphill to a power line and another intersection where Central Trail exits to the right. Follow Laurel Trail uphill and to the left through a forest of oak, maple, pine, and mountain laurel. At

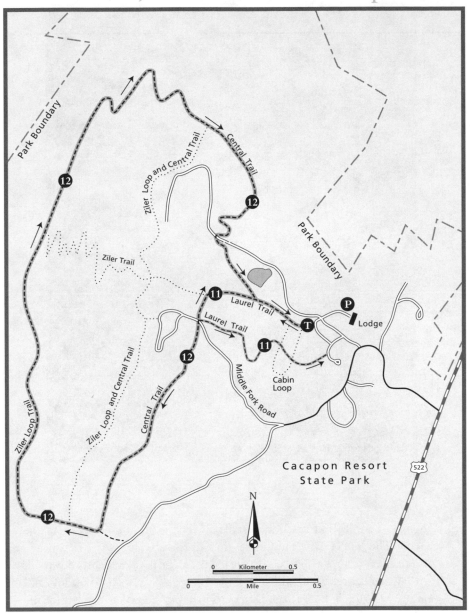

Park Boundary

12

Ziler Loop and Central Trail

Central Trail

12

Ziler Trail

11

Laurel Trail

P

T

Lodge

Park Boundary

11

Laurel Trail

Cabin Loop

Ziler Loop Trail

12

Ziler Loop and Central Trail

Central Trail

Middle Fork Road

Cacapon Resort State Park

522

12

N

| 0 | Kilometer | 0.5 |
| 0 | Mile | 0.5 |

Mountain laurel in full bloom.

0.75 mile, Laurel Trail reaches Ziler Trail. Take some time to rest in the meadow. The trail is short and there is time to spare.

From Ziler Trail, the hike back to the lodge will be predominantly downhill. Turn left on Laurel Trail, which descends gradually from the meadow and soon reaches Middle Fork Road. Don't cross the road. Look to the left for the green blazes. Laurel Trail starts a short, light to moderate ascent as it parallels the road. The trail levels off and passes through a forest in which the groundcover is mostly blueberry plants. A moderate descent leads to another intersection with Cabin Loop Trail. Follow the green blazes through another small meadow, then exit the forest near cabin 25. Turn left, follow the driveway to the road, and turn left again. Walk to the bridge and turn right to reach the lodge parking lot.

12

Laurel to Ziler Loop Trail
Cacapon Resort State Park

Overview: *If you are hiking in the Cacapon area in summer and notice few leaves on the trees or the ground covered with green leaf pieces, look on the branches for a medium-sized, lightly fuzzy caterpillar with red spots. The oaks in the area have been battling gypsy moths, a species brought to the United States in the late 1860s to produce silk. The moth escaped, and by the 1890s defoliation was occurring. Although gypsy moth larvae will feed on many tree species, oaks are their favorite. In areas with severe infestation, trees may be totally defoliated.*

General description: A pleasant loop hike to the crest of Cacapon Mountain, through a forest filled with blueberry, and past the park lake.

General location: 10 miles south of Berkeley Springs

Length: 6.0 miles

Difficulty: Moderate

Special attractions: Mountain and lakeside views, mountain laurel blooming in June.

Maps: Cacapon Resort State Park map and trail guide, USGS quads: Great Cacapon, Ridge

Camping: There is no camping at Cacapon Resort State Park. There are, however, a lodge and rental cabins.

Seasons: Open year-round.

For information: Cacapon Resort State Park, Route 1 Box 304, Berkeley Springs, WV 25411; (304) 258–1022

See map on page 35.

Finding the trailhead: From I–81 in Virginia, take US 522 north 27 miles to the park entrance on the left side of the road. From I–70 in Maryland, take US 522 south 16 miles. The park entrance is on the right, just after the town of Omps. From central West Virginia, take US 50 or US 220 to the small town of Junction. Follow US 50 east out of Junction past Gore, VA. Five miles east of Gore, turn left onto VA 600. Follow VA 600 to US 522. Take US 522 north to the park entrance on the left side of the road. Once in the park, follow the main park road to the lodge parking lot.

The hike: From the lodge parking lot, walk back to the main park road, cross a small bridge, and walk to the cabin area. The signed trailhead for Laurel Trail is near Cabin 24. Laurel Trail is marked by green blazes.

From the trailhead, follow the green blazed trail past the white blazed Cabin Loop Trail. Laurel Trail travels uphill to a power line and another intersection where Central Trail exits to the right. Follow Laurel Trail uphill and to the left through a forest of oak, maple, pine, and mountain laurel. At 0.75 mile, Laurel Trail reaches Ziler Trail and a small meadow. Laurel Trail gradually descends from the meadow, reaching Middle Fork Road at approximately 1.0 mile.

An easterly view near the top of Ziler Trail.

Across Middle Fork Road, the red blazed Central Trail begins near a small stream. Follow the trail past a rental cabin. The trail is rocky as it travels downward through a forest of oak and maple.

The hike follows Central Trail as it bounces across the ridge before traveling to the top of Cacapon Mountain via Ziler Loop Trail. Central Trail travels easily up and down, often through wet and muddy sections. At approximately 2.0 miles, the blue blazed Ziler Loop Trail is reached. Turn right and follow Ziler Loop Trail uphill. (A left at the intersection leads to Bratt picnic shelter.) The trail mixes "side-hilling" with difficult uphill sections as it ascends Cacapon Mountain. At 3.25 miles from the trailhead, the trail crests the mountain.

Ziler Loop Trail travels the crest of Cacapon Mountain for approximately 0.75 mile before beginning the descent of the ridge. The ridge crest is wide and grassy. There is very little middle canopy. At 3.5 miles from the trailhead, Ziler trail heads off the mountain to the right for a steep 2.5-mile hike to the cabin area. In a rainstorm or emergency, it is the fastest way off the ridge. To continue the hike, stay on Ziler Loop Trail as it crosses the ridge top, passing an old barn to the left. Finally, at 4.0 miles, Ziler Loop Trail begins to descend the ridge.

Another 0.75 mile of hiking completes much of the descent of Cacapon Mountain and leads the hiker to Central Trail. In early summer this section of the hike is gorgeous with blooming mountain laurel. The trail becomes rocky and leads through four switchbacks. When the angle becomes easy and the trail widens, the junction with Central Trail is reached. A right continues on Ziler Loop and Central Trails. Take the left fork to follow the lone Central Trail.

Central Trail leaves Ziler Loop Trail and crosses a gravel road. The trail hikes through a stand of pine, and mountain laurel fills the middle canopy. Thick blueberry covers the ground, causing the trail to become very narrow. After passing some large boulders, stone stairs lead to a paved road.

Cross the paved road and follow the trail across a grassy area to the banks of the park lake. At 5.9 miles, Central Trail passes a bench overlooking the lake. Although it is late in the hike for a rest, the lake view makes it tempting. Central Trail travels moderately uphill to the intersection with Laurel Trail. Turn left onto Laurel Trail and hike downhill to the trailhead at cabin 24. Follow the paved road back to the lodge parking lot.

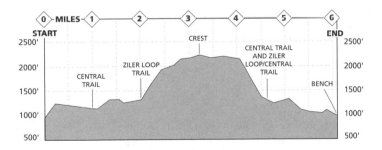

13

Appalachian Trail to Loudoun Heights Trail Loop
Harpers Ferry National Historical Park

Overview: *The Appalachian Trail extends from Georgia to Maine. This section of the trail passes through the picturesque small town of Harpers Ferry, the scene of many historic events. The town itself is at the confluence of two major rivers, the Shenandoah and the Potomac. Harpers Ferry National Historical Park attempts to preserve and interpret the local history of the town, particularly during the time of the Civil War. Within the park is the Redoubt Trail, a short, wheelchair-accessible interpretive trail to the cannon redoubt that was utilized in the defense of Harpers Ferry.*

General description: This hike passes through three states and the town of Harpers Ferry, providing river hiking, ridge crest hiking, and great views.
General location: Harpers Ferry
Length: 12.1 miles round-trip
Difficulty: Difficult
Special attractions: In Harpers Ferry, one can browse the little shops and "rehydrate" for the remainder of the hike.
Maps: Harpers Ferry Official Map and Guide; Appalachian Trail guide maps; USGS quad: Harpers Ferry

Camping: Overnight backpacking is allowed on the Appalachian Trail but not in the park.
Seasons: The Appalachian Trail is open to hiking year-round. The park is open from 8:00 A.M.. to 5:00 P.M. every day, except Thanksgiving, Christmas, and New Year's Day.
For information: Appalachian Trail Conference, P. O. Box 807, Harpers Ferry, WV 25425-0807; (304) 535–6331; Harpers Ferry National Historical Park, P. O. Box 65, Harpers Ferry, WV 25425; (304) 535–6223; www.nps.gov/hafe/home.htm

Finding the trailhead: To reach the Appalachian Trail, take I–81 to exit 12 and head east on WV 9. Travel 22.5 miles to the West Virginia/Virginia border and the Keyes Gap parking area on the left. To reach Harpers Ferry National Historical Park, take US 340 north to the park entrance. Turn left at the light to reach Bolivar Heights.

The hike: At the parking area at Keyes Gap, a short spur trail leads to the Appalachian Trail. There is an information booth located at the junction of the spur trail and the AT. The elevation here is 900 feet. At the information booth, turn north on the AT and follow the white blazes along an old road. The trail is wide, flat, and easy to follow. On the left are the remains of an old stone fence.

After an easy descent of about 0.5 mile, the trail leaves the crest and begins to contour along the east side of the ridge. The trail is rocky in places. Following this flat stretch, there is an easy climb back to the crest, followed by a short descent to a narrow saddle. The trail passes under a power line and

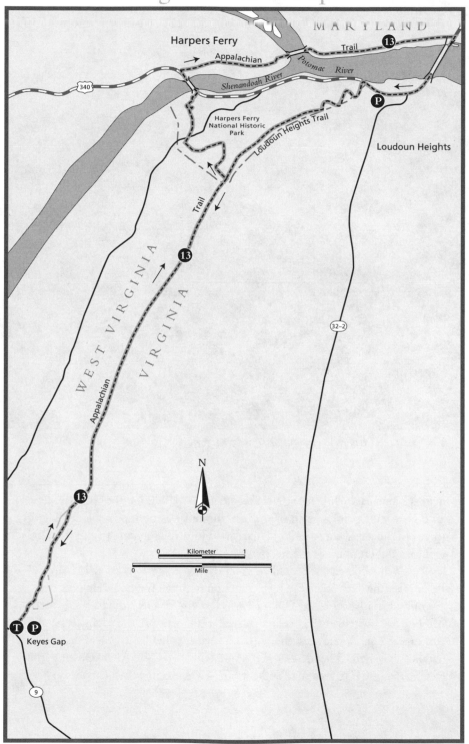

MARYLAND

Harpers Ferry

Appalachian Trail

13

Appalachian

Potomac River

340

Shenandoah River

Harpers Ferry
National Historic
Park

Loudoun Heights Trail

Loudoun Heights

WEST VIRGINIA

VIRGINIA

Appalachian

Trail

13

32–2

13

N

13

T P

Keyes Gap

0 Kilometer 1

0 Mile 1

9

The town of Harpers Ferry can be seen from Jefferson Rock.

begins a long easy climb along the crest to an elevation of just over 1,100 feet. The views along this stretch of trail are limited. At the top of a small knoll, there is a short descent to a second narrow saddle, then a climb to almost 1,200 feet, the highest point of the hike.

After a short descent, the trail enters the Harpers Ferry National Historical Park. Near the park boundary is the junction with the Loudoun Heights Trail, 4.0 miles from Keyes Gap. The AT turns left and begins a moderate descent. After a left switchback, a yellow blazed trail exits to the right. The AT continues a moderate descent through three switchbacks then begins to parallel a trench. The descent becomes much steeper. After crossing the trench, the trail crosses a road and continues to descend into a narrow hollow.

Cross the hollow, climb briefly up the opposite side, and then begin a steep descent to the Shenandoah River.

The trail crosses the river on the US 340 Bridge. On the opposite bank take the Cliff Trail, which exits the road almost immediately after crossing the river. The trail climbs quickly up a steep escarpment and then contours along the bluff on an easy grade. Continue straight at the junction with the AT. A blue blazed trail exits left and heads to the Camp Hill area and the AT headquarters. Continue straight and pause to take in the wonderful view at Jefferson Rock. Composed of sandstone pillars, this is the spot where Jefferson described the junction of the Potomac and Shenandoah Rivers.

The AT winds down into Harpers Ferry where the Shenandoah and Potomac Rivers meet at an elevation of 287 feet. Cross the Potomac and enter Maryland. The trail is wide, flat, and easy, paralleling the C&O Canal for about a mile. At the US 340 bridge, turn left and cross the canal and railroad tracks. Climb the steep bank to the highway; cross the Potomac again. Follow US 340 past the parking lot on the left to the Loudoun Heights Trailhead. The distance from the bridge to the trailhead is approximately 0.2 mile.

There is a small sign marking the trailhead. The trail exits the road on the left and climbs the road bank to an old road. Past a house and a right switchback, the trail becomes a narrow footpath and the climb begins. Five more switchbacks assist in the climb up this moderate grade. Tall beech, maple, oak, and poplar dominate the canopy. The ascent continues to a rock outcrop with a great view of Harpers Ferry and the confluence of the Potomac and Shenandoah Rivers.

After leaving the rock outcrop, the trail enters a narrow hollow and begins an easy climb to the ridge crest. On the crest, the trail is flat and wide. After dropping over to the west side of the ridge, the trail climbs again a short distance to the intersection with the AT. Continue straight at this junction to head back to the parking area at Keyes Gap.

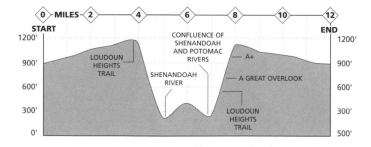

13 Tuscarora Trail (Northeast)
Sleepy Creek Wildlife Management Area

Overview: *The Tuscarora Trail is a 242-mile blue-blazed side trail of the famed Appalachian Trail. The trail was originally built to bypass developed areas in northern Virginia. If the Appalachian Trail had not been protected as a National Scenic Trail in 1968, the path of the Tuscarora Trail my well have become the "new" AT. The Virginia and West Virginia sections of the Tuscarora Trail were known as the Big Blue Trail until 1997 when the two trails were officially unified. The majority of the West Virginia Tuscarora Trail travels through the 22,928-acre Sleepy Creek Wildlife Management Area. The area is managed as a game habitat for hunting and fishing.*

General description: This hike follows a portion of the well-maintained Tuscarora Trail through Sleepy Creek Wildlife Management Area. The trail crosses Pee Wee Point and then travels to Sleepy Creek Lake.

General location: 3.0 miles west of Glengary

Length: 8.0 miles one-way

Difficulty: Moderate

Special attractions: Boggy bottomland, a ridge-top tower, and a lily-pad-covered lake.

Maps: USGS quads: Glengary, Stotlers Crossroads

Camping: Camping is available at the campground near Sleepy Creek Lake.

Seasons: Open year-round.

For information: Potomac Appalachian Trail Club, 118 Park Street SE, Vienna, VA 22180-4609; (704) 242–0693

Finding the trailhead: To reach the southern trailhead, take I–81 to exit 5 near Ironwood and travel west on SR 51 to WV 45 and turn left. (From Martinsburg, take SR 45 southwest.) Past Glengary, WV 45 makes a sharp left-hand turn. In the bend of the turn is an unnamed gravel road. Turn right and follow the road uphill. The road will level out and turn left. On the right, two fire roads intersect the gravel road. The blue blazed fire road straight ahead is the Tuscarora Trail.

The middle of this hike can be accessed from CR 7–13. From Martinsburg, follow WV 45 southwest to CR 7 in the town of Glengary. Turn right and follow CR 7 north to CR 7–13. Turn left onto CR 7–13 and follow it to the

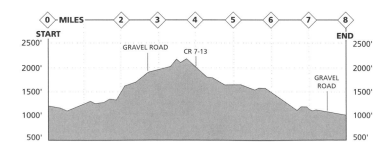

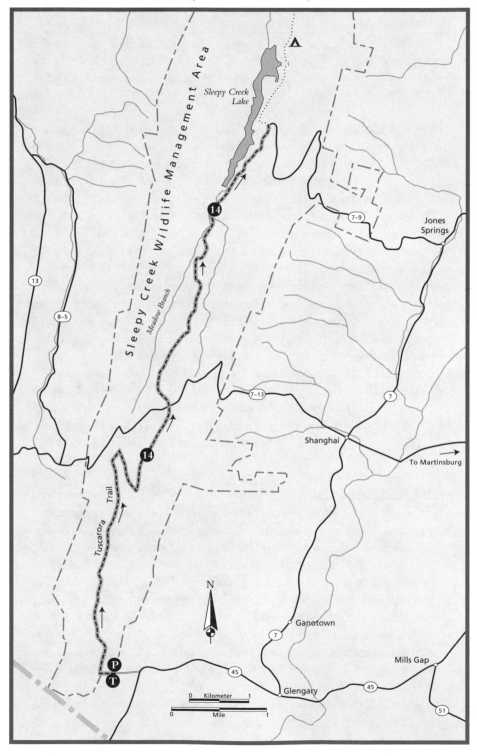

Sleepy Creek Wildlife Management Area

Sleepy Creek Lake

Jones Springs

Meadow Branch

Shanghai

To Martinsburg

Tuscarora Trail

Ganotown

Mills Gap

Glengary

N

Kilometer

Mile

top of the mountain. Park on the right side of the road near the trailhead for the Old Steel Trail, just past the turnoff for Magler Spring Campsite.

To reach the northern trailhead at Sleepy Creek Lake, follow CR 7 past the turnoff for CR 7–13. Turn left onto CR 7–9, which leads to Sleepy Creek Wildlife Management Area. Turn left onto Park Road 827 and travel along the lake, parking near its southern end.

The hike: From the unnamed gravel road at the southern trailhead, follow the Tuscarora Trail along an old forest road. The trail is blazed blue and easy to discern. It bounces over short ups and downs for a while, passing several dugout areas to prevent vehicle traffic from using the road. The trail begins to hike uphill along this old road until it reaches a gravel forest road at 2.75 miles.

On the forest road, continue the uphill hike to a road intersection. A sign points up the road to the right and reads PEE WEE POINT TRAIL. Turn right and continue hiking uphill. The trail contours and cross-contours along the ridge while traveling south. At 3.25 miles, Tuscarora Trail turns left, leaves the fire road, and hikes steeply up the side of Pee Wee Ridge. The trail twists and turns for 0.5 mile, and finally reaches the ridge top. Follow the trail across the ridge top and past an old fire tower. The single-track trail on the ridge top is lined with mountain laurel. Blueberry covers the ground and cherry occupies the canopy. The trail travels another 1.0 mile for a total of 4.0 miles when it intersects with CR 7–13.

At the road, turn right and hike east. Just before reaching the trailhead for Old Steel Trail, follow the blue blazed trail as it enters the woods on the left-hand side of the road. The trail wraps through the woods to an old fire road. This road goes straight to the pull-off at Old Steel Trail, so access can be had at the pull-off or via the trail.

The Tuscarora Trail now travels old logging grades through clear-cut and wildlife management areas. The clear-cuts allow for a lot of direct sunlight, and the trail can be very warm in summer. The trail travels predominantly north at an easy descent. At about 7.0 miles, the trail reaches a boggy area and a pond. The trail in this section is not completely obvious, but blue blazes make route finding easy. At 7.5 miles, Meadow Branch Trail heads off to the left at the junction of two streams. Take the right branch and cross a small creek. There is a wooden footbridge, but lack of maintenance has taken its toll. It may be safer to just stay off of it. Although portions of the hike since CR 7–13 have been damp, this creek is the first decent place to get filterable water.

The trail again widens to a fire road and at less than 7.75 miles reaches a gravel forest road, Park Road 827. Turn left and follow the blue blazes. The trail reaches the southern end of Sleepy Creek Lake at 3.75 miles from CR 7–13 and 7.75 miles from the start of the hike. The park road travels the length of the lake to a camping area on the northern end.

Potomac
HIGHLANDS

Rising abruptly in eastern West Virginia, the peaks and ridges of the Allegheny Mountains create an outdoor playground for the hiker. The same geologic events that pushed the high plain of western West Virginia straight up also tilted and folded the ground of the Potomac Highlands, creating majestic mountains and deep valleys. As the name suggests, the watersheds in the region give rise to the mighty Potomac River, which flows north toward Harpers Ferry. Great expanses of resistant Tuscarora sandstone line ridge tops and provide breathtaking vistas at nearly every turn.

Hiking the Potomac Highlands is very rewarding. Walks range from short, easy boardwalk paths to difficult, extended day hikes. Trails in the area reach altitudes of 4,000 feet, and ecosystems vary greatly as altitude changes. Creek bottoms are lined with birch and hemlock, while spruce dominates the ridge tops. Trails here are managed by state parks or state forests. Camping is permitted in campgrounds, and it is advisable to make reservations. Although much of the land in this region is owned by the federal government and managed as the Monongahela National Forest, trails in the forest itself are described in a separate section of this guide.

In addition to hikers, the Potomac Highlands attracts many other outdoor athletes. Canaan Valley and Snowshoe ski resorts bring both downhill and cross-country skiers from all over the east coast. Summertime sees the ski resorts catering to mountain bike enthusiasts. Every summer, Snowshoe resort plays host to thousands at an increasingly popular twenty-four-hour mountain bike endurance race. Rock climbers enjoy the sandstone cliffs, while white-water enthusiasts flock to the stream banks.

15

Beartown Boardwalk
Beartown State Park

Overview: *Beartown State Park is a small 110-acre park located near Droop Mountain Battlefield State Park. This wild and remote hilltop contains huge rocks and boulders strewn about a dense forest floor. Wind and rain have eroded the deep crevices and walls of rock in an eerie fashion, almost as though they had been carved with a special purpose in mind. Some of the pockets carved out of the rocks are very small, others are large enough to hold a grown man.*

Beartown's name comes from the local legend that claims that colonies of black bear once inhabited the house-sized stone formations that form the maze of this natural area. Also, the many deep, narrow crevices were formed in a somewhat regular crisscross pattern and appear from above like streets of a small town. A boardwalk with interpretive signs directs visitors through this unique park. A 150-foot accessible walk also allows wheelchair users to enter one of the major crevasses of the park.

General description: A short hike on a boardwalk through small rock crevices covered with lush greenery.
General location: 18 miles south of Marlinton
Length: 0.5 mile
Difficulty: Easy
Special attractions: Beautiful fern- and tree-covered rock formations.

Maps: USGS quad: Droop
Camping: Day-use only.
Seasons: The park is open from April to October.
For information: Droop Mountain Battlefield State Park, HC 64 Box 189, Hillsboro, WV 24946; (304) 653–4254

Finding the trailhead: Take I–64 to exit 169 and turn north on US 219. Travel 22 miles and turn right at the park sign. Watch carefully for the turn; it appears quite suddenly. Continue 1.6 miles to the parking area.

The hike: The Beartown Boardwalk is a short interpretive hike. Begin near the information center located in the parking lot. Walk past the sign, and begin a gradual descent through a forest of tall second-growth hardwoods. The boardwalk begins about 150 feet from the trailhead. Once on the boardwalk, the trail enters an area of unique rock formations. Turn left at the loop junction and climb a set of stairs into a stand of tall, straight hemlock. The boardwalk passes over and through numerous small rock crevices. Many of the rocks are covered with elephant ear lichens, some of which are hundreds of years old.

Beartown Boardwalk

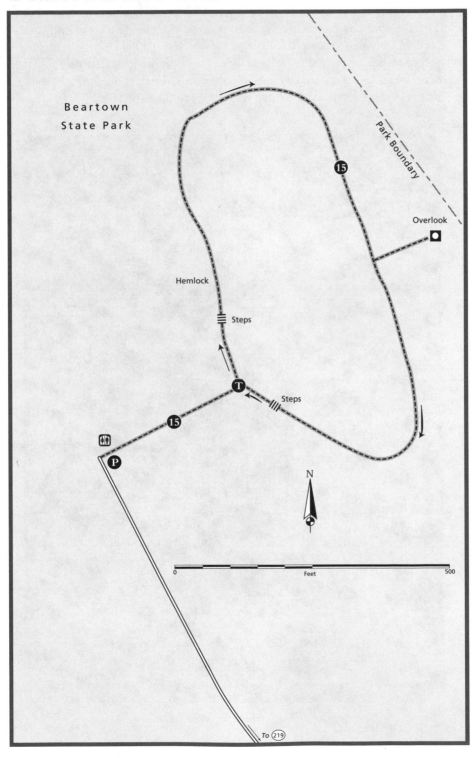

Beartown
State Park

Park Boundary

Overlook

15

Hemlock

Steps

T

Steps

15

P

N

0   Feet   500

To 219

After a short descent, the boardwalk bends right and begins the return trip. The boardwalk is now at the bottom of the rock face. The short cliffs are covered with many small pits, the largest of which could hold a large man. Just before the loop ends, a short boardwalk to the left leads out to a platform that overlooks a beautiful stand of upland hardwoods. The main boardwalk leads back to a short set of stairs and the return trail to the parking lot.

Boardwalks navigate the rocks in Beartown State Park.

16 Elakala to Yellow Birch Trail
Loop / *Blackwater Falls State Park*

Overview: *The 1,812-acre Blackwater Falls State Park is located on the rim of the Blackwater River Canyon. The park offers a host of recreational opportunities. In addition to its 12.5 miles of hiking and cross-country ski trails, the park also offers horseback riding, swimming, and boating. Located within the park boundary is the beautiful five-story Blackwater Falls, which marks the beginning of the immense canyon. The park can also be utilized as a springboard to longer hiking loops in the Canaan Mountain area immediately south of the park.*

General description: The loop trail is an easy hike through upland hardwoods and lush marshy bogs.
General location: 2 miles southeast of Davis
Length: 3.7 miles
Difficulty: Easy
Special attractions: Falls of Elakala, Balanced Rock, and a great view of the Blackwater River Gorge.
Maps: Blackwater Falls State Park map and trail guide; USGS quad: Blackwater Falls

Camping: Camping is available from mid-April to October. The fee is $13 to $17 per night.
Seasons: The park and lodge are open year-round.
Special consideration: The Red Spruce Riding Trail is closed to foot travel from May through October.
For information: Blackwater Falls State Park, P. O. Box 490, Davis, WV 26260; (304) 259–5216

Finding the trailheads: Take WV 32 north out of Davis and turn left on CR 29, Blackwater Falls Road. Travel 1.2 miles to a crossroad, turn left, and continue 1.6 miles to the lodge and the Elakala Trailhead.

The hike: The signed Elakala Trail begins at the end of the Blackwater Falls Lodge parking lot. This trail is for foot travel only, and for good reason. The trail begins with a quick drop to Shay Run. A bridge crosses the run where the Falls of Elakala begins. The water of Shay Run crashes over the side of a steep precipice. On the other side of the bridge, the trail begins an easy climb. Be careful, as the tree roots can be very slippery.

A short descent on stone steps is followed by a short steep ascent with the aid of a set of wooden steps. At the top of this climb, a small clearing provides a great view of the river gorge. Just beyond the view shed is a trail junction. A left turn leads back to the lodge. The loop continues straight, climbing gradually through a forest of yellow birch and spruce. The trail meanders through the woods to the park road at 0.5 mile.

The Elakala Trail ends at the road. The loop continues on Balanced Rock Trail across the road. A sign and several little piles of small rocks mark the

Elakala to Yellow Birch Trail Loop

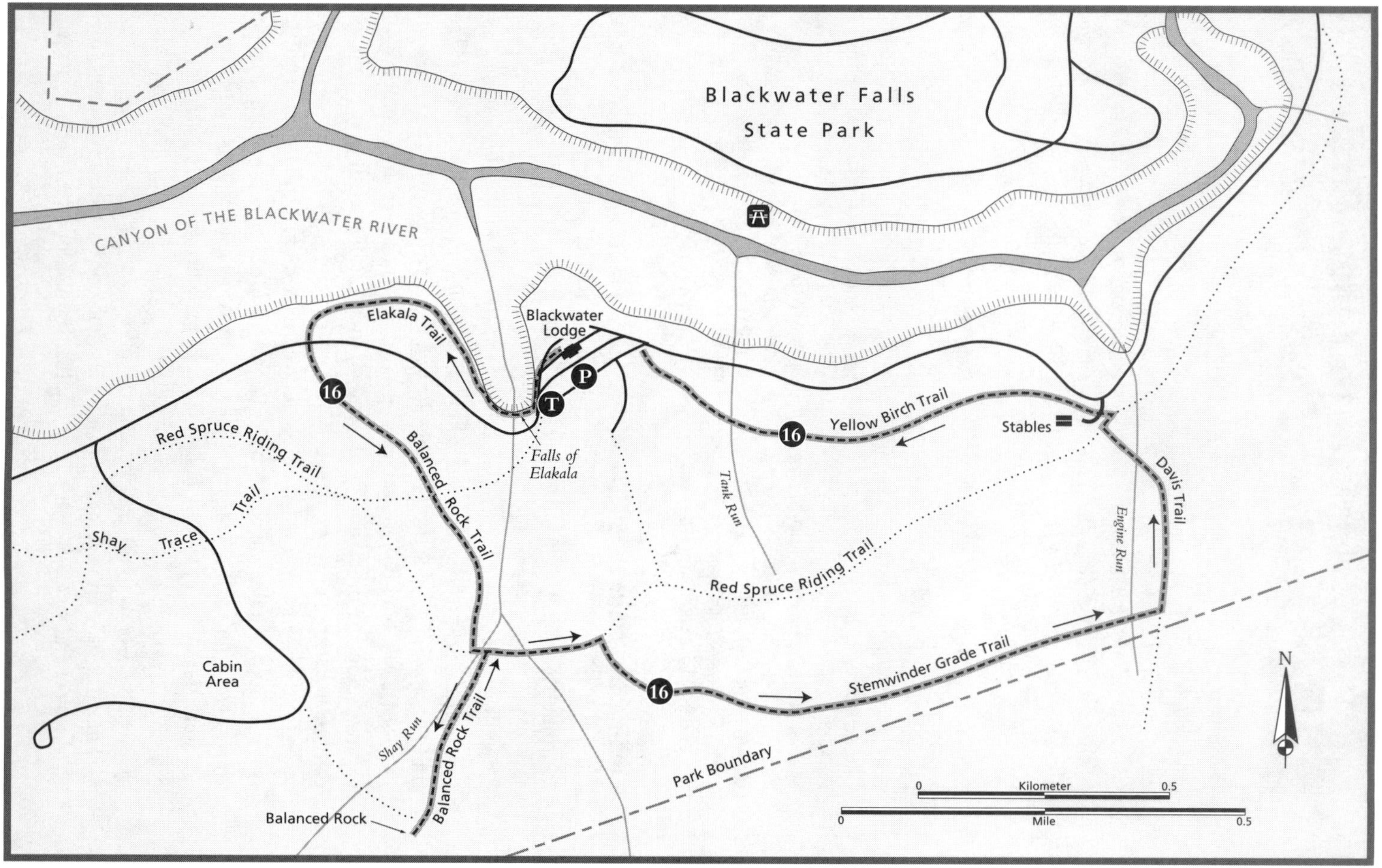

Blackwater Falls
State Park

CANYON OF THE BLACKWATER RIVER

Davis Trail

Engine Run

Stables

Yellow Birch Trail

Stemwinder Grade Trail

Red Spruce Riding Trail

Tank Run

Blackwater Lodge

P

T

Falls of Elakala

Elakala Trail

Balanced Rock Trail

Balanced Rock Trail

Park Boundary

Shay Run

Balanced Rock

Red Spruce Riding Trail

Trail

Shay Trace

Cabin Area

16

16

16

16

N

Kilometer

Mile

0.5

0.5

0

Blackwater Falls.

trailhead. The trail, marked with orange blazes, climbs gradually to the intersection with the blue blazed Shay Trace Trail. Continue straight, and begin an easy descent through a forest of spruce and hemlock trees. This area can be muddy. When the hemlocks give way to hardwoods, Balanced Rock Trail intersects the Red Spruce Riding Trail.

Turn left on the riding trail. Running cedars blanket the forest floor along this section of the hike. There is a short, gradual climb followed by a short descent to Shay Run. Cross the run and, at approximately 0.7 mile, look for a sign for the Balanced Rock Trail and the cabins on the opposite bank. Turn right and begin to parallel Shay Run. The Balanced Rock Trail quickly turns away from Shay Run, and there is a gradual climb into a rhododendron thicket. In the winter, the leafless trees in the canopy present a stark contrast to the dark green foliage of the rhododendron in the understory.

The trail crosses one small clearing, then reaches a trail junction in the second clearing. A right fork leads to the cabins; take the left fork to reach Balanced Rock. The trail climbs 0.1 mile to a large boulder on a rock ledge. Continue past Balanced Rock, making a steep descent back to the trail junction. Stay right on Balanced Rock Trail back to the Red Spruce Riding Trail.

At the Red Spruce Riding Trail, turn right to continue the loop, which now follows a wide road. A short climb is followed by an S-turn descent to a feeder creek. Cross the creek and begin a steady climb. There is an elevation gain of approximately 260 feet. About 200 yards past the creek turn right at the junction with the Stemwinder Trail and continue the gradual climb. This trail follows an old road grade that has been highly reclaimed by nature. The trail can be wet and muddy, and moss seems to grow everywhere.

The climb ends at the powerline, and the trail begins an easy descent to Engine Run. At times during this descent, small feeder streams flow down the middle of the trail, which is also rocky in places. The trail crosses Engine Run and intersects the Davis Trail 3.0 miles from the trailhead.

Turn left on the Davis Trail, which is marked with yellow blazes and is part of the Allegheny Trail system. The trail is a wide flat road. Cross Engine Run again and follow the yellow blazes to the right of the stables to reach the junction with the Yellow Birch Trail, about 3.25 miles from the trailhead.

The loop continues by turning left onto the Yellow Birch Trail, which is marked with yellow dots. The trail climbs a small hill, but the grade is easy. Moss, fern, and rhododendron dominate the understory. About 0.1 mile from the stables, the trail passes some rock boulders and climbs briefly, then becomes much easier. The area is free of undergrowth, but it is boggy in places. A right bend is followed by a left bend, then the trail crosses Tank Run. Continue 0.2 mile to the park road. The lodge is visible from the road.

17 Cranberry Bogs to Overlook Trail Loop
Droop Mountain Battlefield State Park

Overview: *The 237-acre Droop Mountain Battlefield State Park includes the site of one of the largest Civil War battles in West Virginia. The park is situated on a high mountain plateau overlooking the beautiful and vast Greenbrier Valley. Part of the battlefield has been restored and marked for visitors. A small museum contains Civil War artifacts, and a battle reenactment is staged every other year. Recreational opportunities include almost 4 miles of hiking trails, picnicking, and two playgrounds.*

General description: An easy hike through a small bog and along a rocky escarpment.
General location: 15 miles south of Marlinton
Length: 1.25 miles
Difficulty: Easy
Special attractions: A small mountain bog, scenic overlooks, and a walk along a mountain cliff.

Maps: Droop Mountain Battlefield State Park map; USGS quad: Droop
Camping: Day-use area only.
Seasons: The park is open daily. The office and museum hours are 10:00 A.M. to 2:00 P.M. and by request in the winter.
For information: Droop Mountain Battlefield State Park, HC 64 Box 189, Hillsboro, WV 24946; (304) 653–4254

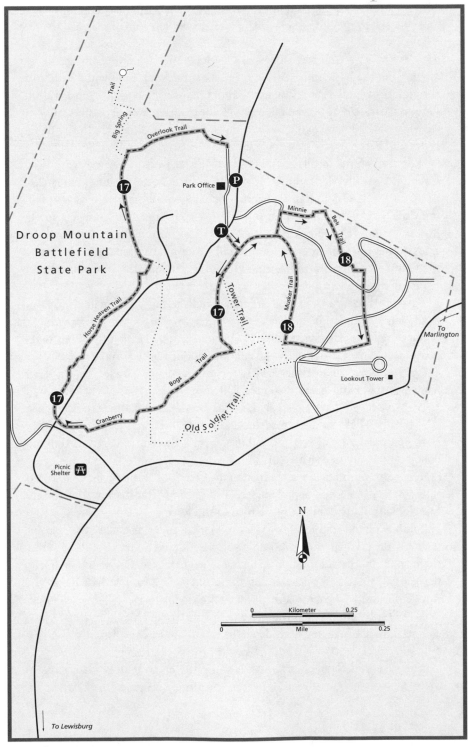

Big Spring Trail

Overlook Trail

Park Office

P

17

Droop Mountain
Battlefield
State Park

Minnie Bell Trail

T

18

17

Tower Trail

Musker Trail

18

Horse Heaven Trail

Bogs Trail

Cranberry

Old Soldier Trail

17

To
Marlington

Lookout Tower

Picnic
Shelter

N

To Lewisburg

| 0 | Kilometer | 0.25 |

| 0 | Mile | 0.25 |

Finding the trailhead: Take I–64 to exit 169 and turn north on US 219. Travel 23 miles and turn left at the park sign. At the T intersection, turn right and proceed to the office and parking area on the left side of the road.

The hike: The Cranberry Bogs to Overlook Trail Loop begins across the street from the park office. A sign marks the trailhead. Follow the wide path through the woods a short distance to the trail junction with the Musker Trail. Continue straight at this junction a very short distance to the intersection of the Tower Trail and the Cranberry Bogs Trail. The Bogs Trail exits to the right, and becomes a narrow footpath.

The trail passes through a stand of second-growth hardwoods with black birch, red oak, maple, and hickory dominating the canopy. The trail is clear of brush and is easy to follow. There is little elevation gain. After about 0.25 mile the Cranberry Bogs Trail intersects a spur trail that connects to the Tower Trail. At this intersection, the Bogs Trail turns right. Just beyond this intersection the trail enters a stand of tall white pine and black birch. This is the Cranberry Bog, a small wetland located in the middle of the natural area. A sign marks the location.

Past the bog, the trail passes under a power line. Mountain laurel and rhododendron thrive in the understory. After crossing a wide old road, Old Soldier Trail, there is an easy climb to a Y intersection. The left fork leads to the picnic area. Take the right fork and continue about 150 feet to the park road.

On the other side of the road is the trailhead for Horse Heaven Trail, named for the cliffs where the horses killed in the Battle of Droop Mountain were disposed of. There is no sign for the trailhead, but the path is obvious. The trail parallels the park road for about 0.25 mile and wanders along the edge of a rocky slope. Near the end of the trail, there is a short side trail to a bench on the end of a small cliff.

The loop continues along the road to the Overlook Trail. At the paved road, turn left and continue approximately 100 yards to the parking lot for the Overlook Trail. The trail exits the road to the left.

The Overlook Trail follows an old road for a short distance. After passing through a rocky gap, the trail begins a short climb. The trail parallels a steep ridge slope and passes through a rhododendron thicket. On the other side of the thicket, there is a sign pointing to an old bear den. Just past the den, a wooden bridge leads out to a small rock outcrop and a great view to the west. This is also the intersection with the Big Spring Trail. This short, steep trail is an out-and-back hike that leads down the mountain to a bold spring. This 0.3-mile side trip is worth the effort, if only for the cool, fresh water.

The Overlook Trail continues east along the crest. The grade is easy. At the next intersection, about 100 yards, continue straight. On the right are the remains of some Civil War trenches. After the trenches, a short, easy, climb leads back to the road. Turn right and continue about 0.1 mile to the parking area.

Heading to Big Spring.

Overview: *Located on the summit of Droop Mountain, this state park offers an assortment of tremendous vistas along its well-maintained footpaths. A small cranberry bog surrounded by tall white pines lies at the heart of this small state park.*

General description: A short hike with a wonderful view to the east from a wooden tower.

General location: 15 miles south of Marlinton

Length: 1.0 mile

Difficulty: Moderate

Special attractions: A small mountain bog, scenic overlooks, and a walk along a mountain cliff.

Maps: Droop Mountain Battlefield State Park map; USGS quad: Droop

Camping: Day-use area only.

Seasons: The park is open daily. The office and museum hours are 10:00 A.M. to 2:00 P.M., and by request in the winter.

For information: Droop Mountain Battlefield State Park, HC 64 Box 189, Hillsboro, WV 24946; (304) 653–4254

See map on page 55.

Finding the trailhead: Take I–64 to exit 169 and turn north on US 219. Travel 23 miles and turn left at the park sign. At the T intersection, turn right and proceed to the office and parking area on the left side of the road.

The hike: The Minnie Bell to Musker Trail Loop begins on the opposite side of the road from the park office. Follow the wide trail to the intersection with the Musker Trail and turn left. Walk about 100 yards to an intersection and turn left on the Minnie Bell Trail.

The Minnie Bell Trail descends to the park road. Turn right and follow the road about 75 feet to a sign for the trail. Turn right and enter the woods. Initially the descent is easy, but after a right and left switchback there is a short, steep descent. At the bottom of the descent, the trail makes a right bend, and the moderate climb to the summit and the tower begins. During the beginning of the climb, water can be heard running under the rocks. The trail crosses a bridge, makes a short climb, and flattens out as it parallels a park road. After crossing another bridge, the trail crosses the park road and begins another short, moderate climb. The trail crosses the park road a third time and makes a short climb to the summit.

On the summit is a tower that was built in the 1930s by the Civilian Conservation Corps, as well as a picnic area, playground, and toilets. The view to the east from the tower is spectacular. The Musker Trail enters the woods

A view east from the CCC tower.

near the playground and drops to cross the park road. The trail is wide and easy to follow. After a right bend, there is a moderate descent into a small hollow dominated by tall cove hardwoods. The trail bends left on the mountain shoulder and drops gradually to the intersection with the Minnie Bell Trail. Turn left and make a gradual climb back to the parking lot.

19

Robert W. Craig Campground Hiking Trails

Jennings Randolph Lake Project

Overview: *This multipurpose project is owned and operated by the U.S. Army Corps of Engineers, and is located on the North Branch of our nation's river, the Potomac. Jennings Randolph Lake was designed to improve the water quality of the river downstream of the dam, to reduce flood damage, and to provide a source of water supply for municipalities and industry downstream. The project also affords the public the opportunities for recreation such as white-water rafting, fishing, boating, camping, hiking, and sight-seeing. The Jennings Randolph Lake Visitor Center has on display the unique waffle rock.*

General description: An easy loop hike.
General location: 15 miles west of Keyser
Length: 2.3 miles
Difficulty: Easy
Special attractions: A beautifully reclaimed quarry, hiking through an upland hardwood forest, and a great view at the Sunset Trail Overlook.
Maps: Robert W. Craig Campground Hiking Trails Map; USGS quads: Kitzmiller, Westernport

Camping: Robert W. Craig Campground has eighty-four sites. Fees for camping are $12 nonelectric, $18 electric.
Seasons: Hiking is allowed only when the campground is open, late April to October.
For information: Reservoir Manager, Jennings Randolph Lake, P. O. Box 247, Elk Garden, WV 26717; (304) 355–2346

Finding the trailhead: At the intersection of US 50 and WV 42, turn north on WV 42 and travel 5.0 miles to WV 46 in Elk Garden. Turn right on WV 46 and continue 5.0 miles to the campground entrance. Turn left and proceed to the entrance station. Parking is available on the right for the trailhead for the Sunset Trail. To reach the High Timber Trail, follow the campground road. At the intersection, continue straight to the signed trailhead at site 69.

The hike: The rocky High Timber Trail, marked with orange arrows, exits site 69 and begins a gradual descent. Several trees along the trail are identified with small signs, such as a huge serviceberry tree on the left at the first right bend. Begin a gradual descent to a small stream, where there is a bench to sit and enjoy the forest.

Cross the stream on a bridge and begin a gradual climb. At a right bend the 0.5-mile Connector Spur Trail leads to the Sunset Trail and is also marked with orange arrows. Turn left on the Connector Spur Trail and descend gradually to the intersection with the Sunset Trail. At the trail junction a right provides a shortcut back to the parking area.

Robert W. Craig Campground
Hiking Trails

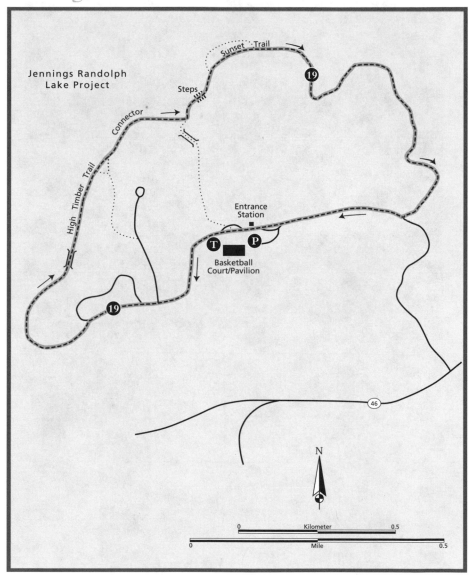

To continue the loop, continue straight on the Sunset Trail. The trail crosses the road, and heads toward the big meadow. Follow the crest of a small ridge to a TRAIL sign, turn right, and drop into the meadow. This meadow is actually a reclaimed quarry, the source of the stone used to build the dam.

Climb to the summit of a small knoll. Actually, it is worth the climb to the

Snow is one of the joys of winter hiking in West Virginia.

top as the view of the meadow is spectacular. Drop down to some picnic tables and a fence at 1.25 miles for a good view of the dam and the state of Maryland.

Continue past the fence, following a mowed trail. Skirt along the steep escarpment a short distance and then begin to cross the meadow. There are three quick, easy stream crossings. After a short climb, bend right and begin paralleling a narrow V-shaped hollow as the trail runs along the edge of the escarpment. At the picnic table, turn left and begin a short moderate climb. The trail turns left again and becomes a footpath as it enters the woods; watch for orange arrows. The grade becomes easier after entering the woods, then climbs the ridge to the road and the guardrail. Turn right on the road and walk a short distance back to the parking area.

20 The Big Loop
Kumbrabow State Forest

Overview: *Kumbrabow State Forest encompasses a total of 9,474 acres. The area is largely undeveloped and truly offers a chance to get away from it all. The forest is wide and rugged with steep slopes and tall stands of cove hardwoods.*

General description: A long loop that can be shortened depending on the route chosen.
General location: 25 miles southwest of Elkins
Length: 13.5 miles
Difficulty: Difficult
Special attractions: The views from the Mill Ridge Fire Trail and Raven Rocks.
Maps: Kumbrabow State Forest map and trail guide; USGS quads: Adolph, Pickens, Samp, Valley Head

Camping: The Kumbrabow State Forest operates a thirteen-site campground, open from April 15 through deer rifle season. The fee for camping is $10. The forest also has four- to eight-person cabins for rent.
Seasons: The hiking trails are open to the public year-round.
For information: Kumbrabow State Forest, Box 65, Huttonsville, WV 26273; (304) 335–2219

Finding the trailhead: At the intersection of CR 219-55 and CR 250-92, head south about 7 miles to the intersection of CR 219-55 and CR 219-16. Turn west on CR 219-16. Travel 3.7 miles to the Y intersection and bear left. The Mill Creek camping area is 2.1 miles on the right. The Raven Rock's trailhead is 2.4 miles on the right. The Meat Box trailhead and picnic area is 2.7 miles on the right. The Park Office and trailheads for the Clay Run Trail and Potato Hole Trail are 4.4 miles.

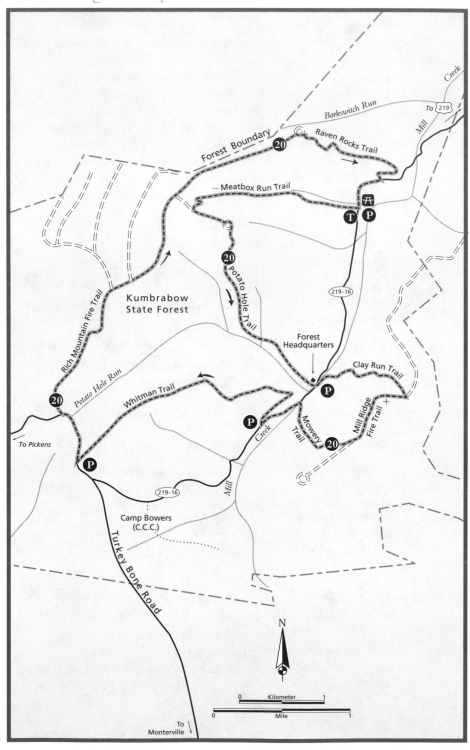

The hike: The Big Loop involves several trails forming one large loop. The size of the loop can vary considerably depending on the route selected. The Big Loop begins at the picnic area and the trailhead for the Meatbox Trail. The elevation at the trailhead is 3,080 feet. The Meatbox Trail, marked with red blazes, parallels the Meatbox Run as the climb up the mountain begins. The trail follows an old road up the left side of the hollow. A short, steep climb through an area of yellow birch is followed by an easy walk through a stand of hemlock and red spruce. Fern thrives in the moist understory.

After crossing a dry feeder stream, the trail passes through an area of significant storm damage on an easy grade. This is followed by a short moderate climb into a wet boggy area. The trail crosses many small feeder streams, then there is a hard push to the ridge crest at 1.5 miles. The trail is steep and the slopes are covered with tall straight hardwoods. On the crest is the junction with the Rich Mountain Fire Trail.

Option: For a shorter hike of about 3.8 miles, turn right on the fire road and walk to the T junction. Turn right and follow the fire road to Raven Rocks Trail. Take the Raven Rocks Trail to CR 219-16, turn right, and follow the road about 0.3 mile to the picnic area.

To continue the Big Loop, turn left. The trail now follows a wide grassy road. There is a short, gradual descent followed by an easy climb to the summit of a high knob. The knob has a small clearing, and was the site of an old fire tower, but there are no views from the knob.

At the end of the clearing, 0.4 mile from the end of the Meatbox Trail, a sign marks the junction with the Potato Hole Trail. The trail is marked with yellow blazes and begins with a steep descent. At a small stream about 0.3 mile from the trailhead, the grade becomes more moderate. The forest floor is covered with running cedar. Small spruces dot the landscape. The trail crosses three small feeder streams and enters a wide area where two larger streams converge. The trail bends left and continues its easy descent, passing a maintenance building and following a road to the park office.

Go past the park offices and cross CR 219-16. The Clay Run Trail parking area and trailhead are on the opposite side of the road. The distance from the top of the mountain to the Clay Run trailhead is 2.3 miles.

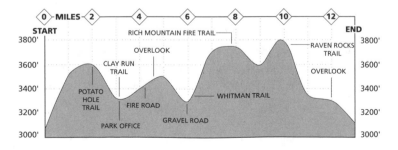

Option: Turn left on the road and walk 1.7 miles back to the parking area. The distance of this loop is 5.5 miles.

The Clay Run Trail is marked with white blazes. It passes through a small field and then crosses the Mill Creek. When the water is high, it is necessary to remove your boots. After crossing, the trail follows an old railroad grade downstream. At 0.25 mile past the road, the trail bends right and leaves the railroad grade behind. The climb is easy at first, becoming more moderate after crossing a small creek. The climb through a forest of small hardwoods continues to the crest of the ridge.

On the crest is the junction with the Mill Ridge Fire Trail (elevation 3,600 feet). There is a sign for the Clay Run Trail at the intersection. The distance from the trailhead to the fire road is 0.75 mile. Turn right on the fire road and climb the ridge on a wide grassy road. The road passes through a small timber harvest. The coppice growth is thick. At 0.25 mile from the fire road, there is a picnic table on the left and a tremendous view to the mountains farther east. The trail continues a moderate climb to the flat ridge crest and tall straight hardwoods. Black cherry and maple dominate the overstory. After a right bend and a big red oak, the Mill Ridge Fire Trail intersects the Mowery Trail. The distance from the Clay Run Trail to this junction is 1.0 mile.

Turn right on the Mowery Trail, marked with orange blazes, and begin a steep descent through a narrow hollow. The grade soon becomes easy. Cross Mowery Run and parallel Mill Creek downstream. After an easy crossing of Mill Creek, climb the steep embankment to the road. The elevation is 3,240 feet.

Turn left on CR 219-16 and walk 0.3 mile to the Whitman Trail, which exits the road to the right. There is a small parking area on the left. The 2-mile Whitman Trail, also marked with orange blazes, begins with a high moderate climb through six switchbacks. At the end of the last switchback, the grade becomes easy as the trail crests the ridge. On the crest the trail is a wide, easy-to-follow footpath.

At a small clearing, there is a boggy area, and running cedar covers the ground. On the opposite side of this small bog, the trail enters a parklike setting. The trees are widely spaced and the ground is relatively free of brush. The trail becomes a little indistinct and hard to follow, but watch for the orange blazes. There is a slight climb and the trail bends left along the crest of Whitman Knob. The elevation is almost 3,800 feet. The trail is a pleasure to walk as it intersects an old road and descends steadily to Turkey Bone Road.

Turn right on Turkey Bone Road and walk 0.4 mile to the intersection with the Rich Mountain Fire Trail, a gravel road that exits to the right. Cross the gate and gradually descend past a small clearing and a game pond. This area is in the upper reaches of the Potato Hole Run drainage. Several smaller roads that exit to the right and left lead to small timber cuts and game clearings.

After a descent into a boggy area with a forest of red spruce and hemlock, the road becomes grassy and climbs to a major fork. Take the right fork and continue

Raven Rocks provides picturesque views.

climbing, following the green blazes. After 0.25 mile of easy climbing, the trail passes a game clearing, then reaches a sign. The road to the right leads to the Meatbox Run Trail and the Potato Hole Trail. The elevation at this junction is 3,780 feet.

Option: Turn right and walk about 100 yards to the intersection of the Meatbox Run Trail. Turn left and descend to the picnic area for a hike of approximately 12.5 miles.

To continue the Big Loop, go straight. There is a sign for the Turkey Bone Road and the Raven Rocks Trail. The road is grassy and makes an easy climb along the crest to a flat region with a forest of hemlock, spruce, and yellow birch. At 3,862 feet, this is the highest point of the loop. After a short drop, the Rich Mountain Fire Trail intersects the Raven Rocks Trail.

There is a sign for the Rich Mountain Fire Trail and Raven Rocks Trail. A concrete marker puts the distance to the camping area at 2.0 miles. The trail begins with a steep descent. There is a left switchback and then a bend to the left, after which the trail begins to descend a finger ridge. This descent ends abruptly in a stand of tall hemlock and red spruce. The flat stretch is short-lived, however. A second short, steep descent through a rhododendron thicket leads to the Raven Rocks and the Raven Rocks Overlook. This small outcrop has a tremendous view of the small, narrow Mill Creek Valley. A moderate descent is followed by a steep descent, then the forest road. The distance from the crest to the road is 1.0 mile. Turn right on the road and walk 0.3 mile to the picnic area.

21

Howards Lick to Copse Cove Trail Loop / *Lost River State Park*

Overview: *This 3,712-acre park offers nearly 25 miles of trails and an almost infinite number of loops. East Ridge and Big Ridge form the eastern boundary of the park, separated by Howards Lick Run.*

General description: This loop utilizes several trails to completely circumnavigate the southern end of the state park. Utilizing other side trails, loops of almost any distance and difficulty can be hiked.

General location: 7 miles southwest of Lost City

Length: 5.50 miles

Difficulty: Difficult

Special attractions: A pleasant hike along Howard Lick followed by a challenging climb up East Ridge.

Maps: Lost River State Park map and trail guide; USGS quad: Lost River State Park

Camping: Backpacking is allowed in the backcountry in the northeast section of the park by permit only.

Seasons: The park is open for hiking year-round.

For information: Lost River State Park, HC 67 Box 24, Mathias, WV 26812; (304) 897–5372

Finding the trailhead: At the intersection of WV 259 and CR 12 in Mathias, turn west on CR 12. Proceed 4.1 miles and turn left on the main park road. Continue 0.1 mile to a parking area on the left.

The hike: To reach the trailhead for the Howard Lick Trail, cross the parking lot and walk along the wide path through the grass past the swimming pool. After 100 feet the trail crosses the road. There is a sign for the orange blazed Razor Ridge Trail and the blue blazed Howards Lick Trail. The elevation is 2,000 feet. The Razor Ridge Trail takes the right fork and begins to climb. Follow the left fork down a short hill and begin to parallel the Howards Lick Run. The path is wide and easy to follow.

The trail crosses the run and then crosses CR 12. After a short distance, the trail crosses the road to the stables and meanders along the left bank of Howards Lick Run on an easy grade. Small rock cliffs adorn the bank to the left of the trail. The creek itself is a series of small, rock shelf waterfalls. Just before reaching CR 12 again, cross the run on a swinging bridge, 1.25 miles from the trailhead. The elevation at this point is 1,840 feet, the lowest point on the hike.

Turn left on the road and walk about 100 feet to the trailhead for the East Ridge Trail, which exits to the south side of CR 12 and is marked with red blazes. Once in the woods, the trail bends right and begins a moderate climb

Howards Lick to Copse Cove Trail Loop, White Oak to Big Ridge Loop

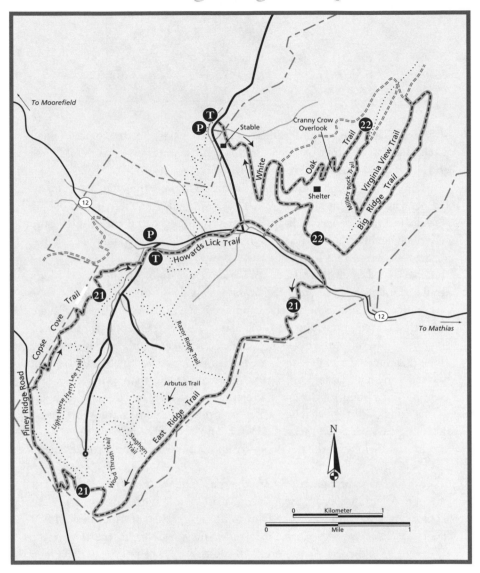

through a forest of old second-growth hardwoods. Tulip poplar, red oak, white oak, maple, and hickory dominate the canopy in this sheltered cove.

After 0.2 mile, there is a left bend and the trail enters a narrow hollow. Cross a dry branch and begin a moderate climb up the right side of the ravine. A right switchback signals the beginning of the climb up the finger ridge,

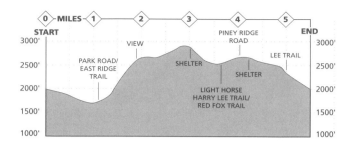

which is steady and at times difficult. The dry ridge crest is home to small pitch pine and chestnut oak. The trail is a heart pounder, but several bends and switchbacks help in the relentless climb to the crest.

After crossing under a power line, the grade becomes much easier. A broad left bend means the big climb is over. The elevation is 2,680 feet. The trail now actually begins to descend a little. The trail drops over to the west side of the mountain, and parallels the crest. About 0.25 mile after reaching the crest, the Razor Ridge Trail exits to the right

Option: To shorten the hike to 3.75 miles, turn right on the Razor Ridge Trail and follow it south until it again intersects the East Ridge trail.

Continue straight at this junction and begin an easy climb on the East Ridge Trail to the second junction with the Razor Ridge Trail. After another 0.25 mile, the yellow blazed Arbutus Trail exits right and descends quickly down the ridge. Continue straight on the East Ridge Trail, passing the Staghorn Trail, marked with blue blazes, which also descends to the right. After passing a clearing and a house on the left, there is a small shelter near the highest point of the climb, 2,900 feet. The shelter is located at the beginning of a long descent. After two switchbacks, the Wood Thrush Trail exits to the right. After two more switchbacks, the trail wraps around a large bowl at the southern end of the park.

After passing through the bowl, the East Ridge Trail ends at a Y trail junction 3.75 miles from the parking area. The Light Horse Harry Lee Trail follows the right fork. The loop continues on the left fork, the Red Fox Trail, which begins a moderate 0.25-mile climb back up to the ridge crest following an old road. At the crest, the Red Fox Trail intersects the Piney Ridge Road; turn right.

As the name suggests, the loop is now following an old road across the top of Piney Ridge. The grade is easy. A short descent is followed by a gradual climb up to a second small shelter at an elevation of 2,680 feet. After a short descent the Covey Cove Trail exits to the right; continue straight. The road descends briefly before coming to a pasture and a gate. There is a sign here for the Copse Cove Trail. Fifty feet beyond the sign, turn left on the yellow blazed Copse Cove Trail.

Initially, the trail follows the fence line. Then there is a moderate descent through four switchbacks. Somewhere along the way, the trail picks up white blazes, but the trail is still marked with yellow blazes. There is another steep descent to a small hollow covered with muscadine grape vines, then a short climb to the junction with the Lee Trail, which exits to the right. Stay on the Copse Cove Trail, which continues its easy descent along the ridge.

After a left bend, the trail enters a small sheltered hollow. It crosses a dry creek bed and then parallels it for a short distance. A second left bend leads the trail into another small hollow. The trail crosses a small creek and then makes a short, steep descent back into the first drainage. A left bend leads to a short climb and a trail junction, where there is a sign that says CABIN 2. The Copse Cove Trail continues straight. Take the right fork and descend toward Cabin 2. Pass the cabin and cross the bridge. The parking area is across the road.

22   White Oak to Big Ridge Loop
Lost River State Park

Overview: *The 25 miles of trails in Lost River State Park range from short and easy to long and difficult. In addition to hiking, the park also offers cabins, swimming, picnicking, and horseback riding, as well as a bit of early American history. It once belonged to Light Horse Harry Lee, the father of General Robert E. Lee.*

General description: This loop climbs to the crest of Big Ridge and offers several wonderful panoramic views to the east.

General location: 7 miles southwest of Lost City

Length: 6.0 miles

Difficulty: Difficult

Special attractions: Big rock outcrops with great views and quiet backcountry.

Maps: Lost River State Park map and trail guide; USGS quad: Lost River State Park

Camping: Backpacking is allowed in the backcountry in the northeast section of the park by permit only.

Seasons: The park is open to hiking year-round.

For information: Lost River State Park, HC 67 Box 24, Mathias, WV 26812; (304) 897–5372

See map on page 69.

Finding the trailhead: At the intersection of 259 and CR 12 in Mathias, turn west on CR 12. Proceed 3.7 miles and turn right on the road to the stables. Travel 0.5 mile to a small parking area and the White Oak Trailhead on the right.

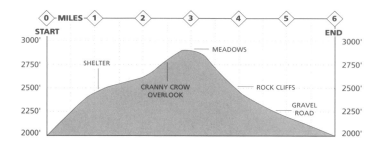

The hike: The White Oak to Big Ridge Loop is an orange blazed trail that begins just past the stables. The trailhead, at an elevation of 1,960 feet, is on the east side of the road. The beginning of the trail is a short climb up the road embankment. After crossing a small feeder creek, the trail passes the stables and begins a gradual climb up the side of the finger ridge. The beginning of the trail suffers from severe erosion.

The forest is composed of pine and chestnut oak. Blueberry and mountain laurel fill the understory. After a left bend, the trail climbs the actual ridge. Cross a road and pass under a power line. The trail is now on the side of the ridge again. In the winter there is a good view back to the southern end of the park. Another left bend puts the trail back on the finger ridge, and the grade is moderate.

After a right switchback and a third left bend, there is a small shelter with an excellent view. The shelter is about the halfway point of the climb, at an elevation of 2,500 feet. The trail really begins to climb the ridge after the shelter. There are several bends and switchbacks during the climb, which is long and difficult.

Near the crest of the ridge is the junction with the Millers Rock Trail, a long trail that extends from one end of Big Ridge to the other. The distance from the trailhead to this junction is 1.5 miles, and the elevation is 2,800 feet. Turn right on the yellow blazed Millers Rock Trail and head south to Cranny Crow Overlook, a stone shelter with a view back to Virginia. The trail descends rapidly to Cheeks Rock, an outcrop that offers another expansive view to the southeast. Continue descending to the Virginia View Trail. Another rock outcrop is visible just beyond the junction with the Virginia View Trail.

Turn left on the Virginia View Trail and begin climbing back up Big Ridge. The trail is marked with red blazes and the grade is easy, climbing gradually for 0.6 mile to Big Ridge Trail.

At the junction with the Big Ridge Trail, turn left and climb up to the meadow, where there is a small shelter, picnic tables, a privy, and an old log cabin built in the 1840s. The added distance (0.6 mile) is worth the effort.

The Big Ridge Trail is a heavily used trail marked with yellow blazes. It begins with a steep descent and then levels out for a short distance, followed by another steep descent down to a road junction. Take the right fork and follow the trail as it bends around the base of Cheeks Rock. The grade near this rock face is easy. Past the rock face, the trail begins a moderate descent to the gravel road. Turn right on the gravel road and make an easy climb about 0.4 mile to the junction with the White Oak Trail. Turn left on the White Oak Trail and descend to the parking area.

23 Scarlet Oak to Hilltop Trail Loop / *Seneca State Forest*

Overview: *Seneca State Forest is 11,684 acres of forestland located in the heart of Pocahontas County. The forest has more than 23 miles of trails and loops for beginners and even the most seasoned hiker. In addition to hiking, Seneca State Forest offers a host of other recreational opportunities, including bicycling, rowboat and canoe rentals, and fishing.*

General description: A short loop hike up one narrow finger ridge and then down another.

General location: 10 miles northeast of Marlinton

Length: 2.5 miles

Difficulty: Easy

Special attractions: A dry upland hardwood forest with a ground covering of blueberry and mountain laurel.

Maps: Seneca State Forest trail map; USGS quads: Clover Lick, Paddy Knob

Camping: The State Forest has a ten-site campground that is open from mid-April to early December. The fee is $10. Free overnight camping by permission of the superintendent is possible at the shelter on the Allegheny Trail/Loop Road. The forest also has cabins for rent.

Seasons: Hiking is available year-round, but the road may be closed in the winter by snow.

For information: Seneca State Forest, Route 1 Box 140, Dunmore, WV 24934; (304) 799–6213

Finding the trailhead: From the intersection of US 219 and US 39 in Marlinton, go east on US 39. Travel 5.4 miles and turn north on WV 28. Proceed 10.3 miles to the Seneca State Forest entrance and office. Continue 0.5 mile to a small parking spot on the left. A Scarlet Oak Trail sign marks the trailhead.

The hike: The Scarlet Oak Trail is across the road from the parking spot. The trail, marked with red squares, begins with a 0.2-mile moderate climb followed

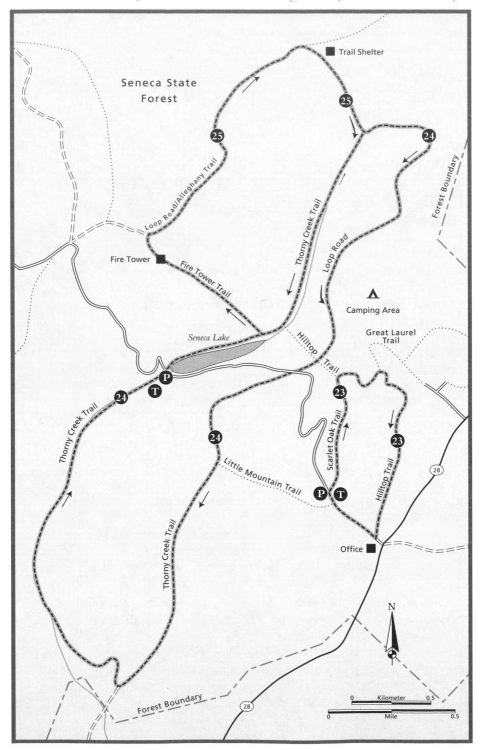

Trail Shelter

Seneca State Forest

25

25

24

Forest Boundary

Loop Road/Alleghany Trail

Fire Tower

Fire Tower Trail

Thorny Creek Trail

Loop Road

Camping Area

Great Laurel Trail

Seneca Lake

Hilltop Trail

Thorny Creek Trail

P
T

24

23

Scarlet Oak Trail

24

Little Mountain Trail

Hilltop Trail

28

23

P T

Office

N

Thorny Creek Trail

Forest Boundary

28

28

| 0 | Kilometer | 0.5 |
| 0 | Mile | 0.5 |

by an easy 0.2-mile section. The trail climbs the finger ridge to the ridge crest. The canopy of the finger ridge comprises a mix of pine and dry upland oaks. The trail enters a small saddle dominated by a large hemlock and many very small white pines. There is one final steep climb to the loop road at 0.5 mile.

At the road, turn right and walk 0.1 mile to the Hilltop Trail, which exits the loop road on both the right and left. Turn right and begin a steep descent along a narrow finger ridge. The trail levels out and then traverses the ridge at an easy pace. At the beginning of the next major descent, the Great Laurel Trail exits left and descends to the State Forest campground.

The Hilltop Trail continues straight and makes a moderate descent to another flat region, then gradually climbs and descends until it reaches a sign. The trail turns right at the sign and starts to drop of the ridge. The descent is moderate. At a left bend, the trail begins to parallel a small stream, entering a sheltered cove dominated by white pine and hemlock. The trail follows the stream to the entrance road. Turn right on the entrance road and walk 0.4 mile back to the parking area.

Thorny Creek Trail
Seneca State Forest

Overview: *Seneca State Forest's 23 miles of trails include sections of the Greenbrier Rail Trail and the Allegheny Trail. The sheltered creek bottom along Thorny Creek Trail is the home to a thriving stand of towering white pine and small hemlock and cove hardwoods.*

General description: A long loop hike through the heart of the state forest.
General location: 10 miles northeast of Marlinton
Length: 6.1 miles
Difficulty: Moderate
Special attractions: The Thorny Creek Trail climbs easily along the Thorny Creek through rhododendron tunnels.
Maps: Seneca State Forest trail map; USGS quads: Clover Lick, Paddy Knob
Camping: The state forest has a ten-site campground that is open from mid-April to early December. The fee is $10. Free overnight camping by permission of the superintendent is possible at the shelter on the Allegheny Trail/Loop Road. The forest also has cabins for rent.
Seasons: Hiking is available year-round, but the road may be impassable due to snow in the winter.
For information: Seneca State Forest, Route 1 Box 140, Dunmore, WV 24934; (304) 799–6213

See map on page 74.

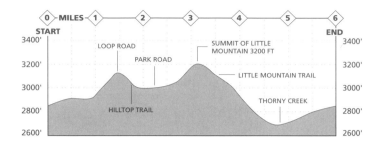

Finding the trailhead: From the intersection of US 219 and US 39 in Marlinton, go east on US 39. Travel 5.4 miles and turn north on WV 28. Proceed 10.3 miles to the Seneca State Forest entrance and office. Continue 1.7 miles to the parking area on the left, just beyond the bridge that passes over the lake spillway. This is the parking area for the Thorny Creek Trail loop and the Thorny Creek to Allegheny Trail Loop.

The hike: The Thorny Creek Trail, marked with blue circles, begins at the boat docks. A sign marks the trailhead. The trail parallels the left bank of Seneca Lake under a canopy of hemlock trees. At the end of the lake (about 0.3 mile), the Fire Tower Trail exits left. The Thorny Creek Trail continues an easy grade. About 0.1 mile from the Fire Tower Trail junction, the Hilltop Trail exits right.

Option: To shorten the loop (about 3.0 miles), turn right and climb 0.2 mile to Loop Road, turn right, and walk 0.2 mile to the entrance road.

The Thorny Creek Trail goes straight and enters the woods, crossing a small feeder creek via a wooden bridge and continuing an easy grade. About 0.5 mile from the trail junction, the trail bends left and crosses the creek, then bends left and follows an old grade through a rhododendron tunnel. Tall white pine, hemlock, and cove hardwoods dominate the canopy. The trail climbs gradually, paralleling Thorny Creek. The creek forks and the trail parallels the right fork. After the fork, the grade becomes moderate. Just before Loop Road, the trail bends right and climbs steeply to the road. The distance to the road is 1.3 miles.

At the road (elevation 3,160 feet), turn right. Loop Road makes a series of easy climbs and descents. Follow the road past the junctions with the Hilltop Trail and the Scarlet Oak Trail.

Option: At the Hilltop Trail, the loop can be shortened considerably. Turn right on the Hilltop Trail and drop down to the Thorny Creek Trail. Turn left and follow the trail to the trailhead for a hike of approximately 2.6 miles.

Rains may quickly fill even the smallest stream to capacity.

The Thorny Creek Trail crosses the entrance road and enters the woods at about 2.4 miles. The trail is wide and easy to follow. The forest is composed of early second-growth hardwoods. The next mile is a series of ups and downs along an old road with a marked increase in elevation. The last climb is a moderate grade to the crest of a small knoll, the summit of Little Mountain (elevation 3,200 feet). After the knoll, the road drops sharply to the intersection with the Little Mountain Trail at 3.5 miles. This trail exits left and drops rapidly to the entrance road. The Thorny Creek Trail continues along the old road in a series of gentle ups and downs. At a sign, the trail bends right and exits the road.

There is a left switchback about 150 feet past the sign, then a short, steep descent to a narrow ridge crest. Follow the crest to a fence, turn right, and begin another steep descent to a small feeder creek. At the creek, make a left switchback and then parallel the small creek a short distance. The trail bends right and climbs over a small finger ridge, then drops down to the Thorny Creek (elevation 2,680 feet) at 4.7 miles. Tall white pine dominates the canopy.

The trail parallels the Thorny Creek on an easy grade. At times the trail passes through rhododendron tunnels, and the remains of a log structure are visible on the right in the creek bottom. The trail crosses the creek via a wooden bridge and bends right. After passing through a small clearing, the Thorny Creek Trail climbs a short distance and then makes a short, steep drop back to a small feeder creek. Cross this creek and follow the trail as it bends right and begins to climb again. At the end of this climb, cross the bridge and climb the hill to the parking area.

25

Thorny Creek to Allegheny Trail
Loop / *Seneca State Forest*

Overview: *Seneca State Forest is under the umbrella of the West Virginia Division of Forestry. The forest management plan is controlled by the concept of multiple use. Therefore, forest management practices attempt to maintain a healthy forest ecosystem for a variety of wildlife, as well as protect and preserve watersheds and water quality. In addition, Seneca State Forest provides a multitude of recreational activities.*

General description: A loop hike with a short brutal climb up a narrow finger ridge, followed by a long gradual descent back to the trailhead.

General location: 10 miles northeast of Marlinton

Length: 4.0 miles

Difficulty: Moderate

Special attractions: An old fire tower surrounded by tall spruce.

Maps: Seneca State Forest trail map; USGS quads: Clover Lick, Paddy Knob

Camping: The state forest has a ten-site campground that is open from mid-April to early December. The fee is $10. Free overnight camping by permission of the superintendent is possible at the shelter on the Allegheny Trail/Loop Road. The forest also has cabins for rent.

Seasons: Hiking is available year-round, but the road may be closed in the winter by snow.

For information: Seneca State Forest, Route 1 Box 140, Dunmore, WV 24934; (304) 799–6213

See map on page 74.

Finding the trailhead: From the intersection of US 219 and US 39 in Marlinton, go east on US 39. Travel 5.4 miles and turn north on WV 28. Proceed 10.3 miles to the Seneca State Forest entrance and office. Continue 1.7 miles to the parking area on the left, just beyond the bridge that passes over the lake spillway. This is the parking area for the Thorny Creek Trail and the Thorny Creek to Allegheny Trail Loop.

The hike: The Thorny Creek to Allegheny Trail Loop begins at the boat docks. A sign marks the trailhead for the Thorny Creek Trail, which is marked with blue circles. The trail parallels the left bank of Seneca Lake under a canopy of hemlock trees. At the end of the lake (about 0.3 mile), turn left on the Fire Tower Trail, marked with green squares.

The Fire Tower Trail begins with a steep climb, followed by a short breather stretch and then another moderate climb as it travels up a narrow finger ridge. At the top of the second climb is an old telephone pole with old glass insulators and wires. More poles form a line all the way to the summit. Another short breather is followed by a third short, steep climb. The forest here is composed

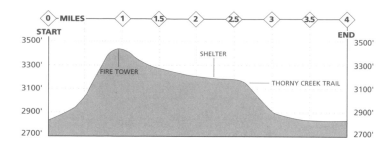

of small second-growth hardwoods. Another short, flat stretch leads to the fourth, final, and worst climb of them all.

At the summit, an old fire tower is surrounded by dark black spruce and hemlock. The trees have grown so tall that they now limit the view from the tower, which still has all its steps intact and is climbable. However, a sign warns that one climbs the tower at their risk. The elevation at the tower is 3,440 feet, the highest point of the loop. The distance from the trailhead is 1.1 miles.

From the tower, the trail follows a road downhill to the right. After 150 feet, the road intersects Loop Road and the Allegheny Trail, which is marked with yellow blazes. Turn right on the Allegheny Trail, following Loop Road northeast in a series of easy ups and downs. After 1.1 miles, there is a shelter on the left. The Allegheny Trail exits the loop road left and begins to climb. Stay on Loop Road, which begins to descend at a moderate grade through an S turn. At the bottom of this descent, turn to the right at the trail sign and follow the blue dot Thorny Creek Trail. The elevation at this junction is 3,160 feet. The distance from the trailhead is 2.7 miles.

The Thorny Creek Trail makes a short, moderate descent to a left bend and a small springhead, which marks the beginning of the Thorny Creek. The trail begins to travel along the left side of the creek. The moderate descent continues to the point where two small streams come together in a narrow hollow. The forest in this area changes from upland hardwoods to sheltered cove species, and rhododendron starts to crowd the trail. The trail follows an old road grade to a creek crossing, which is marked by several blue circles. Watch carefully for this crossing, as it can be easy to miss. After the crossing, the trail continues to parallel the creek.

There is a thick stand of white pine and hemlock at a bridge that crosses a small feeder stream. The Hilltop Trail exits left; the Thorny Creek Trail continues along the right creek bank a short distance back to the junction with the Fire Tower Trail. Continue straight at the Fire Tower Trail to complete the hike.

26 Arrowhead Trail to Jesse's Cove Trail Loop / *Watoga State Park*

Overview: *Watoga State Park, West Virginia's largest state park, encompasses a total of 10,100 acres. The 330-mile Allegheny Trail snakes along the eastern boundary of the park, and the scenic 81-mile Greenbrier River Trail borders its western end. In addition to hiking, the park offers many recreational activities, including swimming, horseback riding, cross-country skiing, tennis, tubing, and horseshoes. The park also has two campgrounds as well as rental cabins for those looking for more comfortable lodgings.*

General description: This loop climbs a high ridge to a wooden tower with a great view to the west. A pleasant walk along a high ridge leads to a steep drop back to the Greenbrier River.

General location: 10 miles southwest of Marlinton

Length: 5.3 miles

Difficulty: Moderate

Special attractions: The Ann Bailey Observation Tower and the hike down Rock Run.

Maps: Watoga State Park trail map; USGS quads: Denmar, Hillsboro, Lake Sherwood, Marlinton

Camping: The park has two campgrounds. The Riverside campground is open from April 1 through the first week of December. The fee for camping is $13 to $17.

Seasons: The park is open for hiking year-round, but the road may be covered with snow in winter.

For information: Watoga State Park, HC 82 Box 252, Marlinton, WV 24954; (304) 799–4087

Finding the trailhead: From the stoplight at the intersection of US 219 and US 39 in Marlinton, proceed south on US 219. Travel 9.6 miles to CR 27. Turn left and continue 3.1 miles to a fork in the road, where there is a state park information sign. Continue straight 0.4 mile to the campground store. The parking area for the Arrowhead Trail is on the left, directly across the road from the store. Water and rest room facilities are available at the campground store.

The hike: A sign at the trailhead marks the beginning of the Arrowhead Trail, which follows an old road into the woods. The elevation is 2,100 feet, and yellow blazes mark the trail. About 100 feet from the trailhead, turn left onto another old road. The grade begins a moderate climb through a forest of small hardwoods and pine. The understory is composed primarily of mountain laurel and blueberry. Follow the road approximately 0.5 mile to an Arrowhead Trail sign; turn left. The trail continues following an old road. Initially, the grade is moderate as the trail begins climbing a finger ridge, but at the

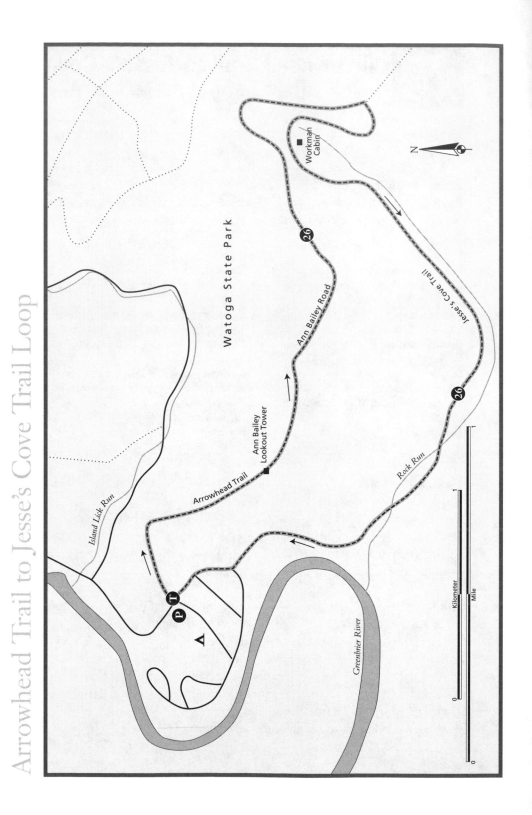

Arrowhead Trail to Jesse's Cove Trail Loop

Patrol cabin on Jesse's Cove Trail.

beginning of a left bend, the climb quickly changes to grueling as the trail climbs straight up the finger ridge to the Ann Bailey observation tower.

The wooden observation tower sits at about 2,900 feet, and offers a splendid view of the Greenbrier River and the mountains to the west. There is a picnic table in the grassy opening in front of the tower. The Arrowhead Trail ends at the tower, but the narrow, grassy Ann Bailey Road continues past the tower and along the ridge. No blazes mark the way, but the direction is obvious. The road descends a short distance and then begins an easy climb to a small meadow 1.2 miles from the tower. The forest is an old second-growth stand of upland hardwoods.

At the beginning of the meadow is the small gravestone of Forest S. Workman, who farmed this area before the land was acquired by the state. The

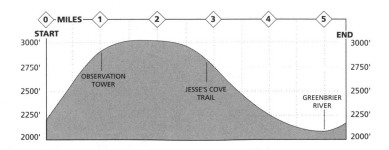

meadow also marks the high point of the climb, slightly more then 3,000 feet. The road parallels the meadow a short distance, and then drops to the junction with the yellow blazed Jesse's Cove Trail. A sign marks the junction; turn right and descend off the ridge.

Jesse's Cove Trail follows a narrow old road and descends at a moderate rate a short distance to a left switchback. After the switchback, the trail drops down to an old log cabin located in a small clearing. There is a privy here. Past the cabin, Jesse's Cove Trail begins to parallel Rock Run. About 0.25 mile beyond the cabin, the road disappears and a footpath takes its place. The Rock Run tumbles down a narrow, steep-walled ravine. Rhododendron, mountain laurel, and hemlock dominate the scenery within the narrow confines of a creek bed. The trail drops sharply down to the creek and follows the creek bed briefly before crossing to the opposite bank. The trail continues along the left bank for a short distance, then crosses back to the other side. The second crossing is much easier.

After the second crossing, the descent moderates. Tall hemlocks line the left side of the creek, while cove hardwoods occupy the right slope. The trail bends right and exits the Rock Run drainage, and the Greenbrier River is now visible. The trail hugs a steep slope then makes a steep descent to the river, turns right, and heads upstream. The grade is flat as the trail enters the Riverside Campground at site 6. Turn right on the road and follow it to the campground store.

Honeybee Trail
Watoga State Park

Overview: *The Brooks Memorial Arboretum Trail System in Watoga State Park is a true delight. Located near one of the cabin areas in the park, the trail system comprises three trails. The Dragon Draft and Buckhorn Trails interconnect with the Honeybee Trail, allowing for loop hikes of various lengths.*

General description: The Honeybee Trail is a long loop trail around the hollow formed by the Two Mile Run.
General Location: 10 miles southwest of Marlinton
Length: 4.5 miles
Difficulty: Moderate
Special attractions: Great ridge-top hiking and a wonderful walk along a lush green creek bottom.
Maps: Watoga State Park trail map; USGS quads: Denmar, Hillsboro, Lake Sherwood, Marlinton

Camping: The park has two campgrounds. The Riverside campground is open from April 1 to the end of deer rifle season. The fee for camping is $13 to $17.
Seasons: The park is open for hiking year-round, but the road may be covered with snow in winter.
For information: Watoga State Park, HC 82 Box 252, Marlinton, WV 24954; (304) 799–4087

Finding the trailhead: From the stoplight at the intersection of US 219 and US 39 in Marlinton, proceed south on US 219. Travel 9.6 miles to CR 27. Turn left and drive 3.1 miles to a fork in the road. Turn left and continue 1.4 miles to a parking area on the right. There is a large sign for the Brooks Memorial Arboretum.

The hike: The Honeybee Trail, marked with red blazes, crosses the bridge and begins to parallel Two Mile Run. About 0.1 mile from the bridge, the Honeybee Trail splits. Continue straight up the creek drainage along the flat, easy-to-follow trail. Signs along the trail identify the surrounding trees. The

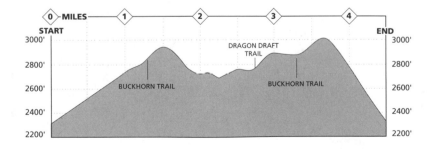

Honeybee Trail

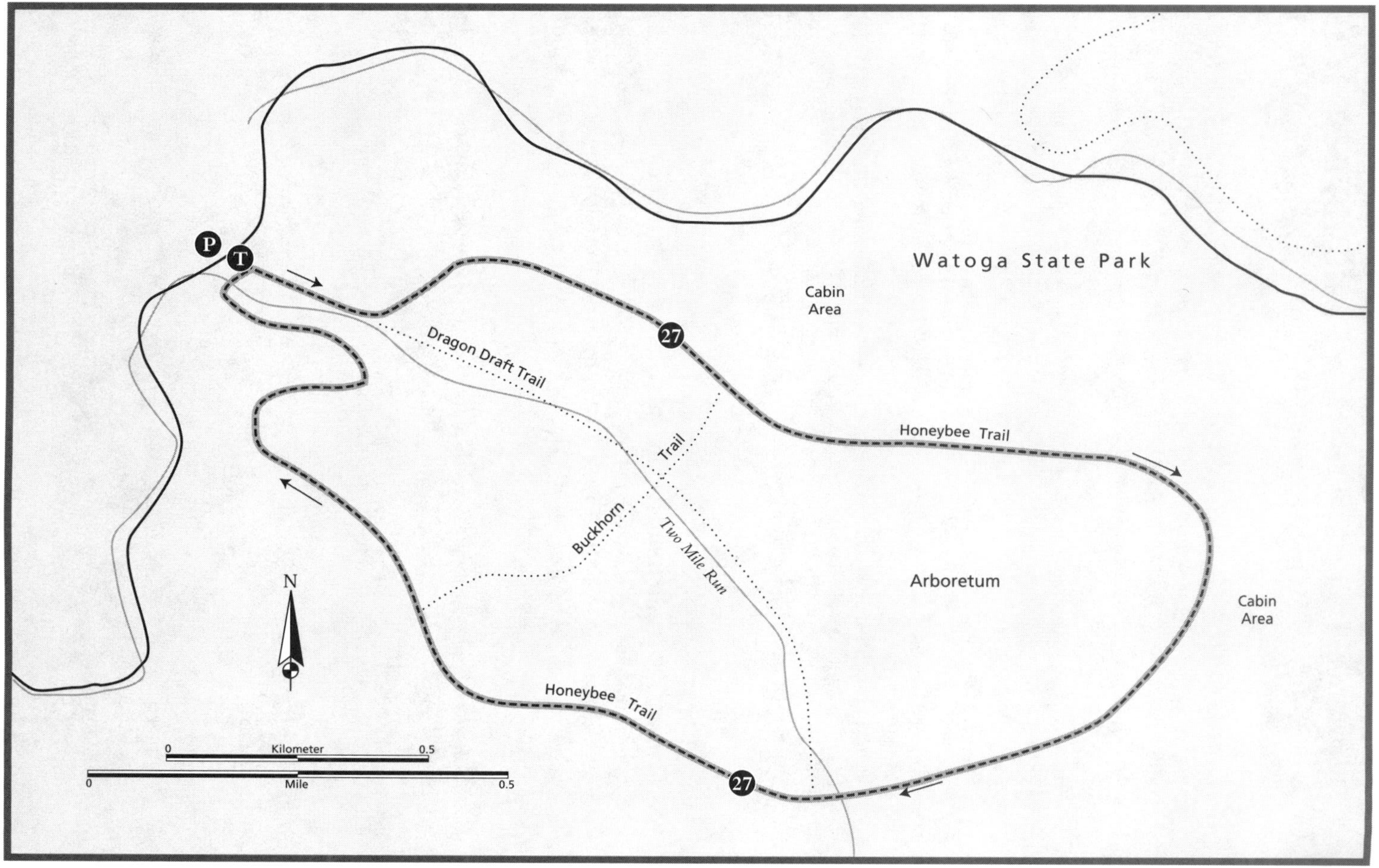

Watoga State Park

Cabin Area

Cabin Area

Arboretum

Honeybee Trail

Honeybee Trail

Dragon Draft Trail

Buckhorn Trail

Two Mile Run

27

27

P T

N

Kilometer

Mile

0   0.5

0   0.5

Shelter in Brooks Memorial Arboretum.

trail crosses the creek via a wooden bridge, after which the Dragon Draft Trail turns right. Stay left to remain on the Honeybee Trail.

The trail makes a right switchback and begins to climb the ridge on the left side of the creek. The climb is moderate for the first 0.4 mile. Near the top of this climb is a small rock overhang and a wooden bench to rest on. The trail continues to climb, but the grade is easy. After climbing almost to the ridge crest, the trail wraps around a bowl. The forest is composed of upland hardwoods. The trail passes around a second bowl and over a finger ridge, where the Buckhorn Trail exits right at 1.3 miles.

At the intersection with the Buckhorn Trail, the Honeybee Trail bends left and continues an easy climb to 2,920 feet. About 0.1 mile from the intersection, the trail drops off the right side of the ridge and descends to a small feeder creek then climbs easily over a finger ridge and across the upper end of another small feeder stream. On the next finger ridge, the trail descends moderately to Two Mile Run and the intersection with the Dragon Draft Trail at 2.7 miles. There is a broken-down shelter at the junction. The Dragon Draft Trail exits right and follows Two Mile Run downstream.

Continue straight on the Honeybee Trail and pass through a rhododendron tunnel. At the end of the tunnel, the trail passes through a small drainage, makes a left switchback, and climbs the ridge. Some of the trees in this area are labeled with brown tags. After a right bend, the trail continues its moderate climb, passes through another bowl and over a finger ridge, and enters a rhododendron thicket. The slope on the right is very steep. Once out of the thicket, the Honeybee Trail again intersects the Buckhorn Trail at 3.4 miles. The Buckhorn Trail exits right and descends.

The Honeybee Trail climbs steeply up the ridge to an elevation of about 3,000 feet. There are two switchbacks during this climb. After cresting the ridge, the trail begins a long, moderate descent. There is a bench just before the final descent back to Two Mile Run, then the trail bends right and descends again. After a left switchback, the Honeybee Trail closes the loop. Turn left to walk back to the parking area.

28 Honeymoon Trail
Watoga State Park

Overview: *Watoga State Park lies in the heart of the Greenbrier Valley. The Greenbrier River forms the western edge of the park. The wooded backland of the park is a recreational paradise. The park's lengthy trail system allows for easy leg-stretcher and long, difficult day adventures. Trails meander along fast moving streams and make long difficult climbs through steep, narrow ravines.*

General description: A trail system on the eastern end of the park that climbs through an upland hardwood forest.
General location: 10 miles southwest of Marlinton
Length: 2.5 miles, with an additional 2.0-mile option
Difficulty: Moderate
Special attractions: A small stand of spruce, once one of the dominant species of the West Virginia forest ecosystem.
Maps: Watoga State Park trail map; USGS quads: Denmar, Hillsboro, Lake Sherwood, Marlinton

Camping: The park has two campgrounds. The Riverside campground is open from April 1 to the end of deer rifle season. The fee for camping is $13 to $17.
Seasons: The park is open for hiking year-round, but the road may be covered with snow in winter.
For information: Watoga State Park, HC 82 Box 252, Marlinton, WV 24954; (304) 799–4087

Finding the trailhead: From the stoplight at the intersection of US 219 and US 39 in Marlinton, proceed south on US 219. Travel 9.6 miles to CR 27. Turn left and continue 3.1 miles to a fork in the road, where there is a state park information sign. Turn left at the fork, continue 4.5 miles, and turn right on Pine Run Cabins Road. Travel 0.3 mile and turn right onto the Pine Cabin Road. Continue past the sign for the Honeymoon Trail, bear to the left at the

Honeymoon Trail

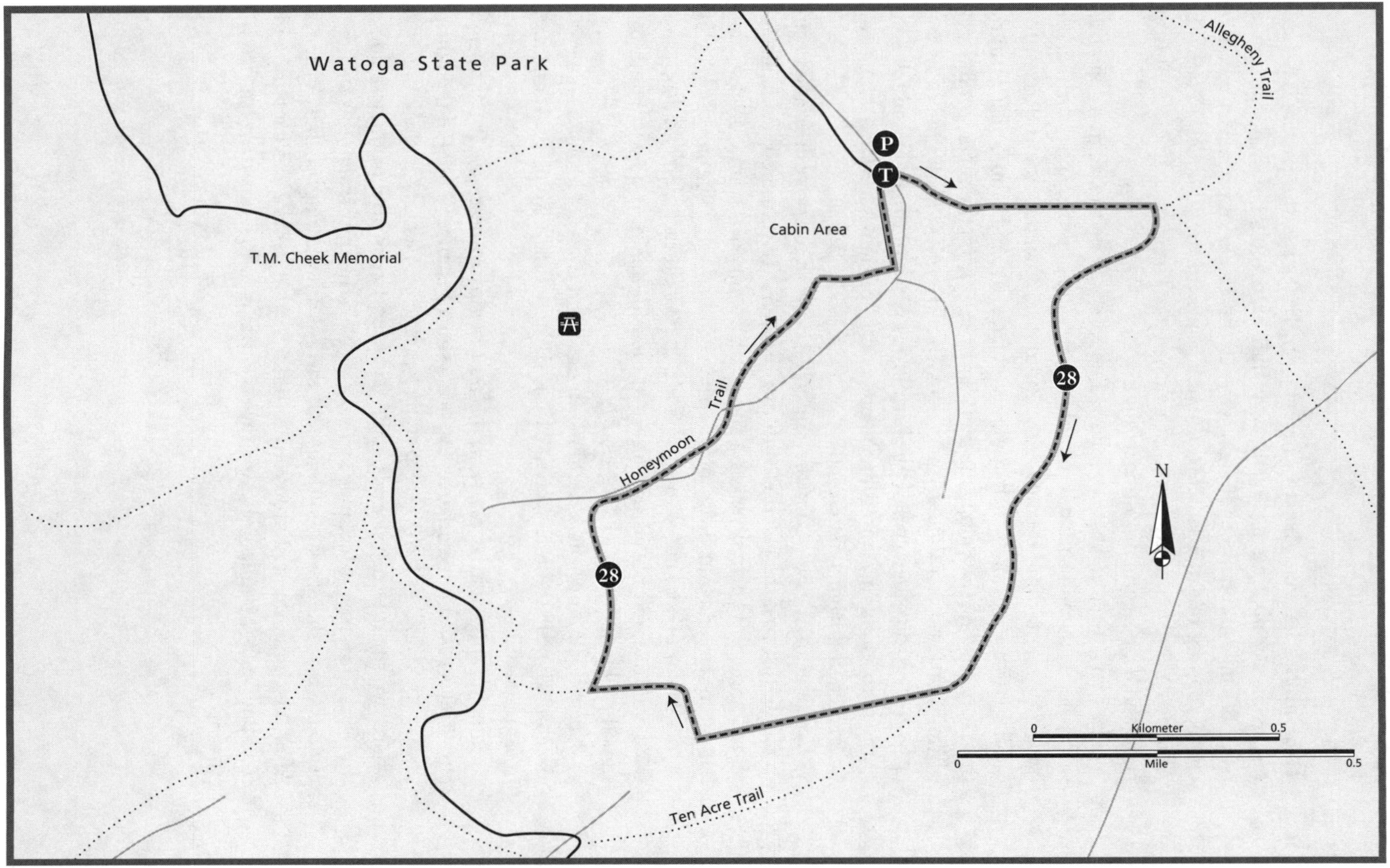

Watoga State Park

Allegheny Trail

Cabin Area

Honeymoon Trail

T.M. Cheek Memorial

Ten Acre Trail

28

28

N

P

T

Kilometer

Mile

0.5

0.5

0

0

Y, and travel 0.1 mile to the end of the road. A sign marks the trailhead for the Honeymoon Trail.

The hike: The white blazed Honeymoon Trail exits the parking area and begins an easy climb along a small creek. Tall white pines dominate the canopy. After 0.1 mile the trail bends right, crosses the creek, and begins a moderate climb, topping out in a saddle at the junction with the Allegheny Trail. The Allegheny Trail continues straight or turns left. The Honeymoon Trail turns right and begins climbing a finger ridge.

The trail is wide and easy to follow. The forest along the ridge is composed of dry slope pine and chestnut oak. Blueberry and mountain laurel thrive in the understory. The climb becomes easy, and the trail begins a short descent to a saddle. Large hardwoods such as red oak, black oak, and tulip poplar form the overstory. Beyond the saddle, the trail climbs steeply up the ridge. On the crest of the next knoll is a sign warning cross-country skiers of the hill. The trail crosses a narrow ridge crest with sharp drops on both the right and left sides of the trail. Along this crest is the junction with the Ten-Acre Trail, which exits on the left and begins to descend.

Continue on the Honeymoon Trail as it stays with the ridge crest and begins to climb. Just past the junction with the Ten-Acre Trail, there is a small stand of red spruce. The trail makes a moderate climb to a rounded crest, then begins to descend and drops off the right side of the ridge down to an old grade. The trail does not follow the grade. Instead, it turns left and drops away from the road and travels past an earth mound. There is a short climb to a signed trail junction.

Option: For a longer hike, continue straight at the sign. This loop comes out at cabin 21 near the intersection of CR 21 and Pine Cabin Road, adding 2 miles to the hike.

After turning right at the sign, the trail begins to descend. It bends right after 100 yards, and the grade is easy for a short distance. The trail then drops sharply through a narrow, steep-walled ravine and enters a sheltered cove where two small feeder streams come together. Cross over to the left side of the creek. Towering white pine and smaller black birch thrive in this sheltered region. Cross the creek two times and then climb the ridge a short distance. After the climb, the trail drops down to the road at cabin 27. Turn left on the road and walk 0.1 mile to the Y. Turn right and follow this road back to the parking area.

Mountain Lakes
REGION

In the geographic center of West Virginia is the Mountain Lakes region. The folded ridges of the Highlands give way to the high plateau, where eons of water flowing over the land have cut deep gorges into the countryside. Streams that flow out of the Potomac Highlands are harnessed and dammed to create the region's many lakes and wildlife management areas.

Trails in this region can be deceiving, even short ones can be very difficult. With so much flat water, it's easy to forget that the ridges can be steep. Take care in planning your trip. Review the trail maps, especially contour lines.

If the day seems too hot for hiking, the Mountain Lakes region is just the place to be. The miles of waterline offer a multitude of swimming or fishing holes. If you're lucky enough to have brought your boat, then a day of water skiing may be in order.

Camping can be found in many of the region's state park campgrounds. One message of warning: During much of the fall and winter, and possibly some of the spring, Wildlife Management Areas are frequented by hunters. Be careful in the woods and check for local hunting seasons.

29

Nature Trail
Audra State Park

Overview: *Audra State Park's 355 acres, located in the northwestern part of the state, were acquired by the state in 1950. Nestled in forests and rhododendron thickets along the Middle Fork River, the park derives its name from a Lithuanian word meaning "thunderstorm," due to the thundering runoff caused by rains and snowmelt coursing through the river's cataracts in spring. This recreation area offers excellent riverside camping and picnicking. In summer, the river beach makes swimming a popular activity. Hiking trails through varied rock formations complete Audra's recreational opportunities.*

General description: A short loop hike through an upland hardwood forest and along the Middle Fork River.
General location: 11 miles northeast of Buckhannon
Length: 2.5 miles
Difficulty: Easy
Special attractions: The Middle Fork River and the "Alum Cave."

Maps: Audra State Park map; USGA quad: Audra
Camping: The campground has sixty-five tent and trailer spaces, and is open from mid-April to October. The cost for camping is $13 per day.
Seasons: The park is open year-round.
For information: Audra State Park, Route 4 Box 564, Buckhannon, WV 26201; (304) 457–1162

Finding the trailhead: Take US 33 east from Buckhannon and turn north on Talbott Road (CR 17). There is a sign for the state park. Travel 2.0 miles and turn left on Chestnut Flats Road (CR 54). At the T intersection turn left. Continue 4.9 miles and turn right into the first picnic area. There are rest rooms at the picnic area.

The hike: To reach the trailhead, follow the road through the picnic area. A sign, TRAIL AND CAVE, marks the trailhead. This trail description follows the trail away from the cave.

The trail begins as a wide path that meanders through a forest of tall upland hardwoods. The grade is easy and the trail is well maintained. After approximately 0.25 miles there is a bench on the left, then the trail contours just below the summit of an unnamed knob on the right. There are small hemlocks and beech trees in the understory. The trail wraps around to the west side of the ridge. On the left is a steep escarpment that drops to the Middle Fork River.

Nature Trail

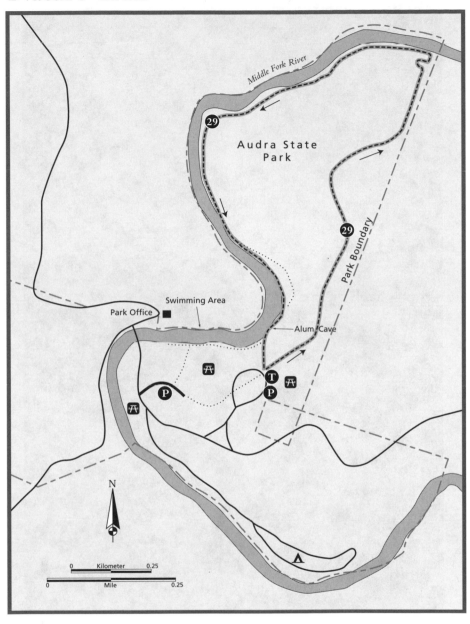

Audra State Park, Alum Cave. COURTESY OF WEST VIRGINIA DIVISION OF TOURISM

The trail now begins a moderate descent to the Middle Fork River. Large boulders dot the steep slope. During the descent, the hardwoods are left behind and tall, straight hemlocks begin to dominate the canopy. Rhododendron thickets crowd the understory. Just before reaching the river, there is a right switchback and the trail passes through a narrow rock crevice.

The trail begins to parallel the wide, swift flowing Middle Fork River. This stretch is very scenic, and small rapids and riffles create a pleasant sound while hiking the riverside. There are many moss-covered rocks and boulders, and tree roots drape a number of the rocks along the stream. Several small side trails lead down to the river.

About 0.3 mile after reaching the river, the trail begins to climb away from its bank. The climb is easy and ends in a small clearing overlooking the river. The trail splits here, with both forks leading to the same location. The lower fork is the proper trail, which descends back toward the river. Near the river, there is a set of stone steps, followed by a massive rock overhang known as the "cave." A boardwalk leads under the overhang to the opposite side.

The trail bends left and makes a very short climb to a trail junction. Continue straight and make a short climb out of the hemlock and back into the hardwood forest. Once in the hardwoods, the picnic area is only a short distance away. The trail ends at the signpost in the picnic area.

30 Park View to Fishermen's Trail Loop / *Cedar Creek State Park*

Overview: *Cedar Creek State Park is a 2,483-acre park named after the creek that flows lazily through its center. Located in the piedmont of West Virginia, the park offers approximately 10 miles of hiking trails. In addition to hiking, there is fishing in both the Cedar Creek and the small fishing ponds located near the creek.*

General description: This trail is a rugged climb to a ridge crest followed by an easy hike along a slow-moving stream.
General location: 7 miles south of Glenville
Length: 2.75 miles
Difficulty: Moderate
Special attractions: Camping, fishing, and trails that pass through beautiful forests. The Park View trail offers a scenic overlook and large, knurled old oak trees.

Maps: Cedar Creek State Park trail map; USGS quads: Cedarville, Glenville, Normantown, Tanner
Camping: Camping is available from mid-April to October. The park has forty-eight campsites from $13 to $17.
Seasons: Hiking is available year-round.
For information: Cedar Creek State Park, Route 1 Box 9, Glenville, WV 26351; (304) 462–7158

Finding the trailhead: At the intersection of US 33 and WV 5 in Glenville, head west on US 33. Travel 4.7 miles to CR 17 (Cedar Creek Road) and turn left. Continue 4.3 miles to the Cedar Creek State Park entrance. Take the park road to the main office. Parking is available here.

The hike: The signed trailhead for the Park View Trail is located near the main state park sign. From the parking lot at the park office, walk back to CR 17. The Park View Trail, marked with blue blazes, begins with a steep climb that has but one purpose: to reach the ridge crest. The first section of the climb leads to a small rock outcrop with a nice view to the south. The trail continues to climb to the crest of a high knoll, gaining 460 feet in 0.6 mile. Small pine, chestnut oak, and cedar line the trail. One old oak has a huge round burl.

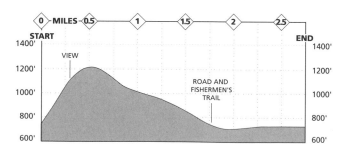

Park View to Fishermen's Trail Loop, Two Run to Stone Trough Trail Loop

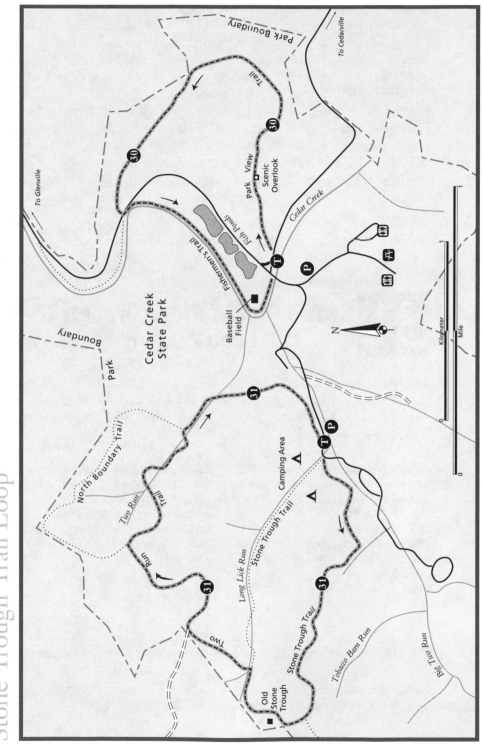

After cresting the narrow knoll, the ridge becomes wider and the trail begins following an old skid road as it starts the long descent back to Cedar Creek. At times the crest is narrow and rocky, other times it is wide and rounded. Large knurled oak trees stand as sentinels along the crest. Near the end of the trail, a series of short, steep descents leads to the road. The distance from the trailhead to the road is 1.75 miles.

Cross the road to the small parking lot and drop down to the river. There is a mowed trail along the riverbank. Turn left on the Fishermen's Trail and begin an easy walk back to the park office. This trail is a little like the creek, it seems in no hurry to get anywhere. It weaves in and out of the small sycamores that line the river, eventually passing the ponds on the left. The baseball field marks the end of the trail. The park office can be seen from the baseball field.

31 Two Run to Stone Trough Trail Loop / *Cedar Creek State Park*

Overview: *The slow moving Cedar Creek is the heart of Cedar Creek State Park. The flat, narrow creek bottom quickly gives way to tree-covered ridges and steep narrow hollows. The rolling mountains of the park offer wonderful opportunities for back woods hiking and solitude.*

General description: This trail is a rugged loop through the backcountry of the park.
General location: 7 miles south of Glenville
Length: 4.0 miles
Difficulty: Moderate
Special attractions: The Stone Trough Trail has steep rugged climbs and a hand-carved stone trough.
Maps: Cedar Creek State Park trail map; USGS quads: Cedarville, Glenville, Normantown, Tanner

Camping: Camping is available from mid-April to October. The park has forty-eight campsites from $13 to $17.
Seasons: Hiking is available year-round.
For information: Cedar Creek State Park, Route 1 Box 9, Glenville, WV 26351; (304) 462–7158

See map on page 97.

Finding the trailhead: At the intersection of US 33 and WV 5 in Glenville, head west on US 33. Travel 4.7 miles to CR 17 (Cedar Creek Road) and turn left. Continue 4.3 miles to the Cedar Creek State Park entrance. Take the park road to the campground gate and park on the left near the gate.

The hike: The Stone Trough Trail begins at site 7 in the campground at an elevation of 820 feet. There are two trailheads; take the trail to the left of campsite 7. The trail is marked with orange blazes and begins with an easy climb along an old road. The road climbs a short distance, and then drops back to the campground at site 3T.

The trail turns left and enters a narrow hollow, then begins a moderate climb up the left side of the hollow. This first climb is short and ends on a wide old road lined with tall tulip poplars. Cross this road and begin a second, much steeper climb up the ridge. Blazes are scant during this climb, but they are there. While climbing, angle upward and in the direction of the campground. After about 100 yards, the climb ends as the trail hits another old logging road.

The grade changes from brutal to easy on the logging road, wrapping around the front of a finger ridge that overlooks the campground and entering another narrow hollow. The distance from the trailhead is 0.6 mile and the elevation is about 1,100 feet. The grade is now easy as the trail contours along the side of the ridge. After a gradual climb, there is a T intersection of old roads. Turn right and climb to a saddle, where the trail bends left and continues an easy climb toward the ridge crest. There is a trail fork during this climb. Take the right fork.

On the crest the grade is easy. This is the highest point of the loop, with an elevation of 1,280 feet. The trail turns right and descends the north side of the mountain. The descent is short and moderate. At the road junction, turn right and follow the road about 100 feet. Turn left and exit the road, descending to a hand-carved, stone watering trough. The trail becomes a footpath and makes a steep descent to Long Lick Run. Turn right and follow the Long Lick a short distance to the junction with the Two Run Trail at 1.5 miles.

Option: For a shorter loop, continue on the Stone Trough Trail 0.8 mile back to campsite 7. The trail parallels Long Lick Run down a narrow hollow to the campground. The distance of this loop is 2.25 miles.

To continue the loop, turn left on the Two Run Trail. This trail is indistinct and the blazes are few and far between. Cross the run and begin angling up and to the right in a northerly direction. The trail climbs to a dry feeder, crosses it, and climbs to the top of the finger ridge. Follow the finger ridge straight up the mountain. Just below the rock ridge crest, the trail intersects a road. There is a sign for the Two Run Trail on a tree, and a small pipeline parallels the road.

Turn right on the road and begin to contour just below the ridge crest. The trail wraps around the crest and enters the drainage for Two Run. There is a small clearing and a gas well at the end of the ridge. Continue on the road until it wraps around to the end of the bowl. Tall straight cove hardwoods dominate the canopy. In an area of muscadine grape vines there is some trail confusion because the trail is not well marked. There is a Y of sorts; take the left fork and

continue following the old road. The trail continues to hug the bottom of the rise. Watch for the big boulder on the left as an indication that you are on the correct path. The trail contours all the way to the signed intersection with the North Boundary Trail just over a mile from the junction of the Stone Trough Trail. The North Boundary Trail continues straight at this junction, wrapping around the north end of the park then dropping steeply to rejoin the Two Run Trail after 1.0 mile.

To continue the loop, take the right fork to remain on the Two Run Trail. Begin a gradual descent as the trail drops off the right side of the finger ridge, wraps around the front of the ridge, and begins following an old road. Watch for the green, red, and white blazes. Here the trail turns right and drops steeply down the side of the mountain toward Two Run. At Two Run, turn right and begin paralleling the creek downstream. After a short distance, the trail descends to a narrow point of land and the junction of two small streams 0.6 mile from the junction with the North Boundary Trail.

Cross over to the left side, and enter a narrow steep-walled hollow. The trail crosses Two Run twice and then crosses a small feeder stream. The North Boundary Trail rejoins the Two Run Trail from the steep ridge on the left. There is a sign for the campground and the North Boundary Trail at this junction.

The Two Run Trail continues past a small pond and then enters a meadow. Follow the woods along the meadow back toward the campground. A road at the end of the meadow parallels the base of the mountain and leads back to site 7.

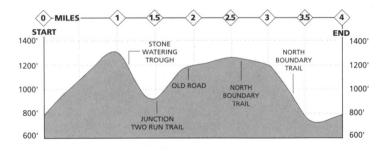

A deep ravine in Two Run Trail.

32 Reverie to Tramontane Trail Loop / *Holly River State Park*

Overview: *Holly River State Park, the second largest park in West Virginia, encompasses 8,101 acres. Ample moisture from the many streams in the park creates a beautiful lush green environment. The park offers an extensive 35-mile trail system with hikes for the beginner as well as trails that will challenge even the most seasoned hiker.*

General description: A wonderful loop hike for experienced hikers.
General location: 32 miles south of Buckhannon
Length: 6.25 miles
Difficulty: Difficult
Special attractions: This loop travels behind a small waterfall, parallels a beautiful free falling mountain stream, and journeys into the past as it travels through an old homestead site.

Maps: Holly River State Park map and trail guide; USGS quads: Goshen, Hacker Valley
Camping: Camping is available from the first week in April through November. The park has an eighty-eight-site campground. The fee is $17 per night, $15.30 for senior citizens.
Seasons: Hiking is available year-round.
For information: Holly River State Park, P. O. Box 70, Hacker Valley, WV 26222; (304) 493–6353

Finding the trailhead: At the intersection of WV 4 and WV 20, travel south on WV 20 about 18.5 miles to the park entrance. Turn left and proceed 0.5 mile to the picnic area. The trailhead for the Reverie Trail is across the road from the picnic area entrance.

The hike: The loop begins on the park entrance road just opposite the entrance to the picnic and camping area. There is a sign for the Reverie Trail, which is marked with yellow blazes and follows an old road into the woods. After 50 feet, the High Rock Trail exits to the right. Big Run is on the left, and rhododendron crowds the trail on the right. There is a gradual climb up a narrow steep-walled hollow. The trail is rocky through this section.

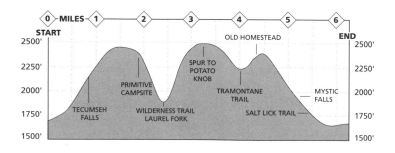

102

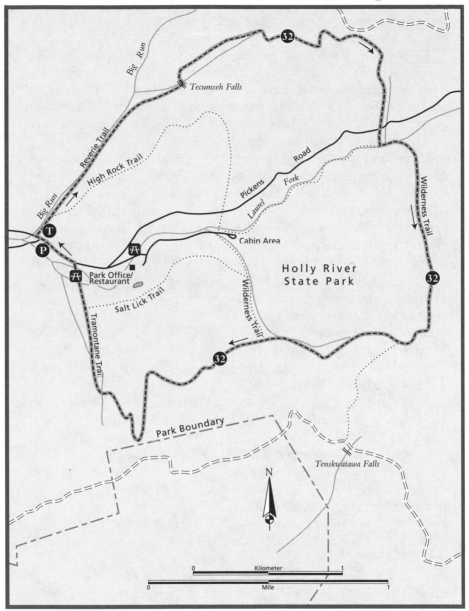

After two quick creek crossings, the trail enters a small meadow called "Dreamers Meadow." Two small streams come together here, and the trail climbs a short steep ridge between them. The climb continues to the intersection with an old road. The road makes a switchback but the trail continues straight. After crossing a small creek, the trail climbs a steep embankment. Steps have been dug into the hillside. After a left switchback, there is a moderate climb to Tecumseh Falls. The waterfall is 0.9 mile from the trailhead.

The trail passes under a rock overhang and behind the falls, then turns right and climbs to the top of the rock overhang. This is a short, moderate climb. Cross the creek and climb to the utility corridor. After two short, steep climbs, the Reverie Trail crests the ridge and passes to the opposite side. Contouring just below the crest, the trail passes through a hollow and around the end of the bowl before climbing back to the ridge.

There is a steep descent down the other side. Several quick switchbacks lead down the ridge to a primitive campsite approximately 2.0 miles from the trailhead. The elevation is 2,400 feet. Here you'll find a privy, fire circle, table, and water supply. A sign points the way to the campground and cabins. At the campsite, it is important to turn right before reaching the road to remain on the trail. Entering a narrow hollow with many small rock overhangs, the trail begins a gradual descent, which quickly changes to a very steep descent. A small creek on the left can be heard madly crashing down the mountainside. At the end of this steep descent is a road. A left leads to Pickens, and a right heads back to the campground and cabins.

Cross the road and drop down to the Laurel Fork (elevation 1,900 feet). The junction with the Wilderness Trail is just beyond the road. To shorten the loop to 3.5 miles, turn right at the trail junction and follow the blue blazes back to the park facilities.

To continue the loop, turn left on the Wilderness Trail and follow the Laurel Fork upstream a short distance. Cross the stream on a bridge and begin paralleling the Crooked Fork, a series of small tumbling cascades. Hemlocks tower overhead and rhododendron crowds the trail and the creek bank. Cross a small feeder creek on a bridge. Many boulders are draped with tree roots and moss here. The trail begins to climb away from the creek to a large rock outcrop. Three switchbacks complete this climb.

At the rock outcrop, the grade moderates, and the trail drops sharply back to Crooked Fork. It meanders along the creek a short distance and begins to climb away from the creek again. After passing under another rock outcrop, there is a trail junction. The left fork leads to the fire tower road and the Railroad Grade Trail. The Wilderness Trail turns right and continues climbing. After a right switchback, the trail powers up to the ridge crest. This climb is about 0.25 mile. Once on the crest, the grade is easy. The trail is clearly marked and easy to follow. Tall hardwoods dominate the canopy.

On the crest, a spur trail leads to the Tenskwatawa Falls and Potato Knob. At the junction is a sign for the park headquarters. Turn right and follow the red and blue blazes. The trail climbs over a small knob with an elevation of

A stone crossing on the Wilderness Trail.

2,480 feet. After an easy climb, the trail drops over the ridge and into a wide hollow. Muscadine grape covers the trees, and large boulders have been dropped everywhere. The gradual descent continues to a small creek. Running cedar carpet the ground. After crossing the creek, the Wilderness Trail intersects the Tramontane Trail.

Option: Follow the Wilderness Trail down the ridge to the park office. The distance of this loop is approximately 6.0 miles.

To continue the long loop, go straight on the Tramontane Trail, marked with yellow blazes. Cross a small feeder creek and look to the hillside on the left, which is covered with green running cedar. Climb gradually to an old homestead. The site has a small cemetery and some great stonework, the remains of an old springhouse. There is even an old holly tree, and several large stumps of old chestnut trees still survive.

Past the homestead, the trail climbs out of the hollow to the ridge crest. Cruise along the crest of the ridge to an area with several trail junctions.

Follow the yellow blazed Tramontane Trail to the U turn and begin a steep descent into the bowl the crest has been paralleling. After several switchbacks, the trail drops to a small creek. The trail parallels the creek a short distance before crossing it. On the left is Mystic Falls. Not far beyond is the junction with the Salt Lick Trail, an orange blazed trail that exits to the right.

Bear left at this junction and continue to descend. The blazes are now orange and yellow. At the next junction, the orange blazed trail that exits to the left goes to the campground. Continue straight, and cross the bridge to the picnic area. Cross a second bridge and then follow the road back to the parking area.

New River/
GREENBRIER
VALLEY

The New River/Greenbrier Valley is what comes to mind when out-of-staters think of West Virginia: gorge country. Southern West Virginia is characterized by high, rocky ridges and deep, white-water filled gorges. Kayakers flock by the thousands to run the region's rapids. Climbers travel from near and far to test the crags of the New River Gorge, the premier climbing area in the eastern United States.

With everything the region offers the outdoor enthusiast, it all seems to exist at two distinct speeds: fast and slow. Although there are miles of fast, world-class white water, the paddler can find even more miles of tranquil, slow moving water. Rock climbers can clamber and sweat their way out of a vertical gorge, while hikers follow the whispers of a trout stream as it crawls out of the gorge more slowly. Ridge-top hikes might meander on the high plain before diving off the ridge with the sole purpose of getting the hiker to the bottom in the least number of steps. The choice is yours. Do you escape from the hustle and bustle, or do you have the need for speed?

Many charming campsites can be found at each of the areas described in this region, which is also home to two of West Virginia's "resort" state parks: Pipestem and Twin Falls. These parks pamper the hiker with restaurants, lodges, golf courses, and fishing lakes—everything the discriminating hiker might need, and then some.

Trips to town in the area will doubtless find one passing through Beckley and Bluefield. The small, quaint towns contain all the necessary services one might require: restaurants, hotels, stores, and so on. Fayetteville, which caters to the rafters and climbers who frequent the New River Gorge, is capable of meeting your outfitting needs. Guides can also be hired here if you would like some professional help with your trip.

One particularly interesting festival occurs in this region. On the third Saturday in October people come from all over the east coast to celebrate Bridge Day along the New River Gorge National River. Visitors crowd onto the 3,030-foot-long structure to celebrate its completion in 1977. Spectators line the river below to watch base jumpers parachute off of the man-made structure. The people, food, music, and scenery combine to make this a wonderful and unique West Virginia experience.

Island in the Sky Trail
Babcock State Park

Overview: *From the perches of Island in the Sky Trail to the cascading Glade Creek, Babcock State Park is a hiker's treasure. Photographers focus on Glade Creek Grist Mill. Anglers drift flies down the creek hoping to entice a hungry trout. From the moment you get out of your car at the parking area, Island in the Sky Trail is an interesting hike. This area is beautiful in early summer when the trail is bright with the pastel pinks of new flowers.*

General description: This is a short hike through a rhododendron thicket to rocky cliff tops and around the base of the cliffs. The park road passes by Glade Grist Mill on the way to the trailhead.

General location: 13 miles southeast of Fayetteville

Length: 0.5 mile

Difficulty: Easy

Special attractions: Clifftop views.

Maps: Babcock State Park map and trail guide; USGS quads: Danese, Fayetteville, Thurmond, Winona

Camping: The State Park has a fifty-one-site campground located off SR 41, north of the main camp entrance. The campground is open from mid-April until the end of October, weather permitting.

Seasons: Although the park's facilities are closed from the end of October through mid-April, park roads and trails can be used during these times. Most park roads are graded to facilitate cross-country skiing during winter months.

For information: Babcock State Park, HC-35 Box 150, Clifftop, WV 25831-9801; (304) 438-3004 or (800) CALL–WVA

Finding the trailhead: Babcock State Park is located west of SR 41 between the towns of Landisburg and Clifftop. From US 60 in Fayetteville, follow SR 41 south. From Beckley, follow US 19 north to SR 41 north at Glenn Jean. There is a large sign at the entrance to the park. Follow the main park road downhill to the gristmill, staying to the left of two intersections along the way. The park headquarters and restaurant are located on the right side of the road at the bottom of the hill. Cross the bridge at the gristmill, turn left, and make a 180-degree right turn heading uphill. The trailhead will be on the right just before a tight left-hand turn.

The hike: The trail leaves the main park road and immediately enters a rhododendron thicket. Above the rhododendron, pine fills the canopy. Pine is one of the few trees hardy enough to eek out an existence on the thin layer of soil that covers this rocky ridge top. The trail travels out toward the edge of the cliff and turns to parallel it. Numerous side trails branch right and take the hiker to the precipitous ledge. The trail travels near the rock's edge until it

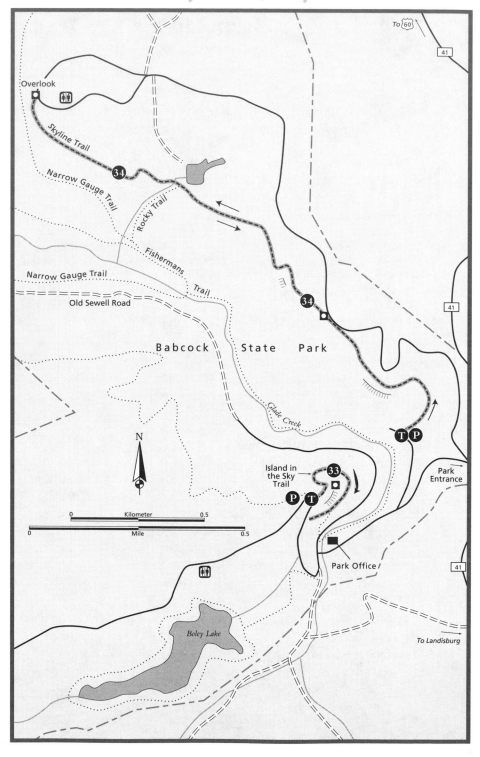

Overlook

Skyline Trail

Narrow Gauge Trail

34

Rocky Trail

Fishermans Trail

Narrow Gauge Trail

Old Sewell Road

B a b c o c k   S t a t e   P a r k

Glade Creek

34

N

T P

Kilometer   0.5

Mile   0.5

Island in the Sky Trail

P T

33

Park Office

Park Entrance

To Landisburg

Boley Lake

To 60

41

41

41

Island in the Sky Trail requires the hiker to scramble through a rock crevice.

reaches a small shelter on a rocky point. There are benches here and the shelter is covered. Although the hike is not long, this is a wonderful place to sit, rest, and take in the beauty of the natural environment.

After your rest, follow the main trail about 10 yards back toward the parking area. Keep on the lookout for a trail entering rhododendron thicket to the right. The trail snakes through the thicket, and then the fun begins. The trail travels down through a hole in some rocks, a maneuver that requires some scrambling, then bends sharply and narrowly to the right and travels down an old wooden bridge that is rickety at best. A sign that reads TRAIL points down. Just after this sign, the trail reaches the bottom side of the cliffs and levels off. The hike continues to wrap around the base of the cliffs you were just on.

At less than 0.5 mile, Island in the Sky Trail reaches a Y intersection. A left at this intersection leads downhill to the gristmill. A right leads uphill and back to the main park road. Take the right, travel a short distance up a moderate climb to the paved road. At the paved road, turn right and hike uphill to the parking area.

34 Skyline Trail
Babcock State Park

Overview: *Babcock State Park's nearly 10 miles of trails take the hiker past the rocky rim of the gorge, down the creek, or around Boley Lake. Early summer finds both Catawba and Rosebay rhododendron blooming in the park. Every turn leads to another vista, another wildflower, another find you're certain is all your own.*

General description: The hike slowly gains elevation as it travels across the ridge near the tops of sandstone cliffs.

General location: 13 miles southeast of Fayetteville

Length: 2 miles one-way, 4 miles round-trip

Difficulty: Easy

Special attractions: Clifftop views.

Maps: Babcock State Park map and trail guide; USGS quads: Danese, Fayetteville, Thurmond, Winona

Camping: The State Park has a fifty-one-site campground located off of SR 41, north of the main camp entrance.

The campground is open from mid-April until the end of October, weather permitting.

Seasons: Although the park's facilities are closed from the end of October through mid-April, park roads and trails can be used during these times. Most park roads are graded to facilitate cross-country skiing during winter months.

For information: Babcock State Park, HC-35 Box 150, Clifftop, WV 25831-9801; (304) 438–3004 or (800) CALL–WVA

See map on page 110.

Finding the trailhead: Babcock State Park is located west of SR 41 between the towns of Landisburg and Clifftop. From US 60 in Fayetteville, follow SR 41 south. From Beckley, follow US 19 north to SR 41 north at Glenn Jean. There is a large sign at the entrance to the park. Follow the main park road downhill toward the gristmill. There are two roads that intersect the main park road from the right. At the second road, turn right and follow the single-lane

Skyline Trail lives up to its name with frequent vistas.

road toward the cabins. The trail will be on the right side of the road before cabin 5. A sign marks the trailhead. There is space to park one vehicle. If necessary, park at the restaurant and park headquarters and walk to the trailhead.

The hike: This trail can be accessed from the Manns Creek Picnic Area or the cabin area near the gristmill and park restaurant. Although there is more parking at the picnic area, this trail description will describe the hike beginning and ending at the cabin area. The forest near the cabin area is much more pleasant than that at the picnic area, thus beginning and ending the hike on a high note.

From the main park road, turn down the very narrow road toward cabins 1–6. The trail begins at a sign designating the trailhead. There is room for one vehicle to park here. If you park at the restaurant parking lot, hike the paved road uphill toward the park exit, and then hike down the cabin 1–6 access road to the trailhead. At the trailhead, a sign warns that this is an area of high cliffs. Because this is a ridge-top hike, make sure you have ample water before beginning.

The yellow blazed trail begins with a moderate climb up through rhododendron. The trail bends to the right, travels up some rock stairs, and then crosses a small footbridge. At about 0.25 mile, the trail levels off as it reaches its first vista. There are picturesque views of Glade Creek to the south. For the next 0.5 mile, the trail parallels the cliffs, offering numerous viewpoints. To enhance an already beautiful hike, travel the trail in early summer when the rhododendron, thick in the understory, is in full bloom.

After passing through a stand of young striped maple, the trail starts a moderate climb. There is a right switchback followed by a left. When the trail reaches the top of a small shoulder, the angle decreases once again to an easy hike. At about 1.0 mile, the trail abruptly exits the forest at an overlook just off the main park road. This is an open grassy area with benches for resting and gorgeous views to the west.

Past the meadow, the trail reenters the forest and starts down at an easy to moderate angle. The trail passes another scenic overlook and travels through the forest for about 0.5 mile before reaching another overlook. About 1.75 miles from the trailhead, Skyline Trail reaches the intersection with Rocky Trail. There is a sign at this intersection. Rocky Trail heads left down the ridge and will intersect with Narrow Gauge Trail slightly up-ridge from Glade Creek. To continue on Skyline Trail, hike straight through this intersection.

Manns Creek Picnic Shelter is not far from the intersection of Skyline and Rocky Trails. Skyline Trail passes to the right of a large boulder and, a few minutes later, the picnic shelter is reached. The total one-way distance is about 2 miles. There is a water fountain near the picnic shelter. Drink up and enjoy the hike back.

Glade Creek cascades past the gristmill.

35

Bluestone Turnpike Trail
Bluestone National Scenic River

Overview: *Nestled between Pipestem Resort State Park and Bluestone State Park is a quiet stretch of the federally designated Bluestone National Scenic River. Managed by the National Park Service, the designation protects the unspoiled nature of the river and the surrounding land. The Park Service has done its job well. The river is wonderfully wild and the ridges of the gorge are so steep that when sitting by the river it appears that there are only two ways out, upstream or downstream. Luckily, both directions lead to top-notch state parks: Pipestem Resort State Park to the south and Bluestone State Park to the north. The Bluestone Turnpike Trail travels the distance between these parks. Birch and sycamore crowd the riverbank and produce deep shade during the heat of summer. If the shade isn't enough to cool you off, there is a constant supply of swimming holes just a few steps away.*

General description: The Bluestone Turnpike Trail follows the banks of the slow moving Bluestone River from Pipestem Resort State Park to Bluestone State Park. The hike is shady and easy.

General location: 17 miles northeast of Princeton

Length: 8.0 miles one-way

Difficulty: Easy

Special attractions: Lazy river, deep swimming holes, and two state parks.

Maps: USGS quads: Flat Top, Pipestem

Camping: Although camping is not allowed along the Bluestone National Scenic River, it is available at both Bluestone and Pipestem State Parks.

Seasons: The Bluestone National Scenic River is open year-round, as are Pipestem Resort State Park and Bluestone State Park.

For information: Bluestone National Scenic River, P.O. Box 246, Glen Jean, WV 25846; (304) 465–0508. Bluestone State Park, HC 78 Box 3, Hinton, WV 25951; (304) 466–2805. Pipestem Resort State Park, Box 150, Pipestem, WV 25979; (304) 466–1800

Finding the trailhead: To access the trail from the south at Pipestem Resort State Park, take exit 14 off I–77 and travel north on WV 20 for 11.2 miles to the entrance to Pipestem Resort State Park. To reach Pipestem from I–64, take exit 139 and travel south on WV 20 for 22 miles. The entrance to Pipestem will be on the right.

After turning into Pipestem State Park, follow the paved road past the camping area and nature center for 2.1 miles to a fork in the road. Take a left at this intersection and follow this road to the Canyon Rim Center. Park in the parking lot and take the tram or the Canyon Rim to River Trail combination to the Mountain Creek Lodge at the bottom of the gorge. At the lodge, follow the river trail downstream (northeast) until it intersects with the Bluestone Turnpike Trail.

Bluestone Turnpike Trail

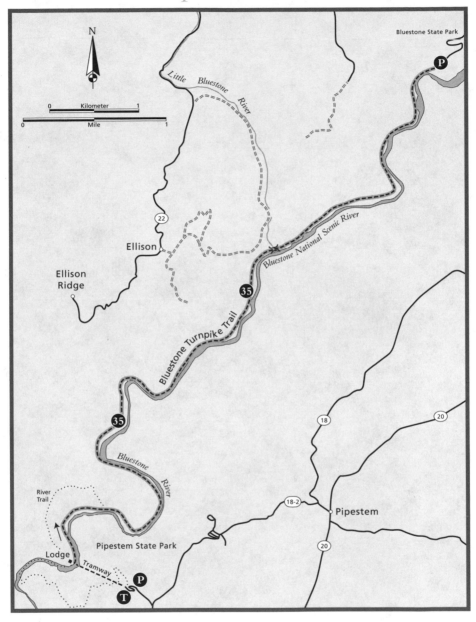

The sleepy Bluestone River.

To access the trail from the north at Bluestone State Park, take exit 14 off I–77 to SR 20. Follow SR 20 north 22 miles to the park entrance. Follow the main park road past the office and gift shop, turn left and follow the road past the Meador Camping Area. Continue to follow the road until it forks at another camping area. Take a right onto the gravel road and follow it to a gate. The trail begins on this old forest road.

The hike: From the Canyon Rim Center in Pipestem Resort State Park, take either the River Trail or the Canyon Tramway down to the Mountain Creek Lodge. At the lodge, follow the River Trail down the Bluestone River. The River Trail leaves the lodge traveling in a northerly direction. The River Trail in this area follows the spacious remains of an old fire road. Sycamore, maple, and beech make up the canopy. Although the ridges that create the river gorge are steep, the river itself flows out of the valley at a lazy pace. The hiker enjoys that same pace while treading the trail.

The Bluestone Turnpike Trail begins at a National Park Service sign approximately 1.0 mile from the Mountain Creek Lodge. Before reaching the sign, a double orange blaze is reached; here the River Trail turns left and starts up the ridge. Continue along the banks of the Bluestone River to an information sign, which announces the boundary of the Bluestone National Scenic River. Camping is prohibited along this trail.

The trail between Pipestem and Bluestone State Parks is wide and easy to follow. It is relatively flat throughout, making it a wonderful path for trail runners. The walk is serene and contemplative. The trail hugs the north bank of the river and there are no stream crossings. This is lucky for the hiker because many pools in the river are deeper than the average hiker is tall. Frequently the hike passes through gaps in the canopy that provide a perfect habitat for thick weed growth. Maintenance of the trail is impeccable, though, and the weeds tend to be cut well back from the trail.

At 5.0 miles from the lodge, a gate is reached. Past the gate, which is used by vehicles, a dirt road begins. Follow the dirt road along the river to a footbridge over a feeder stream. Across the bridge, vehicles do not travel the trail. Pass through another gate and continue. The river begins to widen as it nears Bluestone Lake. At 6.5 miles the only climb of the hike is reached, a moderate ascent that leads away from the banks of the river. A final gate blocks vehicular access to the trail at a small parking area. A dirt road past this gate leads about 0.25 mile to the main park road in Bluestone State Park.

Farley Branch Trail
Camp Creek State Park

Overview: *Camp Creek State Park is a relatively small 550-acre park located just west of Interstate 77. What the Park lacks in size it makes up for in location. First, the proximity to the interstate makes Camp Creek State Park extremely accessible as a destination or as a place to set up camp when passing through. Second, the park borders the 5,300-acre Camp Creek State Forest, increasing the "elbow room" almost tenfold. Two trails traverse the park proper; both are relatively short and easy to hike. There are two sets of waterfalls in the park. Chances are good that you will see fishermen during fair weather because Camp Creek is one of the better-stocked trout streams in the area. The area is also a favorite among hunters; blaze orange is a must during hunting seasons.*

General description: A short, easy stroll across a ridge to a small waterfall.
General location: 24 miles north of Bluefield, 27 miles south of Beckley
Length: 2.25 miles
Difficulty: Easy
Special attractions: Cascading waterfalls and trout-stocked streams.
Maps: Camp Creek State Park map; USGS quad: Odd

Camping: There are thirty-seven campsites at the state park's two campgrounds.
Seasons: State park and campground are open year-round.
For information: Camp Creek State Park, P.O. Box 119, Camp Creek, WV 25820; (304) 425–9481 or (800) CALL–WVA

Finding the trailhead: Camp Creek is very easy to find. From I–77 take exit 20 for Camp Creek. Follow US 19 to the southwest side of the interstate, and turn right onto CR 19-5. Follow the signs for the state park. Once at the park, cross a bridge over the creek and turn left at the fork in the road near the basketball court. The signed trailhead is on the right near this fork. Park at the picnic shelter on the left.

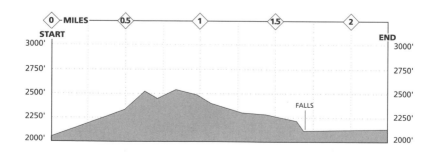

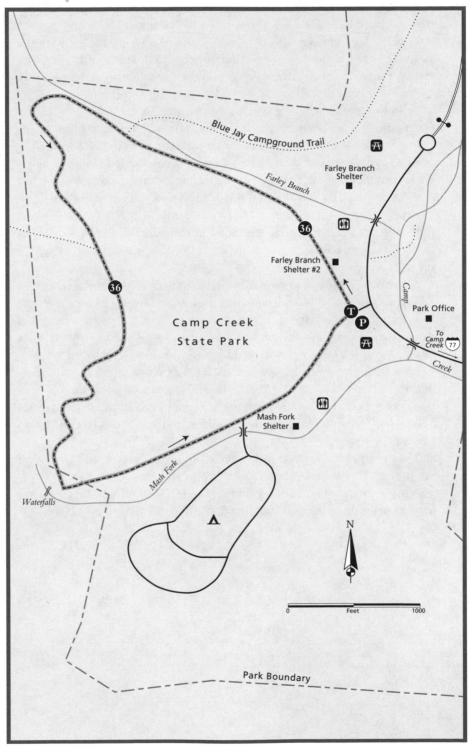

Blue Jay Campground Trail

Farley Branch

Farley Branch
Shelter

36

Farley Branch
Shelter #2

Camp Creek
State Park

36

Camp

Park Office

T

P

To
Camp
Creek 77

Creek

Mash Fork
Shelter

Mash Fork

Waterfalls

N

0   Feet   1000

Park Boundary

The hike: The white blazed trail begins near an information sign just across the road from the basketball court. The sign indicates that Farley Branch is 0.5 miles, Blue Jay Camping Area is 1.4 miles, and Mash Fork Falls is 1.7 miles away. The trail begins with a moderate uphill climb and shortly thereafter crosses a small footbridge over a dry stream drainage. Initially traveling north, the trail will bend to the left and start hiking west up a steep valley.

At just over 0.25 mile, the trail reaches an intersection with the Blue Jay Campground Trail. A right at this intersection will lead the hiker to the campground. Take the left fork and continue uphill on Farley Branch Trail.

At a large slab of sandstone, the trail makes an abrupt left. These boulders are overhanging and could provide shelter during an unexpected rainstorm. Just past the boulders, the trail moves through a rounded, shallow valley and bends left as it travels up the opposite ridge. At this point the trail is trending east. A right switchback points the trail west and a moderate uphill climb follows. The forest in this area is composed of magnolia in the canopy and young chestnut in the understory.

At just over 1.0 mile there is another intersection. A right leads up the ridge and appears to follow the park boundary. Stay to the left and follow the trail as it wraps around the ridge at a lower elevation. The trail starts a moderate descent and enters the first in a series of eight switchbacks. Mash Fork Campground can be seen down the ridge after the fifth switchback.

After the eighth switchback, which is a left-hand turn, a rock stairway leads down to Mash Creek. Mash Creek Falls can be seen to the right. The trail leads down to a gravel road, a parking area, and a small bridge that crosses Mash Creek. A gate blocks the bridge. The land across the creek is Camp Creek State Forest.

To return to your original parking area, follow the gravel road away from the bridge. This road will lead the hiker past the Mash Fork Campground. The paved park road is reached within 0.25 mile. Continue straight and to the left and follow the paved road another 0.25 mile back to the parking area.

37

Greenbrier River Trail

Overview: *The Greenbrier River Trail is the longest rail trail in West Virginia. Beginning at Cass Scenic Railroad State Park, it winds its way 77 miles to Caldwell. The trail, designated as a Millennium Legacy Trail, has a one percent grade from start to finish. Although the trail is long, it is not physically taxing. The trail crosses thirty-five bridges and passes through two tunnels, traveling through small, forgotten railroad towns and green pastures. Camping facilities and water are located all along the trail.*

General description: The first 23 miles of the 77-mile trail are described here. The beautiful and scenic Greenbrier River is a constant companion for the entire length of the trail.

General location: East-central West Virginia between Caldwell and Marlinton

Length: 23.4 miles

Difficulty: Easy

Special attractions: The Greenbrier River and the mountains that rise up on both sides of its banks.

Maps: Greenbrier River Trail map and trail guide; USGS quads: Cass, Cloverlick, Edray, Marlinton

Camping: Along the trail are many designated campsites with privies and running water. These sites are available on a first-come first-served basis.

Seasons: The trail is open year-round.

For information: Greenbrier River Trail Association, HC 64 Box 135, Hillsboro, WV 24926; (304) 653–4722; www.greenbrierrivertrail.com

Finding the trailhead: This is a point-to-point trail; transportation is needed at each end. Remember to make sure the car keys ride along. For the Cass Trailhead, take US 219 to WV 66. Travel east on WV 66 for 11 miles to Deer Creek Road. Follow Deer Creek Road to the parking lot.

For the Marlinton Trailhead, at the intersection of US 219 and WV 39, turn east on WV 39. Proceed 0.5 mile to the train depot located on the left.

The hike: The wide gravel-covered rail trail begins in Cass at milepost 79.4. The trail parallels the Greenbrier River downstream for 5 miles to a shelter at Woods Run Bridge (milepost 74.4). The Woods Run cascades down the mountain from the right.

At milepost 71.2, the trail enters the small community of Clover Lick with its old railroad depot. A small campsite on the left at milepost 69.6 has a privy and clean water supply.

After 14 miles, the 511-foot-long Sharps Tunnel is reached (milepost 65.28), followed by the Greenbrier River Bridge. Exercise caution when

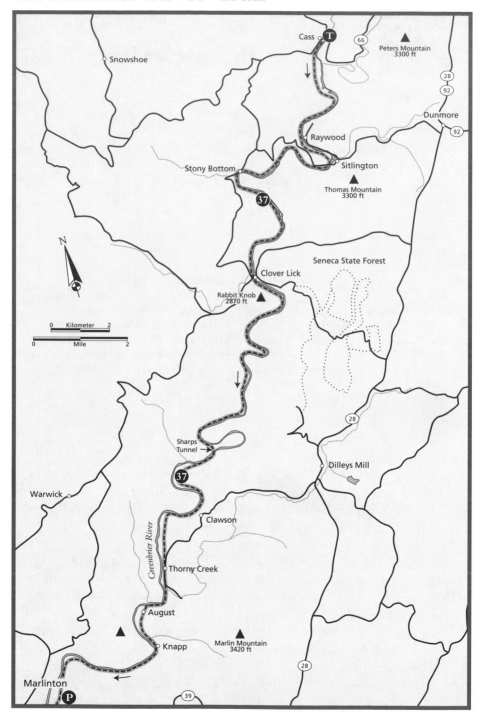

Cass
T
66
Peters Mountain
3300 ft
Snowshoe
28
92
Dunmore
Raywood
92
Stony Bottom
Sitlington
37
Thomas Mountain
3300 ft
N
Seneca State Forest
Clover Lick
Rabbit Knob
2870 ft
0 Kilometer 2
0 Mile 2
28
Sharps
Tunnel
Dilleys Mill
37
Warwick
Clawson
Greenbrier River
Thorny Creek
August
Marlin Mountain
3420 ft
Knapp
28
Marlinton
P
39

traveling through the tunnel. After crossing the bridge, the river is on the right. Another campsite with a privy and a clean water supply is at milepost 63.8.

From the Thorny Creek Bridge (milepost 60.9) to the Halfway Run Bridge (milepost 59.5), there is a lot of beaver activity between the trail and the Greenbrier River. At milepost 56 the trail enters the town of Marlinton and houses begin to line the trail. The hike ends at the Marlinton depot, a yellow single-story building located on US 39. The town offers several fine eating establishments and small shops.

The Greenbrier River passes by Sharps Tunnel. PHOTO BY DON WALLACE.

Kates Mountain Loop
Greenbrier State Forest

Overview: *The Greenbrier State Forest is located in the southeastern corner of the state, encompassing an area of approximately 5,100 acres. The clear flowing Harts Run borders the western region of the forest. Kates Mountain (3,200 feet) is the region's dominant geographical feature. This ridge climbs rapidly from Harts Run to the ridge crest. The forest is composed almost entirely of the eastern deciduous forest species. There are pockets of hemlock and cove hardwoods in sheltered coves.*

Greenbrier State Forest offers a wide variety of recreational activities, including approximately 13.5 miles of hiking trails. Trail difficulty ranges from easy family hikes to very strenuous ridge climbs. All the trails are well marked and maintained.

General description: Kates Mountain Loop offers panoramic vistas and steep, difficult climbs.
General location: 5 miles southwest of White Sulphur Springs
Length: 9.5 miles
Difficulty: Difficult
Special attractions: Kates Mountain Loop is a challenging circuit trail with several excellent views along Kates Mountain.
Maps: Greenbrier State Forest map; USGS quads: Glace, White Sulphur Springs

Camping: The state forest has a sixteen-unit campground, open from April 15 through the first week of December. The fee for camping is $13 to $17. The state forest also has thirteen rustic cabins.
Seasons: The forest is open year-round to hikers.
For Information: Greenbrier State Forest, HC-30 Box 154, Caldwell, WV 24925-9709; (304) 536–1944

Finding the trailhead: Take I–64 to exit 175 and turn south on CR 60/14 to the state forest entrance. There is a parking area on the right for the archery and muzzleloading range and the trailhead for the Old Roads Trail. The Old Roads trailhead, which marks the beginning of the Kates Mountain Loop, is across CR 60/14 near the forest office.

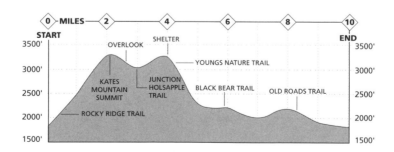

Kates Mountain Loop

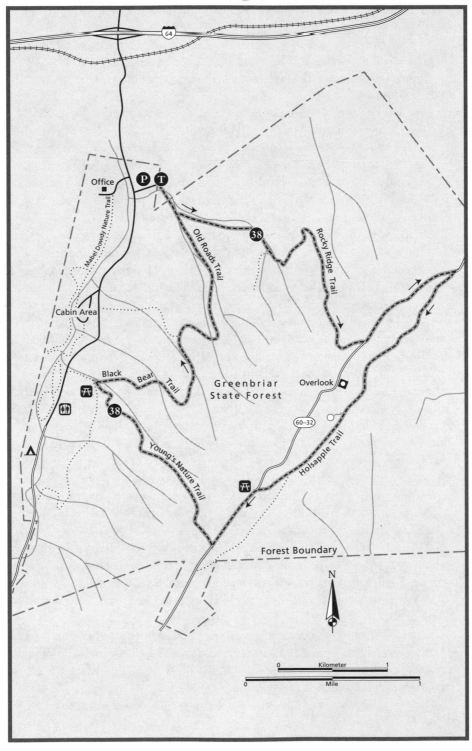

Office

Mabel Dowdy Nature Trail

Old Roads Trail

Rocky Ridge Trail

Cabin Area

Black Bear Trail

38

38

Greenbriar State Forest

Overlook

60–32

Young's Nature Trail

Holsapple Trail

Forest Boundary

N

Kilometer

Mile

The hike: The Kates Mountain Loop is a combination of the Old Roads Trail, Rocky Ridge Trail, Holsapple Trail, Young's Nature Trail, and Black Bear Trail. From the park office, follow the gravel road past the park buildings. The trailhead is located at the base of the mountain at an elevation of 1,825 feet. Begin by following the Old Roads Trail into Dynamite Hollow. At about 0.25 mile turn left on the Rocky Ridge Trail.

The Rocky Ridge Trail climbs from the junction with the Old Roads Trail to the summit of Kates Mountain. This short but demanding trail is well marked with yellow diamonds and is well maintained. It follows an old road for about 0.4 mile and then makes a left turn. A sign marks the turn. After crossing a creek, there is a short, steep climb to another road. Turn right and hike about 100 yards, then follow the trail as it exits the road on the left. There is a gradual climb for approximately 0.5 mile to the crest of a finger ridge.

At the ridge the Rocky Ridge Trail bends right and begins to climb. There are three short, steep climbs followed by short flat sections. The fourth steep climb completes the ascent to the summit of Kates Mountain. This climb is approximately 0.5 mile long and is very steep. The trail is littered with small rocks containing many shell fossils.

At the tree-covered summit of Kates Mountain (elevation 3,200 feet), the trail bends left and descends to CR 60/32. At the road, a left leads to an overlook with a view to the northwest (0.3 mile) and the Holsapple Trail (0.5 mile). A right on the service road leads to an overlook with a view to the southeast (1.0 mile), a shelter (1.5 miles), and the Young's Nature Trail (2.0 miles).

Turn left and follow CR 60/32 about 0.5 mile to the Holsapple Trail. The trailhead is on the left. The Holsapple Trail is a wide, flat, grassy road that travels just east of the ridge crest. After crossing an orange gate the trail becomes a series of gentle climbs and descents. About 1.0 mile from CR 60/32 there is a small spring on the right. Near the 1.4-mile mark, the Holsapple Trail splits. There is a brown post at the junction. Take the right fork and begin a short, moderate climb to CR 60/32.

Turn left on the road. There is a shelter with picnic tables on the right about 100 yards from the junction. About 0.4 mile from the shelter, turn right on the Young's Nature Trail, which makes a rapid descent from the crest of Kates Mountain to CR 60/14. The trail is 1.7 miles long and marked with orange blazes.

Young's Nature Trail begins with a moderate descent to a right bend, then makes three short, steep descents over a distance of approximately 1.0 mile. Another right bend marks the approach to the Black Bear Trail, which exits to the right. The elevation at this junction is 2,200 feet.

Option:: To shorten the hike to 7.8 miles, continue down Young's Nature

Trail to the trailhead on CR 60/14. Cross the road and follow the Mabel Dowdy Nature Trail back to the park office.

To continue the longer loop (9.5 miles), turn right on the 2.0-mile Black Bear Trail, marked with green blazes. The trail follows a creek for a short distance, makes a left bend, and begins a moderate climb to the crest of a finger ridge. It crosses the crest and passes through two hollows on an easy grade. After passing through the second hollow, the trail makes a moderate descent on a finger ridge to the junction with the Old Roads Trail.

This section of the Old Roads Trail is 1.3 miles long; the trail is marked with red blazes. Turn right, pass through a small meadow, and begin a moderate climb to a ridge crest. After climbing the ridge, the trail bends right and follows an old road. Just prior to reaching the trailhead, the muzzleloading and archery range is on the left. The Rocky Ridge Trail is located on the right. Continue on the Old Roads Trail about 0.25 mile to the starting point.

39 Glade Creek to Kates Falls Trail
New River Gorge National River

Overview: *Perhaps better known for white-water rafting and rock climbing, the New River Gorge National River contains more than 70,000 acres of land bordering the waterway. This land, managed by the National Park Service, contains a multitude of hiking trails. Glade Creek Trail is a wonderful hike along the beautiful trout stocked banks of Glade Creek. A hiker who is also an angler will do well to add some "line time" on this hike; the fishing looks that good. A fine idea would be to pack the rod and camp either along the trail or in the camping area. The stream is catch-and-release from the parking area to a footbridge 3.0 miles upstream.*

General description: A picturesque streamside hike from the banks of the New River to the rim of the gorge.
General location: 14 miles east of Beckley
Length: 5.6 miles one-way; 11.2 miles round-trip
Difficulty: Easy to moderate.
Special attractions: New River, beautiful trout stream, deep gorge, wildlife.

Maps: USGS quad: Prince
Camping: Glade Creek Camping Area has five tent sites. Backcountry camping is allowed, and there are many appropriate sites along the creek.
Seasons: Year-round.
For information: New River Gorge National River, Park Headquarters, P.O. Box 246, Glen Jean, WV 25486; (304) 465–0508

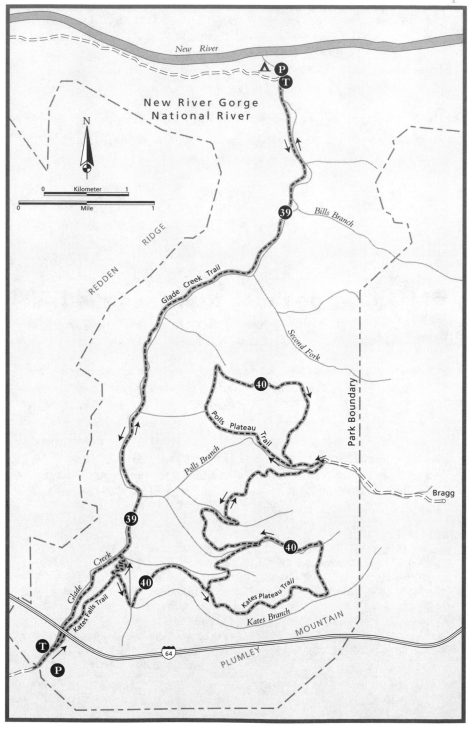

Finding the trailhead: From I–64 east of Beckley, take exit 124 for East Beckley and Eisenhower Drive. Follow US 19 approximately 2.2 miles to the intersection with WV 41 and turn right. WV 41 travels through the hamlets of Tinyview and Stanaford; 6.8 miles from I–64, it turns right and travels down into the gorge. At the bottom of the gorge, 9.45 miles from I–64, WV 41 turns right and travels along the south bank of the New River. At 10.4 miles from I–64 and just before WV 41 crosses the New River, turn right across some train tracks and onto Glade Creek Road. Follow this dirt road 6.2 miles to the northern trailhead and camping area. The trailhead is on the right and is marked by a sign and parking area. The camping area has five tent sites and latrine-style rest rooms.

To reach the southern trailhead, take I–64 to exit 129 east of Beckley. Follow CR 9 south to WV 307; turn left. Turn left again onto CR 22. Follow CR 22 to the gate at Glade Creek Trail. The trailhead is at a gate and is marked by a sign.

The hike: From the lower trailhead parking area, a sign indicates Glade Creek Trail and establishes the one-way trail length as 5.6 miles. The 11.2-mile round-trip is leisurely, though, as there are no steep climbs. Stream trails always seem both energizing and calming at the same time, and this one is no exception. The peaceful babble washes the hiker clean of everyday worries and entices childlike outbursts of rock hopping and puddle jumping.

Tulip poplar, chestnut oak, and sycamore line the trail. Dogwood fills the understory. The trail is wide and easy to follow even though the blue blazes are infrequent. Within 0.5 mile, the stream rewards the hiker with a waterfall. The trail stays to the right of the stream until reaching a footbridge at mile 3.0. This is the only stream crossing. There are a few buckeye in the canopy, which is now dominated by sugar maple, beech, and hickory.

Continue on the Glade Creek Trail as the Kates Falls Trail exits left at 4.0 miles. At about 4.5 miles, the hiker gets a view of I–64 high overhead. A washout to the left is passed and there are good swimming holes in the Glade Creek. The trail ends by a gate at the southern trailhead.

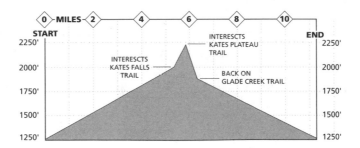

From the southern trailhead, the hiker also has the option of hiking Kates Falls Trail. The trail rejoins Glade Creek Trail at about one mile from the southern trailhead. To access Kates Falls Trail, turn left and hike uphill along the old fire road. The road is wide and grass covered. This is also the Kates Plateau Trail. The trail travels north at a moderate uphill angle, bending to the right at about 0.6 mile. A concrete pillar in this bend marks Kates Falls Trail. Turn left and head downhill along the Kates Falls Trail, a steep single-track trail. Be very careful on this section of trail, which makes a couple of switches as it rapidly descends. A sturdy hiking stick is invaluable. After a set of rock stairs, the trail opens up at the falls, a good spot for a rest.

The tributary of Glade Creek steps down a 5-foot cascade just before a dramatic 15-foot fall. During times of high water flow, these falls are impressive. After enjoying the falls, continue downhill a short distance to the intersection with Glade Creek Trail. Turn right and head back to the northern trailhead. The footbridge is about 1.0 mile away, the trailhead about 4.0 miles away.

Kates Plateau to Polls Plateau Trail Loop
New River Gorge National River

Overview: *Most visitors to the New River Gorge National River congregate near the New River Bridge area, where climbing and rafting dominate, and where cliff-side trails sport magnificent views of the valley. Farther away from the crowds, the "extreme" nature of the gorge is toned down but the beauty of one of the planet's oldest rivers still remains.*

Kates Plateau and Polls Plateau are two loop hikes through upland forest and old farmland. The majority of the hike is along an old farm road. The grade is generally easy; the difficulty lies in staying on the trail. The combination of crisscrossed farm roads and a severe lack of blazes makes route finding in this area a challenge. A rule of thumb: When in doubt, follow the most worn path. It is suggested that only experienced hikers tackle this trail, allowing extra time for the inevitable backtrack after a wrong turn. It wouldn't hurt to take along a flashlight too.

General description: A physically easy hike made difficult by winding, branching trails.
General location: 7 miles east of Beckley
Length: 12.0 miles
Difficulty: Moderate
Special attractions: Quiet forests, rhododendron tunnels.

Maps: USGS quads: Meadow Creek, Prince
Camping: Backcountry camping is allowed in the New River Gorge National River.
Seasons: Open year-round.
For information: New River Gorge National River, Park Headquarters, P.O. Box 246, Glen Jean, WV 25486; (304) 465–0508

See map on page 130.

Finding the trailhead: Take I–64 to exit 129 east of Beckley. Follow CR 9 south, away from the interstate for 0.75 mile to WV 307; turn left. Turn left again onto CR 22 after 0.5 mile. Follow CR 22 1.75 miles to the gate at Glade Creek Trail. The trailhead for Kates Falls Trail is to the right of the gate.

The hike: At the southern trailhead for Glade Creek Trail, a sign points out Kates Falls Trail. The trail follows an old road grade uphill and under the interstate. Hiking is easy along the grass-covered path. At 0.75 mile, the trail reaches a concrete pylon that marks the intersection of Kates Falls Trail and Kates Plateau Trail. Turn right at this marker and follow the old road slightly uphill. There are limited views northward into the gorge. Striped maple and grapevines are slowly reclaiming the road in the name of Mother Nature.

At about 1.0 mile, there is a fork in the road. Stay to the left and follow a path down to a shady creek bed. The trail travels directly in the creek bed for about 50 yards then picks up the old road again. The forest is now composed of lycopodium along the forest floor, rhododendron in the middle canopy, and tulip poplar and chestnut in the canopy.

At 1.75 miles a Y intersection is reached, marking the loop section of Kates Plateau Trail. Take the right fork at this intersection as the trail continues at an easy grade. At 2.0 miles, a side road leads to the right into a meadow. Stay left and follow the trail into a stand of hemlock. After a short, moderate ascent,

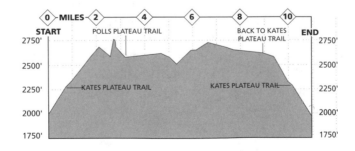

133

an old homestead is reached. The trail passes by a fence, then switches left and travels uphill out of this area. The trail levels off and at just after 3.0 miles passes under a high-voltage power line. An old road leads right and left. A sign indicates Kates Plateau Trail on the left-hand fork. Turn left and continue in an arc on the north side of the power line. The trail returns to the power line and crosses it again.

A short, steep downhill follows the power line along a dry slope. Oaks dominate the forest; sassafras and dogwood occupy the lower canopy. The trail levels out at the intersection with the Polls Plateau Trail. Turn right on the Polls Plateau Trail as Kates Plateau Trail continues to the left.

Polls Plateau Loop Trail is similar to Kates Plateau Trail. There are few climbs as the trail travels through upland forest. Again, be careful of side trails. The main trail is usually easy to see and is the most worn trail. The first leg of the trail, the "out-and-back" part before the loop begins, is fairly straightforward. At just over 5.0 miles, the trail crosses a stream and then reaches an intersection. Turn left to reach the loop section of Polls Plateau Trail. A right travels up the creek through a tunnel of rhododendron to a road that leads to the small town of Bragg.

After turning left, the loop section of the trail starts within 50 yards. At the Y intersection, turn left and travel the loop in a clockwise direction. The loop begins in rhododendron tunnels in the stream valley. The canopy is filled with majestic hemlock, hickory, and oak. A moderate ascent leads to a pasture at about 6.0 miles from the start. The pasture is gorgeous on a warm spring day. Follow the trail to a large white pine, turn ninety degrees to the right, and follow the trail out of the pasture. The trail passes a couple of side trails. Follow the infrequent blazes and the most worn trail. At about 7.0 miles, another trail junction is reached. Follow the trail down and to the right, traveling between high earthen berms on either side. This is the final descent back to the beginning of the loop section of the Polls Plateau Trail. At the close of the loop, walk ahead 50 yards to the next intersection. Turn right and head back to Kates Plateau Trail.

Once back at Kates Plateau Trail, turn right and follow the old road. The remainder of the trail is easy to follow. At about 9.5 miles, the beginning of the loop section is reached. Follow the road back toward the parking area.

At 11.0 miles, Kates Falls Trail is reached. Kates Falls Trail is a beautiful side trail. If you still have some energy, hike steeply down a single track to a picturesque waterfall. This is a wonderful spot for lunch or a nap. From the falls, continue down to Glade Creek Trail, then turn left and hike approximately 1.0 mile to the parking lot.

41

River to Farley Ridge Trail Loop
Pipestem Resort State Park

Overview: *Pipestem Resort State Park is a multidimensional vacation destination that can either test or pamper you. Encompassing the plateau and valley of the Bluestone River Gorge, the state park is ruggedly beautiful. There are 17.8 miles of trails that wind together for hiking, biking, or cross-country skiing trips for all experience levels. Trails vary from 0.2 to 6.2 miles and from virtually flat to aerobically steep. A dip in the swimming pool will be just the thing to relieve those trail-tired muscles. Eighteen-hole and par 3 golf courses will try your skills on nonhiking days. Although many campsites are available, two lodges and restaurants provide romantic evenings when you want to leave your sleeping bag at home.*

General description: This modified loop is a strenuous traverse of the Bluestone River Gorge. The River Trail travels down the eastern ridge, crosses then follows the river, and finally climbs the western ridge. The Farley Ridge Trail brings the hiker back down to the river in a hurry. From the river, the tram can be taken back to the trailhead or you can hike back via the River Trail.

General location: 14 miles north of Princeton, 12 miles south of Hinton

Length: 6.3 or 11.8 miles

Difficulty: Moderate to difficult

Special attractions: Deep river gorge and high, rocky vistas.

Maps: Pipestem Resort State Park map and trail guide; USGS quads: Flat Top, Pipestem

Camping: Pipestem Resort State Park has fifty deluxe campsites with water and electric

hookups, and thirty-two basic campsites. A minimum stay of two nights is required when making a reservation.

Seasons: Pipestem Resort State Park is a four-season resort. The tram at the Canyon Rim Center is seasonal, open on weekends (Saturday and Sunday) in April and daily from May to October. The tram is closed from November through March and also on Tuesday and Thursday afternoons (1:00-4:00 P.M.). A tram schedule may be obtained by calling the park or (800) CALL–WVA.

For information: Pipestem Resort State Park, Box 150, Pipestem, WV 25979; (304) 466–1800.

The Army Corps of Engineers operates a gauge on the Bluestone River that measures water level. A recorded message of the Pipestem Gauge Reading can be heard by calling (304) 466–0156.

Finding the trailhead: From I–77, take exit 14 and travel north on WV 20 for 11.2 miles to the entrance to Pipestem Resort. From I–64, take exit 139 and travel south on WV 20 for 22 miles. The entrance to Pipestem will be on the right. After turning into Pipestem State Park, follow the paved road past the camping area and nature center for 2.1 miles to a fork in the road. Take a left at this intersection and follow this road to the Canyon Rim Center. Park in the parking lot. The trailhead for Canyon Rim Trail is located just north of the Canyon Rim Center.

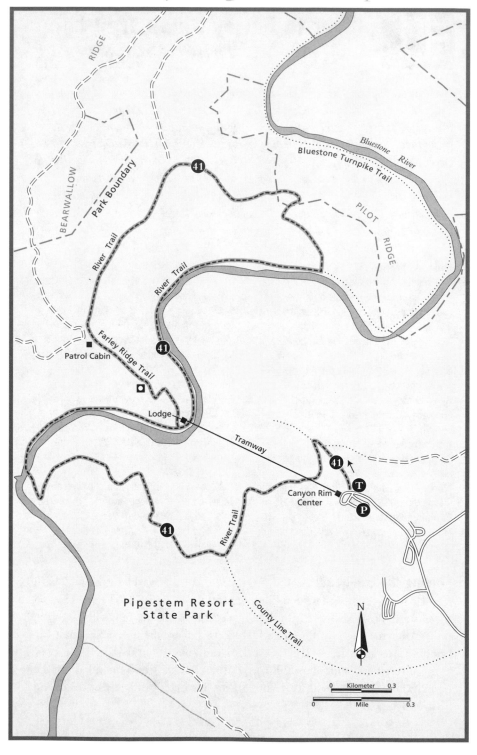

The hike: The River Trail circuit hike begins on the Canyon Rim Trail near the Canyon Rim Center. The upper trailhead for the River Trail is actually near McKeever Lodge about 1 mile away. Choosing to park at the Canyon Rim Center, however, allows the hike to end with a scenic ride up the canyon on the Canyon Tramway.

At the Canyon Rim Center, pass by the northern corner of the structure to reach the Canyon Rim Trailhead. A sign marks the trailhead where the lawn meets the woods, and blue blazes mark the trail. Canyon Rim Trail is wide and lined with tulip poplar, hickory, and dogwood. The trail drops straight and steep to the intersection with the River Trail.

At the trail junction, turn left and follow the River Trail downhill. This section of the River Trail is an old fire road. Although the ridges of the gorge are extremely steep, the trail winds its way into the gorge and drops gently to the Bluestone River. Mountain bikes are allowed on the River Trail, but there is little evidence of their use.

At 1.0 mile the trail passes to the right of a rock river and bends to the north. Shortly after the rock river, the County Line Trail is reached. At this Y intersection, turn right and continue to hike downhill, passing a small meadow where locust trees are filling the gap in the canopy.

The trail passes through two switchbacks and then bends right through a drainage area. It continues an easy descent as the ridge drops off steeply to the right. The drainage is populated with large hemlock and beech.

As the trail bends to the left, the Bluestone River peeks through the trees. A small trail switches back to the right but the River Trail continues straight. A sign and an orange blaze mark the correct path. When the trail reaches the river's floodplain, a right switchback points the trail north. The river is reached at 2.0 miles.

Now it's time to take off the boots and ford the Bluestone River. A sign at the river's edge identifies the River Trail and informs the hiker of the river's current level. At the west bank of the river there is another sign as well as a picnic table. Pass by the sign, hike across a small meadow, and turn right on the gravel road.

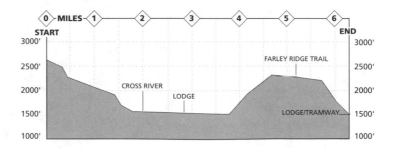

137

The gravel road is not particularly scenic, but it gets you to the Mountain Creek Lodge in about 1.0 mile. The lodge has a restaurant, gift shop, and the lower tram station. Passing the lodge, River Trail reenters the woods. The trail follows the river at an easy grade for 0.5 mile. Sycamore, maple, and beech dominate the canopy.

At 0.5 mile from the lodge, a double orange blaze marks a trail junction. The Bluestone Turnpike Trail travels straight and follows the river for 8 miles to Bluestone State Park (see Hike 35). The River Trail turns left at this junction and heads uphill across a meadow. From the river, the climb to the crest of Bearwallow Ridge is difficult. The trail, however, is an old fire road and is easy to follow. The trail moves through three switchbacks before reaching the crest of the shoulder, but the climb is not over yet. After some difficult ascents, the trail finally levels. A massively thick shade oak is evidence that this ridge top used to be open farmland.

At the oak, turn left and follow the trail to the junction with the Farley Cemetery Spur Trail, a 50-yard walk to a small family cemetery.

Past the cemetery, the trail travels an easy grade for 0.5 mile to a T intersection. The road bends right, but to continue this hike, turn left off the road and walk down to the patrol cabin. There are chairs and a picnic table on the front porch. The cabin marks the end of the River Trail.

From the cabin, the Farley Ridge Trail begins near a sign at the southeastern edge of the meadow. A word of warning: Farley Ridge Trail is steep. Care should be taken to hike downhill slowly. Descending too quickly can overstress the knees. Very quickly, a right switchback is reached. The trail follows a narrow shoulder; the ridges to both sides drop off quickly. There are views to the east.

After hopping down some boulders, there is a sign and a 20-yard spur to Raven Rock Overlook. The views to the south are outstanding. After resting at the rocky outcrop, continue following the trail downhill. After a right switchback, the trail travels past the rocky base of the overlook then switches back to the left. The tram station is now visible down to the right. The lodge is reached after another right switch.

From the lodge, backtrack and hike the River Trail and Canyon Rim Trail back to the parking area. If you're not interested in finishing the hike with a 2.5-mile uphill walk, you can ride the tram back to the Canyon Rim Center. Tram tickets are sold at the gift shop. At the time of this writing, a ticket for anyone who hiked down was $1.50. The tram travels a length of 3,600 feet and takes the passenger from an elevation of 1,542 feet to 2,639 feet at the upper station. The views from the tram are magnificent.

Hiking down Farley Ridge Trail.

42

Cliffside Trail

Twin Falls Resort State Park

Overview: *Nestled in the Allegheny Plateau is Twin Falls Resort State Park. The rugged mountainlike topography was created over millions of years as streams cut deep, steep valleys into the high plateau. The adventurous can camp in the campgrounds and hike the 19.7 miles of trails. Once the adventure is over, pamper yourself in the lodge and set a tee time at the golf course. The lodge and cottages are open year-round; the golf course operates seasonally. The area usually sees several feet of snow each year, and winter temperatures frequently drop below zero.*

General description: A low-angle out-and-back hike to two sets of rocks, with magnificent views of the valley below.

General location: 26 miles southwest of Beckley

Length: 3.0 miles round-trip

Difficulty: Easy

Special attractions: Steep valley ridges viewed from two separate rock outcrops.

Maps: Twin Falls Resort State map and trail guide; USGS quads: McGraws, Mullins

Camping: A fifty-site campground is open from Easter through the end of October.

Seasons: The park is open year-round.

For information: Twin Falls Resort State Park, Route 97, P.O. Box 1023, Mullens, WV 25882; (304) 294–4000

Finding the trailhead: To reach Twin Falls from Beckley, take exit 42 off I–64/I–77. Turn south onto WV 16/97 and continue about 4.0 miles to the intersection with WV 54. Turn right onto WV 54/97. Follow this road to the town of Maben, and turn right onto WV 97 west. Follow WV 97 to a stop sign and turn left onto Bear Hole Road (Park Road 803). There is a Twin Falls sign at this intersection. Take the park road to an intersection across from the pro shop and swimming pool. Turn right and follow the road uphill toward the campground. As you enter the campground, turn right just past the registration booth at a sign that reads DOGWOOD FLATS SITES 16 THROUGH 46. Turn left at the SITES 41 THROUGH 46 sign. The trailhead is at a gate near the rest room facilities. There is a sign at the trailhead for the Cliffside Trail.

The hike: Cliffside Trail leaves the camp road and a cramped parking spot in front of a wooden gate. The trail is wide and appears to be an old fire road. Mountain biking is allowed on this trail. A sign indicates that the trail is severe and rocky with a total hike distance of 3.0 miles. The red blazed trail travels west through an oak, hickory, maple, and hemlock forest. The initial part of the trail hikes up and down at light angles. Sections of the forest floor are covered with running cedar. At just under 0.5 mile a sign points to the left and

Cliffside Trail, Falls Trail

Steven Carroll at Canada Cliffs.

reads BEAR WALLOW TRAIL. Continue straight to follow Cliffside Trail. The forest here has little understory, which belies the jungles to come.

The easy hike continues through the forest. At about 0.75 mile the trail reaches another Y intersection. This is the beginning of a triangular loop with overlooks at two of the points. Turn right at this intersection. The trail travels down slightly to a drainage and then back up before beginning an abrupt descent. Rhododendron fills the understory, making off-trail hiking out of the question. Another intersection is reached; a right leads 30 yards to Canada Cliffs and picturesque views of the Cabin Creek below.

After soaking in the view, continue on the loop toward the second vista. The trail makes a right switchback around a large boulder, then bends left and contours across the ridge. An intersection with the third side of the triangle is reached. Turn right and enjoy the views from Buzzard Cliffs. The large stone slabs offer wonderful views to the south, and the roar of the state park's twin falls can be heard far below.

From Buzzard Cliffs, follow the trail back up the ridge to the apex of the triangle. The climb from the cliffs is steep but short. After closing the loop, it's a leisurely walk back to the parking area.

43

Falls Trail
Twin Falls Resort State Park

Overview: *Named for two waterfalls on the property, Twin Falls Resort State Park has managed to showcase and tame the rugged beauty of the Allegheny Plateau. The 19.7 miles of trails here provide hikes of various lengths and degrees of difficulty. A good indication that a hike is going to be easy is when it starts off as a paved pathway. Although this is not a hard-and-fast rule, it certainly is the case with the Falls Trail, which leads to the park's two waterfalls.*

General description: A beautiful streamside hike to Cabin Creek Falls and Black Fork Falls.
General location: 26 miles southwest of Beckley
Length: 1.25 miles
Difficulty: Easy
Special attractions: Views of the park's namesake twin falls: Cabin Creek Falls and Black Fork Falls.

Maps: Twin Falls Resort State Park map and trail guide; USGS quads: McGraws, Mullins
Camping: A fifty-site campground is open from Easter through the end of October.
Seasons: The park is open year-round.
For information: Twin Falls Resort State Park, Route 97, P.O. Box 1023, Mullens, WV 25882; (304) 294–4000

See map on page 141.

Finding the trailhead: To reach Twin Falls from Beckley, take exit 42 off I–64/I–77. Turn south onto WV 16/97 and continue about 4.0 miles to the intersection with WV 54. Turn right onto WV 54/97. Follow this road to the town of Maben, and turn right onto WV 97 west. Follow WV 97 to a stop sign and turn left onto Bear Hole Road (Park Road 803). There is a Twin Falls sign at this intersection. Once in the park, turn right onto a small paved road. A small sign on the main park road indicates the Falls Trail. Follow the road to a gate and a circular parking area.

The hike: From the parking area, hike past the metal gate and onto the blacktop. The trail begins traveling east, with Marsh Fork down to the right. There are mountain laurel and rhododendron in the understory and maple and hemlock in the canopy. The roar of the falls becomes louder with each step. At a Y intersection the pavement stops. Turn to the right and look over the creek bank. Cabin Creek Falls can be seen cascading 12 to 15 feet from a large rock slab.

To continue the hike, return to the intersection and take the right fork, which follows more closely to the creek bank. The trail angle is nearly flat and the hiking is very easy. This section of trail travels over a century-old logging road Occasionally the remnants of cross ties from the old logging

operation can be seen. The trail follows Marsh Fork and then bends to the left to follow Black Fork. At about 0.5 mile, the trail reaches Black Fork Falls, similar in height to Cabin Creek Falls but narrower. The rock, however, overhangs more, and Black Fork Falls crashes noisily into the crystal clear pool below.

The trail continues past Black Fork Falls and soon reaches a trail junction. To the right, Hemlock Trail leads out of the Bearwallow Fork drainage uphill to the camping area. To the left and straight is the green diamond blazed Nature Trail. Make a U-turn to the left to continue on the Falls Trail. A sign points out all trails at this junction. After the U-turn, the Falls Trail will be traveling west. There are very large hemlock in this area.

At just under 1.0 mile, Falls Trail reaches another intersection as the Nature Trail goes to the right. Continue straight to follow the Falls Trail. Shortly after the intersection there is a gap in the canopy, and an earlier part of Falls Trail can be seen down toward the left. The trail crosses a small meadow and reaches the paved pathway from the beginning of the hike. Enjoy another look at Cabin Creek Falls and then follow the paved pathway back to the parking area.

Black Fork Falls, one of the "twin falls."

Metro
VALLEY

Encompassing the most populated region of West Virginia, the Metro Valley contains the economic corridor between Charleston and Huntington and the land to the southwest. All the creature comforts can be found in the two major cities: hotels, restaurants, universities, college sports, nightlife. With nearly one-third of the entire population of West Virginia living in the Metro Valley, the region is surprisingly rural. The majority of the residents make the two urban areas and the I–64 corridor their home.

The land in this region is characterized by flat-topped hills and short, sometimes steep ridges. Hikes here will often climb quickly out of the valley, but steep climbs are not sustained. Streams may topple noisily to a shallow valley, flowing lazily once they reach it. On the ridge crests, the hiking is easy. Many hiking destinations are located minutes away from the region's urban centers. On particularly nice spring and fall days, expect to see other hikers. To disperse use, try to hike areas near the cities during the week or during off-peak seasons.

Undoubtedly the most curious hike in the region, and possibly in the entire state, is the Kanawha Trace Trail. This trail travels linearly 31.7 miles and almost entirely across private property. Advanced notice is required if you want to hike this trail, and an extremely nominal fee of 50 cents is collected. The trail is well managed by Boy Scouts, who will even guide you on your trip. The managing body will often ask hikers to carry a two-way radio to keep in touch. You won't find this kind of treatment on any other hike in the state.

Overview: *Beech Fork State Park contains 3,144 acres of rolling hills and the headwaters of Beech Fork Lake. The park has more than 8.5 miles of hiking trails. Beech Fork Lake offers excellent opportunities for fishing. The big trophy is the tiger muskie, but bass, catfish, saugeye, and bluegill are a sporting challenge.*

General description: The longest trail in this state park, Lost Trail, is a figure-eight-shaped trail that travels the beautiful banks of Beech Fork Lake and the hills that touch its shores.

General location: 8.5 miles southeast of Huntington

Length: 3.0 miles

Difficulty: Moderate

Special attractions: Beech Fork Lake, bird-watching, lake views, fishing

Maps: Beech Fork State Park map; USGS quad: Winslow

Camping: The park has 275 campsites, all with electric hookups, grills, and picnic tables. Forty-nine sites in the Old Orchard area also have water and sewer hookups. Seventy-two sites are available for reservations, and the Old Orchard area is open year-round.

Seasons: The park is open year-round.

For information: Beech Fork State Park, HC 35 Box 150, Clifftop, WV 25831; (304) 438–3004

Finding the trailhead: From I–64, take exit 11 for WV 10 and downtown Huntington. At the bottom of the exit ramp, turn south onto WV 10. At 3.7 miles from I–64, turn right onto CR 43, Hughes Branch Road. There is a Beech Fork State Park sign at this intersection. At 7.4 miles from I–64, turn left at a sign for Beech Fork State Park. Continue 2.2 miles, turn right, and enter the park near the park headquarters. Pass by the headquarters and the Old Orchard camping area. Turn right onto Moxley Branch, cross a small bridge, and take the first right, then the first left. The trailhead is near Moxley Branch camping lots 34 and 35. Limited parking can be found at the trailhead. There is plenty of parking at the park headquarters Parking at the headquarters will add approximately 0.2 mile to the hike, round-trip.

The hike: The first thing that is evident on the Lost Trail is the mountain bike tracks. Many mountain bikers use this trail, especially the low-angle sections along the lake. It is generally accepted that pedestrians have the right-of-way over bikes, but exercise caution and watch out for bikers.

From the camp lot 34, the trail crosses a small bridge over a wetland. There are yellow blazes, and a sign points out Lost Trail near a second bridge. A left

Lost Trail

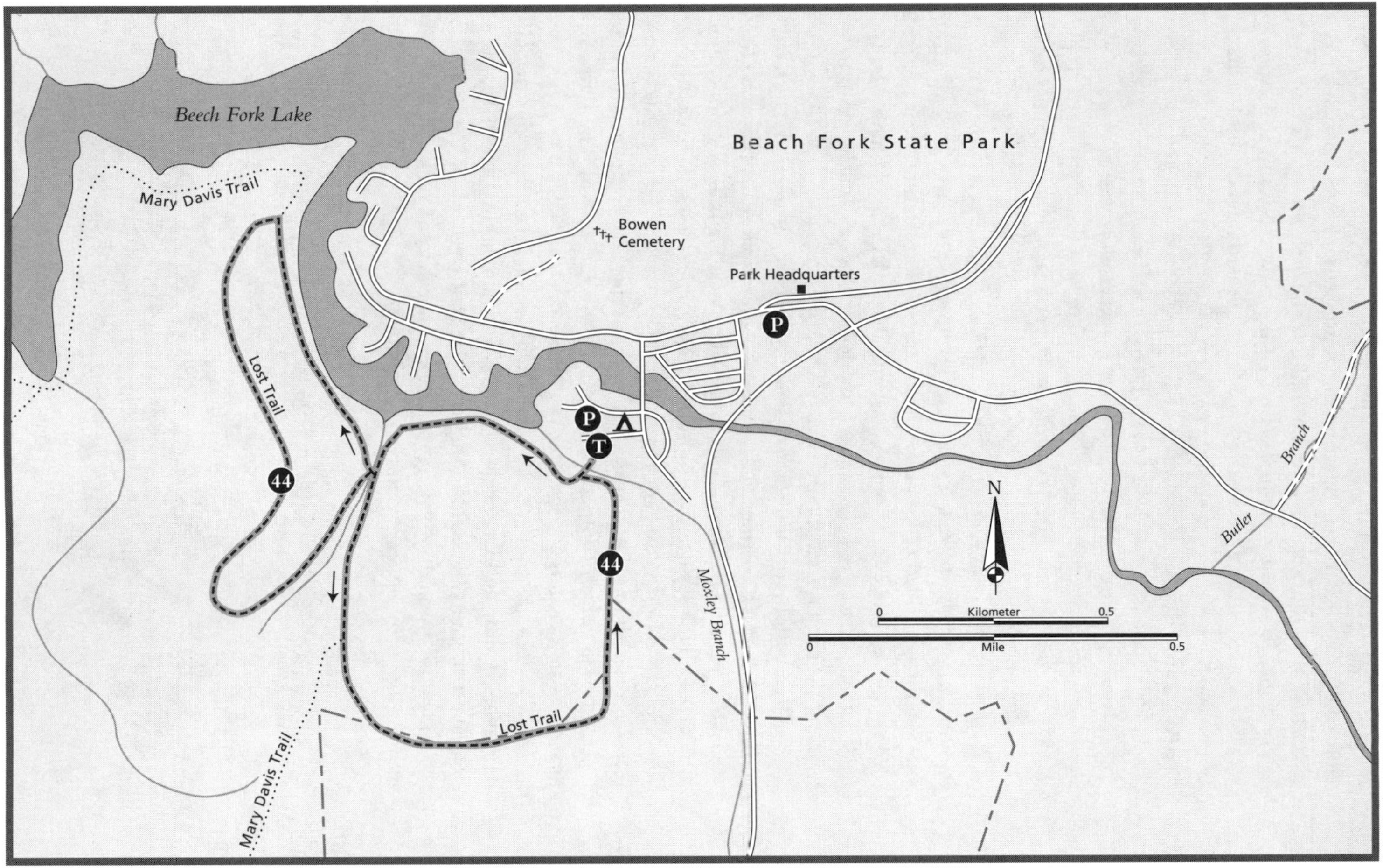

Beach Fork State Park

Beach Fork Lake

Bowen Cemetery

Park Headquarters

Moxley Branch

Butler Branch

Lost Trail

Lost Trail

Mary Davis Trail

Mary Davis Trail

N

Kilometer

Mile

0   0.5

0   0.5

or a right can be made at this sign. Turn right and follow the nearly flat trail along the lakeshore. A small bench offers good views of the lake.

Shortly after the bench, there is a trail intersection, the center part of the figure eight. To continue along the bank of the lake, cross a small footbridge and follow the trail to the right. The views are pleasant and the bird-watching can be good.

At 0.5 mile, Lost Trail turns left at the intersection with the Mary Davis Trail and heads up the ridge. The Mary Davis Trail is a mountain bike trail that follows the lake, turns and travels up Mary Davis Hollow, and ties back in with the Lost Trail at the ridge top. The total distance on the Mary Davis Trail is about 7.0 miles. At the time of writing, however, the trail was not fully blazed or maintained.

As the Lost Trail turns left, it starts its first climb to the ridge top. The climb is moderate and short-lived, leveling off at the ridge top. In winter there are views of the lake-filled valley below. At 1.5 miles, Lost Trail begins its descent near a trail sign. The trail points down and to the left; an old, unblazed trail leads straight. Lost Trail then takes a moderate angle down the ridge to the lake and the center of the figure eight.

The trail bottoms out in a stand of young sycamore. At the trail intersection turn right, cross a footbridge and turn right again. Follow the trail away from the lake in a south-southeasterly direction. The next 0.5 mile is a moderate to difficult climb to the next ridge top, about 100 vertical feet taller than the first. The trail levels off, starts up again, and at 2.5 miles reaches the second intersection with the Mary Davis Trail. A left at this intersection continues on the Lost Trail, which contours just south of the ridge crest. The forest is a mixed-age stand and is a great place to spot white-tailed deer.

At 2.75 miles, the trail makes a left switchback and starts quickly downhill. The angle is difficult; hike slowly to minimize strain on the knees. Cross a fire road and continue down and to the left. The trail levels off at the bottom of the ridge in a stand of young sycamore, beech, and oak. At the next intersection, turn right and return to campsite 34.

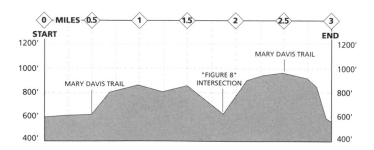

45 Sleepy Hollow to Martin Ridge Trail Loop / *Cabwaylingo State Forest*

Overview: *Named after four nearby counties—Cabell, Wayne, Lincoln, and Mingo—Cabwaylingo State Forest is a gem in western West Virginia. Deep hollows and thickly forested ridge tops combine to make trails magical. There are 12.5 miles of hiking trails to explore. Springtime in the forest brings anglers to the trout-stocked waters of Twelvepole Creek, while hopeful hunters pack the cabins during the various hunting seasons. The Civilian Conservation Corps originally built up the 8,123-acre forest in the 1930s. Many of the structures the CCC built, including the Tick Ridge Fire Tower, still exist today.*

General description: This is a wonderful hike along a mountain stream that has a hidden waterfall and an amphitheater of sandstone cliffs.

General location: 35 miles south of Huntington

Length: 3.5 miles

Difficulty: Easy to moderate

Special attractions: Waterfall, cliffs, deep sleepy canyons, white-tailed deer.

Maps: Cabwaylingo State Forest map and trail guide; USGS quads: Kiahsville, Radnor, Webb, Wilsondale

Camping: Cabwaylingo has twenty-one campsites, each with a fireplace and firewood, electricity, water, shower house, and picnic table. Campsites are on a first-come,

first-served basis. There are also fourteen log cabins that can be reserved. Large groups such as youth organizations can take advantage of the one-hundred-person group camp area, which consists of a dining hall, two buildings that sleep fifty each, and a shower house.

Seasons: Although trails can be hiked year-round, camping areas have a shorter season. The group camp area is open from May to November, the cabins from April through October, and the twenty-one-site campground from April through November.

For information: Cabwaylingo State Forest, Route 1 Box 85, Dunlow, WV 25511; (304) 385–4255

Finding the trailhead: From Huntington, follow US 152 south about 27 miles past Dunlow and turn left onto CR 35. Follow CR 35 for 3.9 miles and turn left at the Sweetwater Picnic Area. The trailhead is across the road from Cabin 1. There is extremely limited parking at the trailhead for Sleepy Hollow Trail. The best bet would be to park at Sweetwater Picnic Area and walk up the road to the trailhead.

The hike: Sleepy Hollow Trail begins with an easy to moderate ascent in a stand of beech and hemlock. Downed timber and boulders are covered with moss, and the stream drops away to the right. The trail is wonderful from the start.

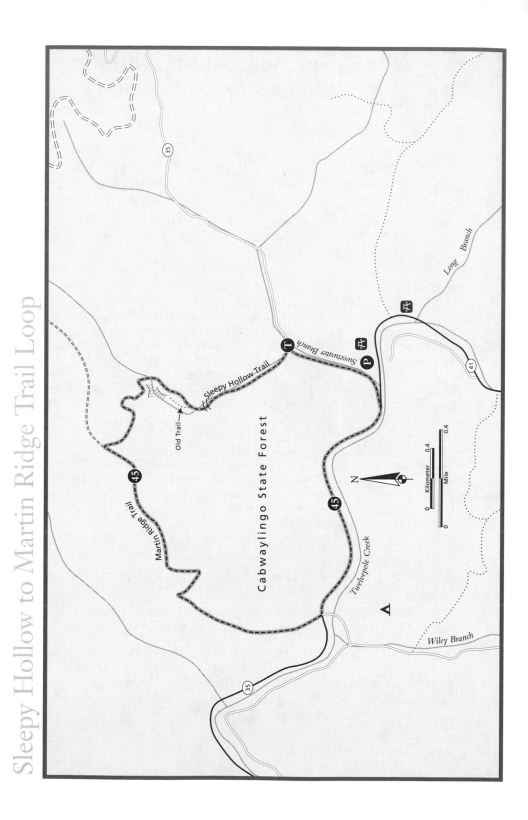

The trail levels off and passes by yellow blazes. The valley is shady with steep ridges on both sides. The trail bends through a couple of drainages, then drops down to the stream, crosses it, and continues up. Before climbing, however, take a short detour by turning right and hiking downstream. On the way up the trail, an observant hiker will notice the sound of a waterfall down the steep ridge to the right. A short and easy hike downstream reaches this hidden waterfall that drops 10 to 15 feet. The seclusion of the falls makes it seem as though no one else in the world knows of their existence.

Travel back upstream to the trail and follow it uphill. The forest is filled with enormous hemlocks. About 0.7 mile from the stream crossing, stay to the right as Sleepy Hollow Trail passes by an old trail that travels down and to the left. Sleepy Hollow Trail soon enters another magical place. As the trail levels off, a gorge of sandstone cliffs will come into view to the left. Cliffs drop off 20 to 30 feet as the stream snakes up through boulders. The shady mini gorge is green with moss. Although the streambed is inaccessible from above, the adventurous hiker can reach the bottom of this canyon by bushwhacking the aforementioned side trail. The side trail is littered with down timber, so be prepared to crawl on your belly and scramble over logs. Because the view from the bottom may be better than that from above, the reward is well worth the effort.

Sleepy Hollow Trail continues past the cliffs by crossing the stream, where it climbs out of the bowl and then crosses to the opposite ridge, providing a 180-degree view of this area. On the opposite ridge, the trail starts up again, traveling west. The trail bends right, and is wide and well marked. There is mountain laurel in the understory. Upon reaching a fire road, turn right, walk toward a natural gas pipeline, and look for the trail continuing uphill to the left. A short, moderate ascent leads to the end of the trail at another well-worn fire road.

A sign for Martin Ridge Trail points left. Turn left and follow the fire road about 0.5 mile. There will be several side roads; stay on the main road by following the markers for the gas line. Look for another small sign on the left pointing out the Martin Ridge Trail. This trail is pleasant but relatively mild compared to Sleepy Hollow.

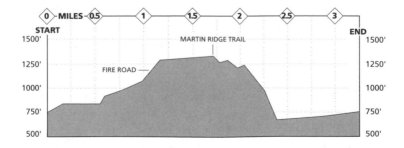

The trail enters the woods and then starts up slightly. It wraps to the right around a point and starts down traveling to the west. There is laurel in the understory and a stand of hemlock. The trail bends left through a drainage and begins traveling south, heading downhill to CR 35. The trail is easy to follow and frequently is flanked by earthen berms 8 to 10 feet tall. At 0.75 mile from the fire road, the trail opens up at a picnic area across the road from the swimming pool. Turn left and follow CR 35 about 1.6 miles to the Sweetwater Picnic Area.

Tulip Tree to Gentle Oak Trail Loop

46

Huntington Museum of Art National Recreation Trail and Bird Sanctuary

Overview: *The Huntington Museum of Art is the state's largest accredited arts museum, offering exhibits in the folk arts, turn-of-the-century American and European paintings, prints, sculpture, and glass. The museum also has a wonderful plant conservatory. Admission to the museum is free, but donations are accepted. The trails are free to the public.*

General description: A short loop through a beautiful sheltered cove.
General location: Huntington
Length: 1.25 miles
Difficulty: Easy
Special attractions: The art center and a beautiful hollow filled with large cove hardwoods. The Tulip Trail is also a self-guided interpretive trail.

Maps: Huntington Museum of Arts trail map; USGS quad: Huntington
Camping: None
Seasons: Open year-round, 10:00 A.M. to 5:00 P.M. Monday through Saturday; noon to 5:00 P.M. Sunday.
For information: Huntington Museum of Arts, 2033 McCoy Road, Huntington, WV 25701; (304) 529–2701

Finding the trailhead: Take I–64 to exit 8 and turn north on WV 527. Take the first right and proceed 1.4 miles to a T intersection. Turn left and take the next left to enter the parking lot for the Huntington Arts Center. There is parking at the trailhead, which is on the right side of the building.

The hike: At the iron posts and lintel that supports an eagle, begin following a gravel path into the woods. At the end of the fence is a right switchback. The junction with the Gentle Trail is just past the switchback. The Gentle Trail exits left and makes a flat, easy 0.25-mile loop back to the parking area.

Tulip Tree to Gentle Oak Trail Loop

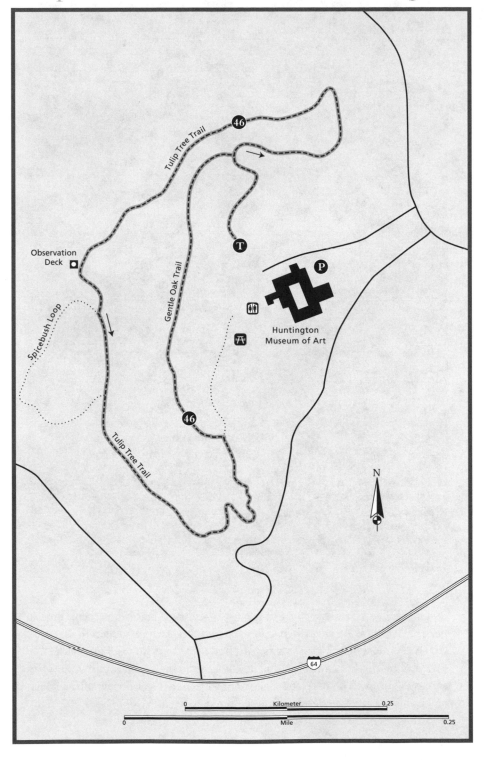

Tulip Tree Trail

46

Observation
Deck

Gentle Oak Trail

Spicebush Loop

P

Huntington
Museum of Art

T

46

Tulip Tree Trail

N

64

| 0 | Kilometer | 0.25 |
| 0 | Mile | 0.25 |

A rock crevice on Tulip Tree Trail.

The Tulip Tree Trail turns right and begins a gradual descent into a beautiful hollow. At a left bend, the trail begins a more moderate descent, which even includes a set of stairs. After crossing over three small bridges, a side trail on the left climbs the hill and intersects the Gentle Trail. Continue an easy descent to an overlook on the left. There is a good view of the small creek and the tall hardwoods of the sheltered cove.

The trail continues its easy descent to an amphitheater and wooden overlook near the halfway point of the trail. Continue past the overlook to the junction with the Spicebush Loop, a short trail that descends to the creek and then climbs back up the hill to rejoin the Tulip Tree Trail.

The Tulip Tree Trail continues straight. The path is wide and level. The second junction with the Spicebush Loop is reached about 100 yards beyond the first. The Tulip Tree Trail contours along the hillside just below a rocky bluff. Just before the stone column and the gate, the trail turns left, exits the road, and begins a short, moderate climb. There is one switchback during the climb.

The trail begins to angle toward the rocky bluff and climbs through a narrow rocky crevice. At the top of the bluff, the grade is easy. Turn left on the Gentle Trail, which exits to the left. This trail travels along the top of the rocky bluff and returns to the Tulip Tree Trail on an easy grade. At the junction of the Tulip Tree Trail, turn right and make a short climb back to the parking area.

Overlook Rock Trail
Kanawha State Forest

Overview: *Located just minutes from Charleston, Kanawha State Forest is busy with outdoor activity. The 9,300-acre forest has more than 25 miles of trails enjoyed by hikers, mountain bikers, and horseback riders. Trails travel from rocky ridges to wooded coves. Summer brings swimmers to the pool, while winter draws cross-country skiers to the trails. Every season is enjoyed in Kanawha State Forest.*

General description: A short hike up the ridge to a small rock outcrop and then back down a neighboring shoulder.
General location: 7.0 miles south of Charleston
Length: 1.5 miles
Difficulty: Easy to moderate
Special attractions: Rocky outcrop with views.
Maps: Kanawha State Forest map and trail guide; USGS quads: Belle, Charleston East, Charleston West, Racine

Camping: The forest has forty-six campsites, twenty-three may be reserved.
Seasons: The state forest is open year-round. The campground is open from mid-April to early November.
For information: Kanawha State Forest, Route 2 Box 285, Charleston, WV 25314; (304) 558–3500

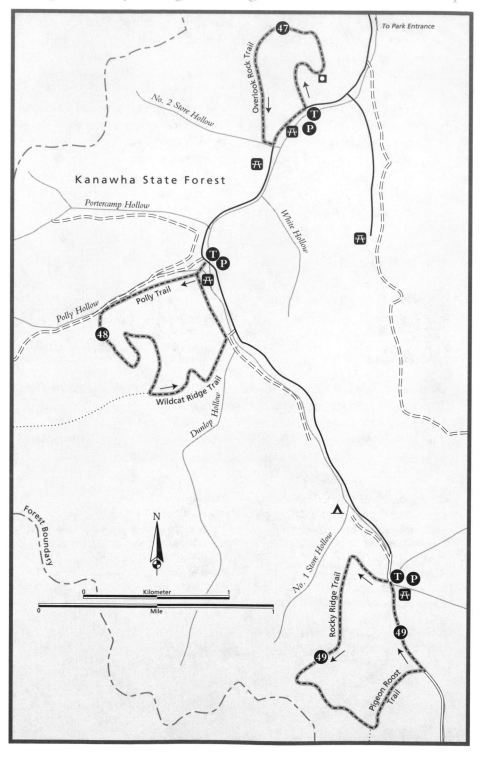

47

To Park Entrance

No. 2 Store Hollow

Overlook Rock Trail

T
P

Kanawha State Forest

Portercamp Hollow

White Hollow

T
P

Polly Hollow   Polly Trail

48

Wildcat Ridge Trail

Dunlop Hollow

N

Forest Boundary

0   Kilometer   1

0   Mile   1

No. 1 Store Hollow

Rocky Ridge Trail

T
P

49

49

Pigeon Roost Trail

Finding the trailhead: From I–64 in Charleston take exit 58A and turn south on US 119, following it for 0.25 mile. Take a left onto Oakwood Road and continue for 1 mile; then take a right onto Bridge Road, which eventually turns into Loudon Heights Road. Take a right onto Connell Road and follow it for 2 miles before turning left onto Kanawha Forest Drive. Follow the park road past the main picnic and swimming area. The trailhead is located on the right side of the road near a small sign just past the main picnic area. There is limited parking on the opposite side of the road.

From I–77, take exit 89 and turn south on WV 94. Follow this approximately 5 miles to CR 44 and turn right. It's another 4.5 miles to the trailhead. CR 44 will change to a dirt road. Continue past Johnson Hollow Picnic Area and the camping area. The trailhead is located on the left just past #2 Store Hollow before reaching the main picnic area and swimming pool. There is limited parking opposite the trailhead.

The hike: Overlook Rock Trail leaves the small parking area and enters the forest. The trail, marked by infrequent gold blazes, heads uphill at a moderate angle. The path leads to a small drainage that is free of water most of the year. The trail continues steeply uphill, passing some boulders. It crosses through the drainage and then bends to the left. Another difficult climb leads to the top of the shoulder.

At the crest of the shoulder, the trail reaches a junction less than 0.5 mile into the hike. A right leads a short distance to a scenic outcropping of rocks, the trail's namesake, where there are views to the south. A left at this intersection leads up the shoulder to the ridge crest. At this point the difficult climbs are over.

The next portion of the hike is along the top of this small hill. The trail continues up at a light angle as it makes its way across the ridge crest. There are limited views in winter along this section of the trail. Turn to the northwest (left) and continue along the crest through a forest of chestnut oaks with briars in the understory.

At just under 1.0 mile, the trail reaches a sign and another junction. There is a double yellow blaze at the sign, which reads OVERLOOK ROCK TRAIL. The trail turns left and heads downhill to the south-southeast, making its way at easy and moderate angles toward the bottom of the valley below. There is one short, difficult section as the trail passes by moss-covered boulders.

The trail bends right then makes a left switch and drops into the western side of the ridge. This valley is shaded and cool in the morning hours. The trail makes a few switchbacks and finally reaches the drainage at the valley floor. The switchbacks in this section of trail are badly eroded by "cutters," hikers who don't follow a switchback all the way through its turn but instead travel steeply downhill several feet before the switchback. The trail suffers greatly, as this steep cut section becomes badly eroded by surface-water runoff during heavy rains. Following switchbacks out completely helps preserve the very ground we hike on. Please respect the trail.

Upon reaching the valley bottom, Overlook Rock Trail exits the forest. There is a sign marking the trail and a picnic table and shelter. Walk down to the road, turn left, and hike back to the original parking area. The road hike will take approximately five minutes.

48 Polly to Wildcat Ridge Trail Loop / *Kanawha State Forest*

Overview: *Located in the figurative "back yard" of the state capital is the 9,300-acre Kanawha State Forest. In addition to 25 miles of trails, the State Forest has a playground for the kids, picnic areas for meals, and a swimming pool to relax in after a fun hike. The shooting range will help you prepare for the upcoming hunting seasons. With all that Kanawha State Forest has to offer the nearby metro population, it's no wonder it is a popular outdoor destination.*

General description: This hike travels up Polly Hollow past several rock outcrops to the top of Wildcat Ridge then down to Davis Creek before looping back around the ridge to the starting point.

General location: 7.0 miles south of Charleston

Length: 2.5 miles

Difficulty: Easy to moderate

Special attractions: Rock outcrops and hardwood forest.

Maps: Kanawha State Forest map and trail guide; USGS quads: Belle, Charleston East, Charleston West (location of hike), Racine

Camping: The forest has forty-six campsites, twenty-three may be reserved.

Seasons: The state forest is open year-round. The campground is open from mid-April to early November.

For information: Kanawha State Forest, Route 2 Box 285, Charleston, WV 25314; (304) 558–3500

See map on page 158.

Finding the trailhead: From I–64 in Charleston take exit 58A and turn south on US 119. Take a left onto Oakwood Road and a right onto Bridge Road, which eventually turns into Loudon Heights Road. Take a right onto Connell Road then turn left onto Kanawha Forest Drive. Follow the park road past the main picnic and swimming area. The parking area is located on the left just past the bridge over Davis Creek. The trailhead for Polly Trail is on the opposite side of the road.

From I–77, take exit 89 and turn south on WV 94. Follow this approximately 5 miles to CR 44 and turn right. From here it's about 3.75 miles to the trailhead.

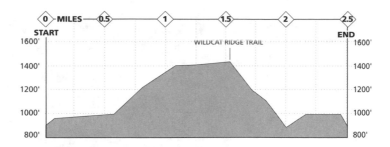

CR 44 will change to a dirt road. Continue past Johnson Hollow Picnic Area and the camping area. The parking area is on the right just before the bridge over Davis Creek. The trailhead for Polly Trail is on the opposite side of the road.

The hike: The hike begins across the road from the parking area. Follow the fire road, cross the creek, and turn left. The trail can be seen heading up the ridge to the right. A small sign identifies the trail and shows that blazes will be red diamonds. The trail travels west up a short-lived moderate to steep grade. As the trail levels out, the loop section of the hike is reached. Turn right and travel the loop in a counterclockwise direction. Oaks and beeches provide shade as the trail passes over a drainage via a small footbridge. Down and to the right are a fire road and a stream.

At about 0.5 mile, the fire road has caught up with the trail in elevation. The trail, road, and stream travel together for several hundred feet. At a double red blaze, the trail bends left, leaving the fire road and stream behind as it starts uphill it. Polly Trail climbs at a moderate angle through first a left then a right switchback. After the second switchback, the trail levels out and travels over a rocky path through a forest of chestnut oak and hemlock. Although the trail appears to be little used, the path is well blazed and easy to follow.

Toward the head of the wide valley the trail has been traveling, a left turn is made near a sofa-sized boulder. A steep ascent follows the turn. With the down side of the ridge now to the left, the trail continues its hike to the ridge crest at the base of sandstone rock outcrops at about the 1-mile mark. There are some wide, low overhangs that could provide shelter during an unexpected storm. The trail levels off and travels at the base of more rock outcrops. At one point it is necessary to scramble down between boulders to continue the trail. The trail reaches what appears to be a trail intersection, but it is not. Following the weak path downhill, it becomes clear to the hiker that this is not a trail at all. It peters out after about fifty yards. At the northwest terminus of the rock outcrops, turn right and follow Polly Trail between two large boulders and up to the top of the rock face. Stop and drink from your water bottle while absorbing the views to the west. This area is ablaze with blooming mountain laurel in May and June.

Mountain bikers often build up smaller logs to help cross a larger log.

Polly Trail leaves the rocks and travels due east across a wide, flat ridge top to the intersection with Wildcat Ridge Trail. A sign at the intersection points directions and names trails. Wildcat Ridge Trail travels both left and right at the junction. Turn left and follow the trail downhill as it begins the long, moderate descent off the ridge. Wildcat Ridge Trail is open to mountain bikers, but you can probably attribute the lack of tire marks to the steepness of the grade.

Wildcat Ridge Trail spends the next 0.5 mile descending the ridge. At 1.5 miles from the start of the hike, the trail bends to the right, then turns left at a double blue blaze near a wooden bench. At this turn an old trail travels at a steeper angle down the hill; keep left. Wildcat Ridge becomes steep and the trail travels through first a right then a left switchback. Hemlock dominates the canopy as the trail turns through another right switchback. This is a tough hike in the downhill direction, twice as tough if you choose to hike this loop in the opposite direction. The trail bends to the left and finally opens into a pasture and recreation area.

More signs point out Wildcat Ridge Trail. Walk toward the swings and another sign pointing out Polly Trail. Red blazes mark the trail as it starts up. The climb is light to moderate, leading around the ridge to the intersection with the spur trail to the original parking lot. Turn right at this intersection, follow the spur downhill, and continue across the creek to the parking area.

49 Rocky Ridge to Pigeon Roost Trail Loop / *Kanawha State Forest*

Overview: *Whether you like to hike, mountain bike, ride horseback, or just lie around the pool, Kanawha State Forest has you covered. Although the state forest is located just south of Charleston it seems worlds away from the high-density, metro population. The hiker will find wildflowers blooming along the trail, birds gliding from tree to tree, and deer grazing in the meadows. Kanawha State Forest provides an escape from the hustle and bustle of the Metro Valley.*

General description: This is a short hike to the crest of the aptly named Rocky Ridge and then back down to the main park road.
General location: 7.0 miles south of Charleston
Length: 2.75 miles
Difficulty: Easy to moderate
Special attractions: Rock outcrops and a 180-degree vista.
Maps: Kanawha State Forest map and trail guide; USGS quads: Belle, Charleston East, Charleston West, Racine

Camping: The forest has forty-six campsites, twenty-three may be reserved.
Seasons: The state forest is open year-round. The campground is open from mid-April to early November.
For information: Kanawha State Forest, Route 2 Box 285, Charleston, WV 25314; (304) 558–3500

See map on page 158.

Finding the trailhead: From I–64 in Charleston take exit 58A and turn south on US 119. Take a left onto Oakwood Road and a right onto Bridge Road, which eventually turns into Loudon Heights Road. Take a right onto Connell Road then turn left onto Kanawha Forest Drive. Follow the park road past the main picnic and swimming area and past the camping area. Park in the parking lot for Johnson Hollow Picnic Area. The picnic area is on the left. The trailhead for Rocky Ridge Trail is on the opposite side of the road at the south end of the parking area.

From I–77, take exit 89 and turn south on WV 94. Follow this about 5 miles to CR 44 and turn right. From here it's approximately 2.5 miles to the trailhead. CR 44 will change to a dirt road. Continue to the Johnson Hollow Picnic Area on the right. Park in the parking lot for Johnson Hollow Picnic area. The trailhead for Rocky Ridge Trail is on the opposite side of the road at the south end of the parking area.

The hike: The trail begins near a sign across the road from the picnic area at Johnson Hollow and Log Town Hollow. Rocky Ridge Trail is blue blazed and travels north, away from the main state forest road. The first section of the

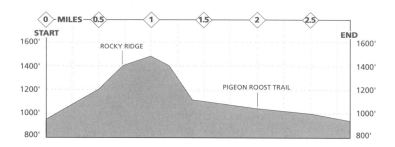

trail climbs gradually to the ridge top, making several bends as it trends northwest. At about 0.5 mile, the trail turns left and travels directly up the ridge. This short, steep climb leads to the ridge top and the trail's namesake, a rocky knob, with a 180-degree view from north to south. The trail continues to pass sandstone outcrops along Rocky Ridge.

The trail travels south across the ridge before climbing to the top of another knob, then levels off and follows the ridge crest. At about 1.0 mile the trail begins to descend and a double blue blaze alerts the hiker to a trail junction. A sign gives directions. Turn left and follow Rocky Ridge Trail downhill. The trail initially drops steeply off the ridge along a rocky path. The angle changes to moderate, though, and the trail passes through four switchbacks. After the final right switch, the grade becomes easy.

Rocky Ridge Trail intersects with Pigeon Roost Trail at about 2.0 miles; a sign points directions. Turn left and follow the red blazed Pigeon Roost Trail downhill to the southeast. There is a washout about 50 yards from the intersection, and evidence of mountain bike activity can be seen in the mud. Pigeon Roost Trail is a hiking/biking trail that has been both maintained and improved by local mountain bikers. Pass by a large tree across the path; logs have been stacked up on either side of it to create a stairway over the obstacle. This part of the hike is almost level. At about the 2.25-mile mark, Pigeon Roost Trail starts down and then widens to a fire road. The main state forest road can be seen ahead. At the main road, turn left and follow the gravel road a short distance back to the parking area.

50

Kanawha Trace Trail
Kanawha State Forest

Overview: *The 31.7-mile Kanawha Trace Trail is managed by the Tri-State Area Council of the Boy Scouts. The trail runs entirely on private land. For permission to hike the trail, contact the Tri State Area Council (see below). For a nominal group fee of 50 cents per person, the council will ferry gear to the two shelters, and provide a guide, a ride to the trailhead, and a ride back at the end of the hike. Individuals also pay 50 cents, but may be required to pay for fuel.*

General description: This rugged trail climbs and descends many ridges from the trailhead near Barboursville to the end at Fraziers Bottoms. The Blacks Creek Shelter is available to hikers on a first-come, first-served basis.
General location: Barboursville to Fraziers Bottom
Length: 31.7 miles
Difficulty: Difficult
Special attractions: Small rock cliffs, trickling waterfalls, and tall cove hardwoods.

Maps: A guidebook with maps is available from the Tri State Area Council in Huntington. USGS quads: Barboursville, Glenwood, Mount Olive, Milton, Winfield
Camping: There are two camping shelters along the trail.
Seasons: The trail is open year-round.
For information: Tri State Area Council, 733 Seventh Avenue, Huntington, WV 25701; (304) 523–3408

Finding the trailhead: Take I–64 to exit 20A (West Mall Road). At the stoplight, turn south and proceed to US 60. Turn left on US 60, travel 1.3 miles to the stoplight for Blue Sulphur Road, turn left, and proceed 1.5 miles to CR 17/4 (Boy Scout Camp Road). Turn right and continue 0.5 mile to Camp Arrowhead. Transportation to the trailhead is available at the Boy Scout camp.

The hike: The Kanawha Trace Trail begins near the junction of Merrick Creek and the Mud River. For the first 1.5 miles, the trail follows a paved road. The eastbound route is marked by a yellow blaze with a white rectangle above and below it. The westbound blaze is white with yellow rectangles.

The best starting place is where the trail exits the right side of the road and enters the woods, beginning a short, steep climb to the crest of a small ridge. There is a trail register after the fourth switchback, then two more switchbacks. On the crest, the trail begins to follow an old road. The climb continues but the grade is easy. The top of this climb is near milepost 2 at an elevation of almost 900 feet.

Kanawha Trace Trail

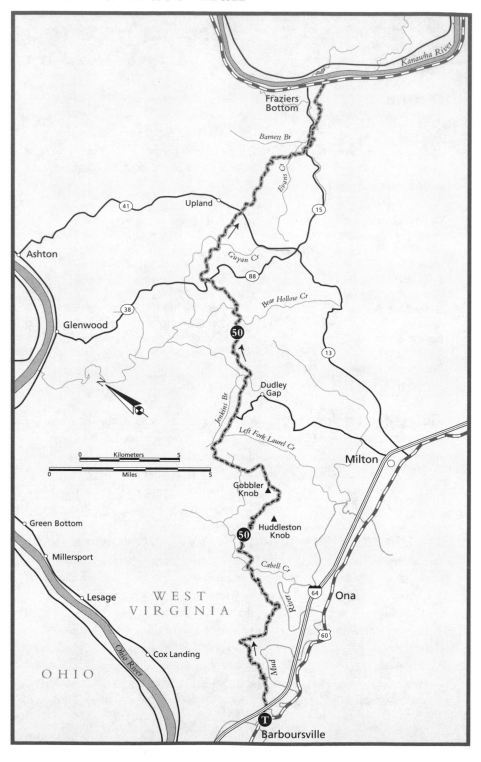

The trail continues the easy grade until it passes under a power line. It exits the old road it has been following and drops sharply to the east side of the ridge. After bottoming out in a narrow sheltered cove, cross two small streams and then head straight up the opposite ridge. The trail rolls over the crest and does another short, steep descent into Newman Hollow. There is a sign at the bottom of the hollow. Cross the creek and pass the remains of an old stone chimney. There is an easy climb out of the hollow, which is dominated by a beautiful stand of hardwoods.

While climbing out of the hollow, the trail passes milepost 3, then wraps around the left side of a small knoll and enters a meadow. The area is flat and the grade is easy. Along the crest, the trail follows an old road and passes milepost 4.

When the road forks, take the left fork. The trail soon leaves the road and drops off the left side of the ridge, crossing a fence via a stile and dropping sharply. After three switchbacks, enter Tag Hollow, which is signed, and follows the little creek down to Blue Sulphur Road. Turn left on the paved road and travel about 150 feet, then turn right off the road and begin paralleling Little Cabell Creek. A series of easy ups and downs leads past milepost 5.

After crossing Little Cabell Creek on a swinging bridge, the trail follows a wide old road. Turn right away from the house at the first fork and then left into a narrow hollow at the next fork. Follow a small feeder into a little rock canyon where there is a small waterfall. *These rocks can be slick, so exercise caution.* Climb out of the canyon and head to the Williams Shelter, which has a privy and water. This Adirondack shelter is one of two places through-hikers can spend the night. The Old Baldy Trail exits to the left of the shelter. Bear to the right, make a short moderate climb to a T intersection, and turn left.

The Old Baldy Trail rejoins the Kanawha Trace Trail near milepost 6. Climb to the crest of a ridge and follow an old road along the crest. Just past the junction of two logging roads, the trail exits the road to the left and contours just below the crest for a short distance. It drops down to and crosses a gravel road, then continues the descent through a gap in a small rock face to a small creek. Cross the creek. The trail parallels the stream past milepost 7.

Cross the creek a second time on a small bridge. Continue downstream to an old home site and follow a grassy road past an old barn to Big Cabell Creek. The trail crosses the creek on a swinging bridge. At the gravel road, turn right and parallel Big Cabell Creek. The elevation in this area is 580 feet. At the fork, head left and continue to follow the creek. The trail enters the woods and the road becomes grassy and a bit indistinct. Watch for the blazes. After crossing a feeder, make a left bend and follow the feeder downstream toward Big Cabell Creek. Just before the reaching the creek, the trail turns right and

The Kanawha Trace Trail is well maintained and well blazed throughout.

begins a short moderate climb. There is a big beech tree on the hillside. At the end of the climb, contour along the ridge just below a rock face.

Pass milepost 9 and climb up to the rocks. Make a right bend around the rock, and begin an easy descent to a meadow. The trail crosses the meadow and a small creek. Turn right on the paved road, walk about 150 yards, and exit the road to the left between the old barn and the white house. Walk straight up the hill and into the woods.

This wooded section is known as Wilson Woods. The trail enters a small cliff-lined hollow, a pleasant spot to sit and relax. There is a small waterfall at the end of the cliff. Walk under the overhang and behind the falls. The trail makes a short, steep climb and intersects the Adahi Trail, which now runs concurrent with the Kanawha Trace Trail. The trail wraps around the end of a bowl, turns right off the logging road, and climbs a short distance to the top of a finger ridge. On the ridge, the trail powers up the hill and then levels out on a narrow saddle at milepost 10.

Contour just below the crest to the junction with a logging road. Turn right, climb up the ridge to the paved road, and turn left. Follow the road past a gate and into the woods. About 100 feet past the gate, turn left and begin a gradual descent past milepost 11.

The trail crosses a narrow ridge and then makes a short, steep descent to McComas Branch. Cross the branch and the road. The elevation at the road is 780 feet. On the opposite side of the road, follow a logging road up the next ridge. This long climb leads to the summit of Gobbler Knob and the highest point on the trail (elevation 1,016 feet). Once on the crest, begin an easy stretch of almost flat hiking past milepost 12.

Follow the gravel road into a meadow and turn left at the paved road. Turn left again on the first road to the left. There is a blaze on a fence post. When the fence ends, begin a short, steep drop to the woods. Remember to go down the middle of this grassy bowl. The trail enters a narrow steep-walled hollow and passes milepost 13.

The trail drops steeply to the creek and follows a footpath along the left bank. Cross a stile and cross Big Cabell Creek. The trail traverses a meadow and climbs the embankment to the road. On the other side of the road, a short, steep climb leads to the ridge crest. Three switchbacks aid the climb. Once on the crest, begin a series of easy ups and downs along a narrow saddle.

Milepost 14 is passed just before a power line. The trail follows an old road through this area. Just before the meadow, turn right off the road and begin a short descent on a new rerouting of the trail. Pass through an area thick with sumac, climb to a paved road, and turn right. At the junction with Left Fork Baker Ridge Road, turn left and follow the road about 0.25 mile to some power poles on the right. Cross the electric fence at the orange hoses, pass through the meadow, and cross the electric fence again. *Be careful not to touch the fence.* On the other side of the fence, the trail enters the woods and passes milepost 15.

The trail is now paralleling Jenkins Branch and begins a long, gradual descent. There is a huge tulip poplar tree about 0.1 mile after entering the woods. This monster is the largest tree along the entire length of the trail. The trail crosses Jenkins Branch several times as it meanders downstream. Milepost 16 is passed near a small meadow.

Follow the footpath over several small feeder streams and cross over a fence on a stile. The trail enters a long narrow meadow. It is necessary to open a gate in the meadow; *remember to close it behind you.* A sign asks people to walk along the creek bank. Pass through a livestock fence and to the ford at Jenkins Branch near milepost 17.

Staying to the left of the creek, climb uphill through the blackberries and drop down into another meadow. Turn right on the road to a T intersection, turn left, and follow the paved road past milepost 18 to the pipeline that climbs up the hill on the right. The elevation here is 610 feet. The trail turns to the right just past the pipeline and begins to climb. After three switchbacks, cross over the pipeline route and begin to contour along the ridge. Tall second-growth hardwood dominates the canopy. Cross a feeder stream and power up the side of the hill and past milepost 19.

The trail is flat for a short distance as it passes around the end of a wide bowl. Cross over the top of a rock overhang and bend left. Climb out of the bowl up to the paved Dry Ridge Road. Turn left and follow the road to the red gate, cross the gate, and follow the gravel road to a second red gate. Cross this gate to enter the meadow at the Blackjack School near milepost 20.

The Blackjack School is an old one-room schoolhouse built in 1883. The building is the second stopover point on the trail. The schoolhouse has eighteen bunks and a woodstove. There is potable water in the cistern as well as a privy.

The trail turns left just past the schoolhouse and begins to descend into Bear Hollow, following a logging road down the hill to a saddle. In the saddle, the trail exits the logging road on the left, climbs a small knoll, and then descends back to the logging road. The road forks; follow the grassy fork a short distance. A footpath exits to the left and descends sharply to Bear Creek. There are five switchbacks in the descent. Jump the creek, turn right, and follow the creek upstream to a small feeder. Turn left and head upstream. Pass through the meadow, cross a stile, and follow the abandoned state road as it passes milepost 21.

The road climbs gradually to a paved road. The elevation at this intersection is 750 feet. Turn left on the paved road and begin a long descent past milepost 22. At the intersection of Meadow Hollow Road, turn right and begin a long stretch on a gravel road. Four dogs reside at the first house on the right.

The road parallels the Guyan Creek upstream past mileposts 23 and 24. At the T intersection, turn right and follow Guyan Creek Road. There is a short moderate climb followed by a short moderate descent past milepost 25. The road bottoms out along a small creek and then climbs to a paved road. Turn right on Upland Mason Road and then left on Mt. Zion Road. Follow the road past the church and milepost 26. This is a gradual climb.

Stay on the road to the logging road that exits to the left. There is a cable across the road. The trail exits to the left just past the logging road and climbs into the woods between the two roads. A short climb is followed by a short moderate descent back to the road. Milepost 27 is passed near the crest of the climb.

Cross the road and continue to descend to an old clear-cut. Begin a series of short, tiring ups and downs. The trail exits the clear-cut and follows and old road to a power line. Turn right and cross under the power line to a wide grassy road that descends to a gravel road. Cross the gravel road and traverse the meadow to a narrow hollow. Begin climbing out of the hollow on an old logging road. Milepost 28 is in this hollow.

The trail makes a short moderate climb to a flat ridge. The ground is covered with ferns and running cedar. The wide old road passes under a forest of tall evergreens. Make a left bend on an old skid road and begin a long gradual descent into a clear-cut. Parallel the woods to the logging road. Turn left on the logging road and climb gradually. After a left bend, the trail exits the logging road on the right and climbs to the 800-foot mark. Cross over a narrow saddle near milepost 29.

Begin a steep descent down to Barnett Branch. Several well-built switchbacks aid in the descent. Cross the creek and turn right. After about 100 feet, turn left and cross a boggy area. At the next ridge, begin climbing the Devil's Stairway, a long moderate climb that gains about 260 feet in 0.25 mile. The climb begins with several switchbacks to a finger ridge. Wrap around the ridge and climb to the top of a small rock outcrop. Continue climbing the ridge to the logging road, cross the road, and enter a stand of small hardwoods. The trail parallels the road a short distance through a series of easy ups and downs. Turn left and begin a moderate descent to the end of a narrow ridge, then make a short, steep drop down to the creek. Parallel the creek downstream. After crossing a small feeder stream, the trail passes milepost 30.

Begin a series of short ups and downs as the trail slowly gains elevation. Climb over a stile and parallel the fence to the ridge. On the crest, turn right and follow an old logging road down the ridge. At the loop, continue straight. There are some old cedars growing in the woods in this area. Make a sharp descent off of the left side of the ridge, cross a small creek, climb the other side, and begin another descent between two old fences. The trail turns right and begins another short climb to an old road. Turn right, walk a short distance, turn left off of the road, and descend to a meadow. Many thick old sycamore trees thrive at the end of this meadow. Cross a stile and pass through a wet marshy area as the trail follows a small stream on an easy grade. After crossing a second stile, the marshy area develops into a small stream on the right. The stream empties into the Five and Twentymile Creek.

Just before the bridge, pass milepost 31. Turn right on the paved Stave Branch Road and walk to the intersection of US 35 in Fraziers Bottom at 31.7 miles.

Mid-Ohio
VALLEY

Like the slow moving Ohio River for which this region is named, the Mid-Ohio Valley is a laid-back, slow moving, rural delight. In this region, rolling hills and shallow canyons give way to the mighty river to the west. The river defined life here, and its influence is still felt today. If the river is queen in the region, then craft is king. Many glass factories and craft shops cater to shoppers.

Hikes here are relaxed and leisurely, with minimal elevation gains and losses. On the North Bend Rail Trail, it is often difficult to discern whether you are traveling uphill or down. One hike in this section even requires a ride on a stern-wheeler—now that's easy on the feet! Wildlife management areas provide prime wildlife viewing, and some hikes can make you feel miles from civilization.

Many hikes incorporate the flavor of the people into the hiking experience. The North Bend Rail Trail passes through charming small towns throughout its course. Likewise, Blennerhassett Island incorporates a mansion and wagon rides into its "heritage" experience. Camping is treated as a social activity, and an interesting character and his Harley-Davidson are often parked at the next campsite.

In the Mid-Ohio Valley, all roads lead to Parkersburg, the metro center of the region. The city sits on the banks of the Ohio River and offers most services one might need. Victorian architecture dots the city, and stern-wheelers travel the river. A joy to visit in its own right, Parkersburg can serve as a plush spike camp for hikes in the Mid-Ohio Valley.

51

Island Road
Blennerhassett Island Historical State Park

Overview: *The 500-acre Blennerhassett Island is located near the confluence of the Ohio River and the Little Kanawha River. Blennerhassett Island is owned by E. I. DuPont de Nemours and Company but is held in a long-term lease by the state. The fifth largest island on the Ohio River, it is less than a quarter mile wide, but is 3.8 miles long. The state of West Virginia is developing the eastern end of the island as a historical site. The Blennerhassett Mansion has been reconstructed on the original site. The hike begins by climbing aboard a stern-wheeler for a short trip down the Ohio River. Landing on Blennerhassett Island is something akin to stepping back in time. The park has the second largest tulip poplar on the east coast and several historical buildings, as well as a snack stand and bicycle rentals.*

General description: A short, easy loop hike on the fifth largest island on the Ohio River.

General location: Parkersburg

Length: 1.5 miles

Difficulty: Easy

Special attractions: A stern-wheeler ride to the park, mansion tours, and wagon rides.

Maps: Blennerhassett Island Historical State Park map; USGS quad: Parkersburg

Camping: Day-use-only area.

Seasons: The Island is closed from October 29 to April 1 and on Monday throughout the remainder of the year. It is also closed on Wednesday from September 4 to October 28.

Permits and fees: The cost to ride the stern-wheeler to Blennerhassett Island is $7.00.

For information: Blannerhassett Island Historical State Park, 137 Julianna Street, Parkersburg, WV 26101-5331; (304) 420–4800

Finding the trailhead: Take I–77 to exit 173 and follow the signs for CR 95. Go west on CR 95 for 2.9 miles to the fifth stoplight. Turn right on WV 14, continue 0.9 miles, and turn left on Market Street. Turn right on Second Street. The museum is located at the intersection of Second Street and Juliana Street. Parking is located behind the museum and at any spot with a white "M". The landing for the stern-wheeler is just north of the museum beyond the floodwall. The trip to the island takes approximately 20 minutes. There are rest room facilities on the island.

The hike: After disembarking the stern-wheeler, follow the gravel path past the huge tulip poplar tree. This tree has an 8-foot diameter and a circumference of 24 feet. The tree originally stood some 76 feet high before the top was knocked out in a storm. Just past the tree, the gravel path forks; take the right fork.

174

Island Road

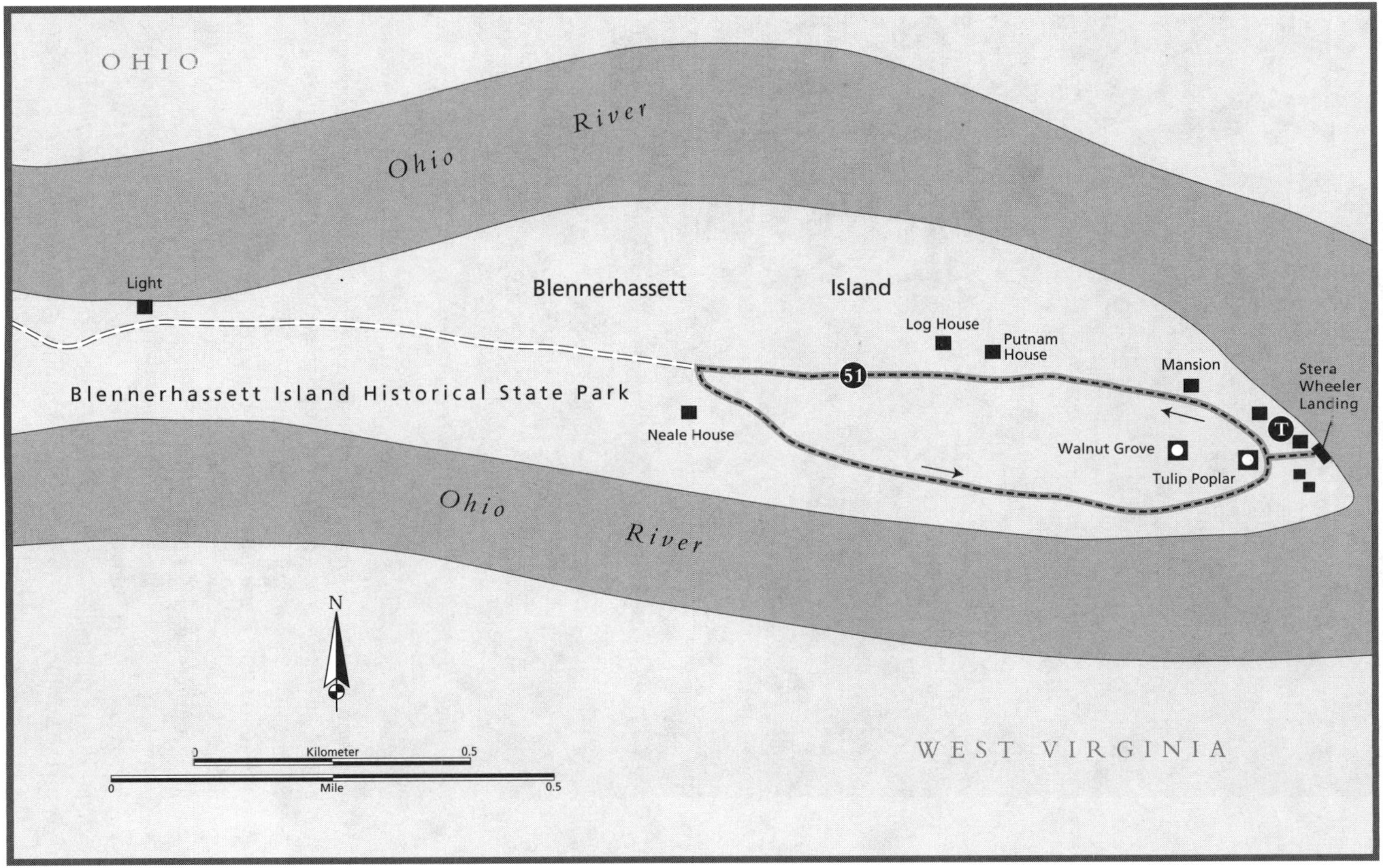

OHIO

Ohio River

Blennerhassett Island

Blennerhassett Island Historical State Park

Ohio River

Light

Neale House

51

Log House

Putnam House

Mansion

Walnut Grove

Tulip Poplar

Stera Wheeler Lancing

T

WEST VIRGINIA

N

Kilometer   0   0.5

Mile   0   0.5

A carriage ride on Blennerhassett Island's main road.

The reconstructed Blennerhassett mansion is on the right. On the opposite side of the path is a large black walnut plantation, planted in the early 1930s. On the right are several more structures that have been rebuilt on the island. The gravel path bends left at the halfway point of the island. There is another old brick structure, the Neale House, on the left. Walt Whitman stayed in this house during the winter of 1849.

Once around the bend, the path enters a large meadow and begins to make its way back to the point of the island. Deer and turkey are plentiful along this portion of the trail. Near the end of the meadow is a massive silver maple. Just past the maple, the path bends left and returns to the starting point.

52

McDonough Trail Loop
McDonough Wildlife Refuge

Overview: *The refuge is a small 277-acre area managed for wildlife. The Vienna Department of Parks and Recreation oversees management. Wildlife that may be encountered include white-tailed deer, turkey, red and gray fox, and coyote. Migratory waterfowl inhabit two ponds found within the refuge. The refuge offers several trails and loops of various lengths. All of the trails are easy to follow and they are well maintained.*

General description: The McDonough Trail passes through wetlands and a forested hillside.

General location: Vienna

Length: 2.1 miles

Difficulty: Easy

Special attractions: Deer, turkeys, geese, and ducks are a common sight along the trail.

Maps: McDonough Wildlife Refuge map; USGS quad: Parkersburg

Camping: There is no camping in the refuge.

Seasons: The refuge is open for hiking year-round.

For information: McDonough Wildlife Refuge, Director of Parks, P.O. Box 5097, Vienna, WV 26105; (304) 295–4473

Finding the trailhead: Take I–77 to exit 179. Turn south on WV 68 (Emerson Avenue) and proceed 3.0 miles to a stoplight at Rosemar Avenue. Turn right on Rosemar and continue 5.2 miles to the refuge entrance on the right. Proceed 0.2 mile to the parking area. The trailhead is located at the end of the parking area.

The hike: There are two trailheads for the McDonough Trail. This description begins with the trailhead that exits the parking area to the left. The trail begins with a brief descent down a set of stairs to two small game ponds. These steps can be slippery when wet, so use caution.

The McDonough Trail crosses between the two ponds and reenters the woods. The trail is wide and easy to follow. About 150 feet after entering the woods, the trail bends left at a trail junction. The 0.7-mile Marsh Run Trail continues straight, paralleling a small creek drainage back to an intersection with the McDonough Trail. The Marsh Run Trail shortens the length of the loop by about half.

Turn left to stay on the McDonough Trail as it begins a short moderate climb through a stand of young oak and shagbark hickory. Wooden steps assist the climb. At the top of the stairs, the trail bends right and the grade is easy. Soon the 0.4-mile White Tail Trail exits right and climbs to a small meadow

McDonough Trail Loop

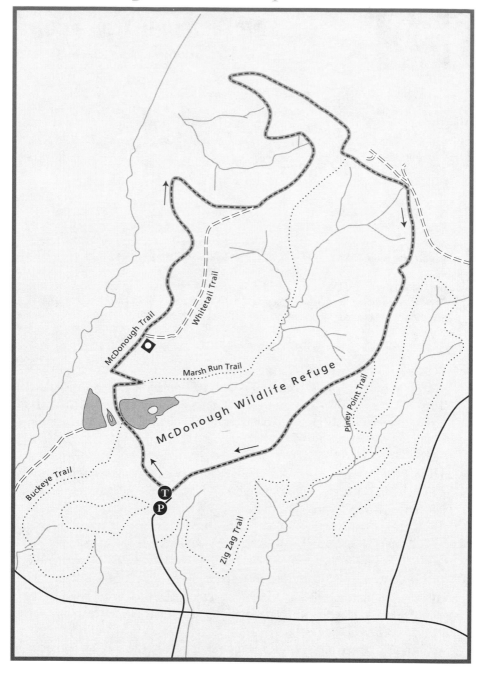

where there is a game observation platform. The White Tail Trail continues past the platform and reconnects with the McDonough Trail.

After the first intersection with the White Tail Trail, the McDonough Trail contours just below the ridge crest. The second intersection with the White Tail Trail is reached at 0.8 mile. The McDonough Trail begins a gradual climb with a right switchback near a small shelter. The trail climbs to the summit of the ridge. A small field in the early stages of forest succession lies at the top of the climb, and the trail becomes flat and easy.

At 1.4 miles the Marsh Run Trail exits right. Houses crowd the scenery on the left side of the trail. Soon the trail becomes wide and grassy and is lined with short evergreens. Not long after entering this area, the trail drops back down to the parking area.

McDonough Trail passes through a small meadow.

53

North Bend Rail Trail

Overview: *In the northern part of West Virginia, roughly parallel to US 50 between the towns of Parkersburg and Clarksburg, lies the 72-mile-long multiuse North Bend Rail Trail. The trail is a reminder of times gone by. You can almost hear the train whistle blow as you hike through dark tunnels and across old railroad bridges. This is not a wilderness hike; small towns dot the trail like beads on a necklace, adding to the trail's charm.*

General description: A wonderful hike through true Americana, the rail-trail travels through tunnels, across bridges, and past old train stops long forgotten. The trail is also open to bicycles.

General location: Linear trail runs from Parkersburg to Wolf Summit. The access at North Bend State Park is 25 miles east of Parkersburg and 55 miles west of Clarksburg.

Length: The entire trail is 72 miles. North Bend State Park to Pennsboro is 10.0 miles one-way. North Bend State Park to Cairo is 3.0 miles one-way.

Difficulty: Easy

Special attractions: Small towns, dark tunnels, bridges spanning the Hughes River.

Maps: The *Track Record Commercial Atlas*; USGS quads (for the section between Cairo and Pennsboro): Cairo, Harrisville, Ellenboro, Pennsboro.

Camping: Camping is permitted along the trail. There are picnic tables and campsites at various intervals.

Seasons: The trail is open year-round.

For information: North Bend Rails-to-Trails Foundation, P.O. Box 206, Cairo, WV 26337; (304) 643–2500. North Bend State Park, Route 1 Box 221, Cairo, WV 26337; (304) 643–2931

Finding the trailhead: Access to the North Bend Rail Trail can be found at numerous locations along the trail, from the western terminus in Parkersburg to the eastern terminus in Clarksburg.

The hikes described here begin at North Bend State Park. To reach the park, travel first to Cairo, located on WV 31 south of US 50, approximately 50.7 miles west of Clarksburg and 21.7 miles east of Parkersburg. From WV 31, turn left onto Low Gap Run Road (CR 14). Follow CR 14 3 miles to the park and follow the signs for the Rail Trail. At the campground, turn left and cross a bridge over the Hughes River. Take another left into the "International Sports Jamboree." Pass the volleyball courts and park in a gravel lot near the picnic shelter. The wide Extra Mile Trail leads northwest to the intersection with the North Bend Rail Trail.

The hike: The North Bend Rail Trail is wide and easy to follow. Most of the trail is double-track and is surfaced with small gravel, and it is as flat as West

North Bend Rail Trail

White-tailed deer warm themselves in the morning sunlight.

Virginia hiking can be. Hikes of varying lengths can be created using the trail map and mileage log. Unless you have two vehicles, all hikes on the rail trail are out-and-back. Thus, a 4-mile one-way is already an 8-mile day. The flat, easy-hiking nature of this rail trail, however, will allow you to hike a longer, faster day than just about anywhere else in West Virginia.

From the parking area, follow the Extra Mile Trail away from the picnic shelter to where it intersects with the North Bend Rail Trail.

To travel the trail east, turn right and immediately hike through a tunnel. The trail travels through several tunnels before crossing under US 50 just before reaching Ellenboro, about 4.0 miles from the park. An interesting landmark in Ellenboro is the glass factory. The rail trail passes through the parking lot of the factory, and the cherry red glow from the heat can be seen in the furnaces.

Continuing east, the rail trail travels through rural America on its way to Pennsboro, about 10.0 miles from the state park. The trail passes over creeks and streams and through another tunnel on its way. Be sure to see the Old Stone House in Pennsboro, an old stagecoach inn that is now a museum.

If hiking west from North Bend State Park, turn left at the intersection of the rail trail and the Extra Mile Trail, and immediately cross a bridge over the Hughes River. The trail crosses the Hughes several more times and passes through the crossroads of Cornwallis during the 3.0 miles to Cairo. Have lunch in Cairo and then a leisurely walk back to the state park. If you're looking for a quick getaway, rent a bike from Country Trails (304–628–3100) and ride back.

Nature Trail
North Bend State Park

54

Overview: *Tucked away in the rolling hills of northern West Virginia is North Bend State Park. Named for the bend in the North Fork of the Hughes River, the park offers natural beauty and modern accommodations. The North Bend Lodge and accompanying restaurant are open year-round to pamper the hiker who appreciates the finer things in life. Cottages that sport telephones, televisions, and fireplaces can be a rustic, romantic alternative to the campground, which is closed in winter. Swimming pools, miniature golf, game courts, and a fishing pond add to the activities list. The park contains approximately 15.5 miles of trails and is bordered by the 72-mile North Bend Rail (see Hike 53).*

General description: A circuit hike that loops through the entire North Bend area.
General location: 25 miles east of Parkersburg, 55 miles west of Clarksburg
Length: 4.5 miles
Difficulty: Moderate
Special attractions: Hardwood forests, rock outcrops, and the banks of the Hughes River.
Maps: North Bend State Park map and trail guide; USGS quads: Cairo, Harrisville

Camping: Seventy-six campsites are available at the state park, fifteen may be reserved.
Seasons: Mid-April through November.
For information: North Bend State Park, Route 1 Box 221, Cairo, WV 26337; (304) 643–2931

Finding the trailhead: To reach North Bend State Park, travel first to Cairo, located on WV 31 south of US 50, approximately 50.7 miles west of Clarksburg and 21.7 miles east of Parkersburg. From WV 31 turn onto Low Gap Run Road (CR-14). Follow CR 14 3 miles to the park and follow the signs to the campground. The trailhead is located on the left side of the road near campsite 47. There is no parking at the trailhead. Continue straight to find parking. At the campground, turn left and cross a bridge over the Hughes River. Take another left into the "International Sports Jamboree." Pass the volleyball courts and park in a gravel lot near the picnic shelter.

The hike: The orange blazed Nature Trail drops down off the north side of the main park road near campsite 47. The trail leads to the edge of the North Fork of the Hughes River before bending left and hiking steeply up the ridge. The short ascent is not sustained; the trail bends right and begins to contour. The height of the ridge affords views of the river below. At about 0.5 mile the trail starts down and works its way back to the river. As the trail levels out again an intersection is reached. A right at this intersection leads northeast toward

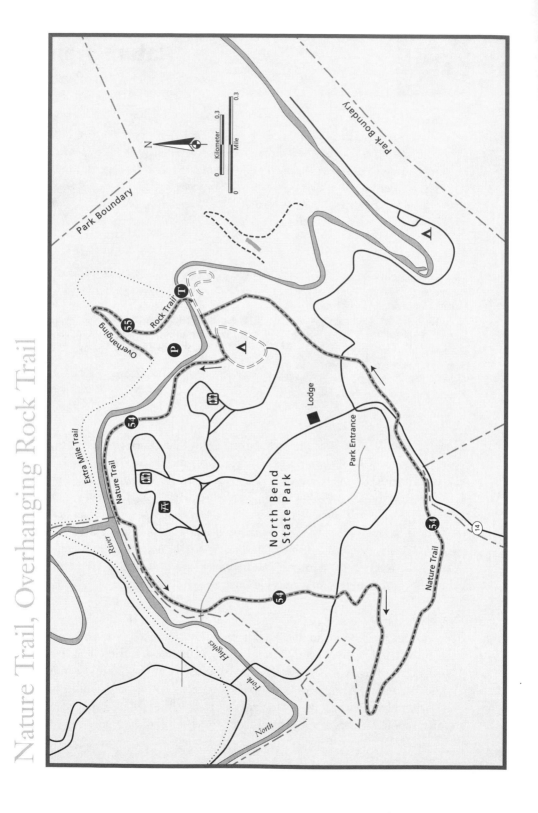

the river. To continue the Nature Trail, follow the left fork across a shallow, muddy drainage, following the orange blazes.

The Nature Trail now travels in the floodplain of the river. In the summer the trail is choked with weeds. At just under 0.75 mile, the trail bends left and starts up the ridge again. Rocks and stones are arranged into a staircase. Weeds prosper in the sunny forest gaps left by numerous downed trees. Soon, however, the forest becomes dark in the shade of gigantic tulip poplars. The Nature Trail passes through the first of three picnic shelters, then starts downhill in a stand of hemlock trees.

At just over 1.0 mile, the trail bends to the right through a dry drainage and then climbs again to the second picnic shelter. Walk toward the rest room and then look to the right for the trail to start a moderate descent. The trail in this section is in need of maintenance. It is evident that storm water drains straight down the middle of the trail. At the base of this ridge, the trail crosses the small feeder stream then passes through thick weeds under a power line. From here, Nature Trail begins its ascent of the ridges.

The first climb begins along the edge of the power line near a small feeder stream. The stream is pleasant and trickles over sandstone slabs. Soon, however, the trail leaves the stream behind and begins a moderate to difficult climb of the ridge. The trail climbs for about one-eighth of a mile, levels off, and then climbs again to the ridge crest. At the crest, the first climb is conquered.

Nature Trail meanders slightly downhill to a road crossing. The trail is picked up across the road near a sign. The path snakes through the forest and bends right toward a large rock outcrop. A large bowl is cut out of the rock. At the front of this rock, turn left and follow the trail uphill. This is important because the trail appears to follow the front of the rock face. This is not the case. The trail makes a left switchback at the very beginning of the outcrop and begins a moderate ascent that leads to the second crest of the hike.

A few "tabletops," areas where steeper sections of trail are broken by nearly flat sections, are passed on the way to the ridge crest. As the trail reaches the ridge top, it turns left and begins hiking straight across the crest. Nature Trail in this area is wide and appears to be an old road. The chestnut oaks that occupy

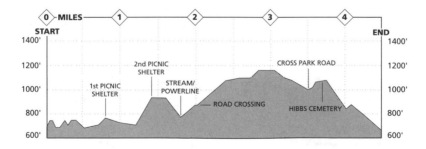

the canopy are testament to the harshness of the ridge top environment. At about 3.0 miles, another moderate ascent leads past a utilities junction box.

Not long after the junction box, the trail begins to descend toward another park road. As the road nears, Nature Trail drops off the ridge to the left. A clearing dotted with spruce is reached, and wooden stairs lead up to a road crossing. Cross the road and then follow the trail across the shoulder. Another moderate descent leads back to the road.

Directly across the road, Nature Trail reenters the forest and leads down to a slate-bottom stream. The small footbridge is quaint. A moderate ascent leads to Hibbs Cemetery and another large rock outcrop. This time the trail is on top of the rocks. During busy months, children can be heard at the campground below. The trail drops off the rocks and travels down to the campground. Nature Trail exits the forest near the campground sign-in station.

55 Overhanging Rock Trail
North Bend State Park

Overview: *North Bend State Park has so much to offer that visitors have to make choices. First, the hiker has to choose a trail: one of the 15.5 miles of trail in the park or some of the 72 miles of the neighboring North Bend Rail Trail. If you plan to spend the night in the park, you must decide between star-filled sites at the campground, camp cottages which give you a roof over your head and a bed to lie down in, or a night in the lodge which can satisfy the most discriminating sleeper. When it's mealtime, guests of the park can decide to cook on their camp stoves or dine in luxury at the lodge restaurant. Fishing, swimming in the pool, putt-putt golf, and playing sports at the "Jamboree" all vie for your time and attention. It's certain the visitor will not be at a loss for something to do, but may have trouble deciding what to do next.*

General description: This hike is an easy stroll up a deep, cool ravine. Water pouring down the canyon for thousands of years has carved unique formations in the underlying bedrock.

General location: 25 miles east of Parkersburg, 55 miles west of Clarksburg

Length: 0.5 mile

Difficulty: Easy, but steep in sections

Special Attractions: Cool gorge and interesting rock formations.

Maps: North Bend State Park map and trail guide; USGS quads: Cairo, Harrisville

Camping: Seventy-six campsites are available at the state park; fifteen may be reserved.

Seasons: Mid-April through November.

For information: North Bend State Park, Route 1 Box 221, Cairo, WV 26337; (304) 643–2931

See map on page 184.

Finding the trailhead: To reach North Bend State Park, travel first to Cairo, located on WV 31 south of US 50, approximately 50.7 miles west of Clarksburg and 21.7 miles east of Parkersburg. From WV 31 turn a left onto Low Gap Run Road (CR-14). Follow this road 3 miles to the park and follow the signs for the campground. At the campground, turn left and cross a bridge over the Hughes River. Take another left into the "International Sports Jamboree." Pass the volleyball courts and park in a gravel lot near the picnic shelter.

The hike: From the parking area and the picnic shelter, follow the road back to the entrance of the International Sports Jamboree. The trail begins at a sign near the entrance to the Jamboree. Overhanging Rock Trail is blazed with a white star. Follow the trail as it travels just inside the forest edge, paralleling the sports area. When the trail splits, be careful to follow it to the left. The trail to the right will immediately climb very steeply as it bends back to the right. The left fork continues to move away from the trailhead at the moderate angle. As the hike gains a few feet of altitude, the trail becomes rocky. Large slab boulders line the trail's borders. Overhanging Rock Trail reaches the edge of a steep shoulder and then turns right to travel along the edge of a deep ravine.

As you hike, the overhanging rocks will come into view down and to the left. Over thousands of years, the stream eroded this valley. Softer rocks were worn away and the harder, more resistant sandstone was left behind. These leftover rocks became rounded from the weathering. The streambed is lined with this rock, and has molded it into a half tunnel. The overhanging rocks are rounded like half of a tube, often tall enough for a short person to stand under.

The trail hikes up the valley past the rocks, then turns right and descends to the streambed. From here the trail travels downstream in the streambed, giving you a hands-on introduction to the rock. After about 75 yards, the trail turns right and ascends the opposite bank, then travels downhill much nearer the valley floor than the hike up the ravine.

Overhanging Rock Trail follows the stream to its intersection with Extra Mile Trail. From this point, follow Extra Mile Trail back to the original trailhead, or pass through the small meadow to the parking area near the picnic shelter.

Monongahela
NATIONAL FOREST

Since 1915, when the first 7,200 acres were purchased, the Monongahela National Forest has grown to more than 900,000 acres. This land is a dream for the outdoor enthusiast. Trout streams cascade off of ridges, rock climbers cling to the lofty crags of Tuscarora sandstone, and the whoop of white-water rafters can be heard in the valleys. More than 500 miles of hiking trails travel the land. So many miles, so little time.

Hikes in the Monongahela are rugged. Of the thirteen hikes described in this section, eight are listed as difficult. Four of the remaining five hikes are moderate. Elevations in the forest range from 900 to 4,800 feet. Hikes to ridge crests are steep and sustained, and creek bottoms are deep and shadowed. Five federally designated wilderness areas provide the promise of solitude, bringing with it added personal responsibility. When hiking in the Monongahela, special care should be taken to ensure self-sufficiency. Take extra clothes, food, and a map and compass (see the essential gear list in the introduction). If you become lost or hurt in the Monongahela, it could be quite some time before you are found. Don't count on another hiker happening by in your time of need.

Camping possibilities are limitless in the Monongahela. Although campgrounds dot the land, this is the place to don the backpack and camp in the backcountry, where beautiful streamside or ridge-top campsites can be found. The sheer joy of being utterly alone and looking out your tent into a flawless, star-filled sky cannot be underestimated.

The area surrounding the Monongahela is, in a word, rural. Enjoy the small towns that line the county routes, but be sure you are well equipped before leaving for your trip. Trying to find an outfitter to replace a worn-out hip belt on your backpack will not be an option.

Finally, exercise caution during hunting seasons, which generally, but not exclusively, occur during the fall and early winter. Before heading out on your hike, please review local hunting regulations and be aware of any hunting season that is open. If you choose to hike during a hunting season, wear blaze orange and stick to well-marked, well-traveled trails.

56 Cranberry Bog Boardwalk
Cranberry Glades Botanical Area

Overview: *The Cranberry Glades Botanical Area protects 750 acres of mountain bogs. Bogs are black, acidic soil wetlands that are more commonly found in northern boreal forests. The ecosystems found here are holdovers from the glacial age of 10,000 years ago. The bog ecosystem is very fragile. Please stay on boardwalks where present.*

General description: The high elevation of the Cranberry Glades Botanical Area protects many unusual plant species that migrated here during the last glacial period. Walking through the glade is similar to walking through the bogs of upper New York State.

General location: 17 miles west of Marlinton

Length: 0.6 mile

Difficulty: Easy

Special attractions: A wheelchair-accessible trail through a beautiful high bog.

Maps: USGS quad: Lobelia

Camping: Camping is not permitted in the Cranberry Glades Botanical Area.

Seasons: The road can be impassable in the winter due to snow.

For information: District Ranger, USDA Forest Service, P.O. Box 110, Richwood, WV 26261; (304) 846–2695

Finding the trailhead: At the intersection of WV 219, WV 39, and WV 55 south of Marlinton, turn west on WV39 and WV55. Proceed 7.0 miles and turn right on FDR 102. There is a sign for the Botanical Area at this intersection. Proceed 1.7 miles to a parking area on the right.

The hike: At the beginning of the hike, a Forest Service interpretive board provides information about the Cranberry Glades area. The boardwalk is an interpretive trail in a wet marshy area drained by the Yew Creek. This description is in a clockwise direction. After the loop junction, the trail enters an open 28-acre area called Round Glade. Sphagnum moss and cranberry vines thrive in this moist environment.

After a right bend, the boardwalk crosses Yew Creek and enters Flag Glade. Pitcher plants, orchids, and reindeer lichens can be found in this region. The trail crosses Yew Creek two times. Near the end of the loop, a 300-year-old yellow birch survives in the moisture of the Cranberry Glades.

Cranberry Bog Boardwalk

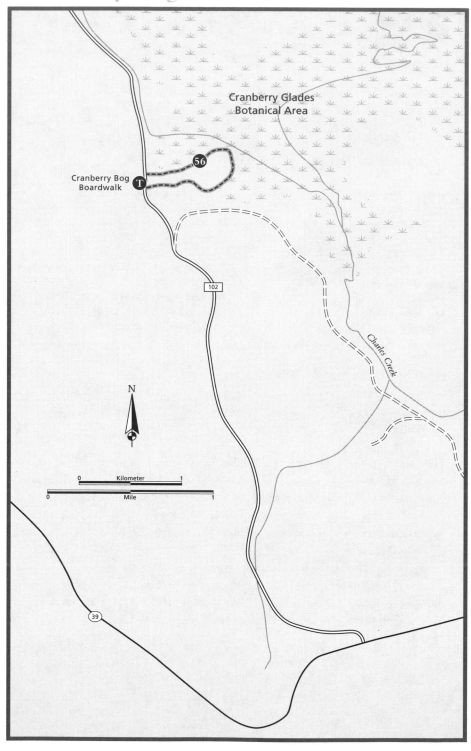

Cranberry Glades
Botanical Area

Cranberry Bog
Boardwalk

56

T

102

Charles Creek

N

Kilometer
0   1

Mile
0   1

39

Cranberry Glades.

57 Middle Fork to Big Beechy Trail
Loop / *Cranberry Wilderness*

Overview: *Wallace Stegner viewed wilderness as "a part of the geography of hope." The true understanding of what Stegner meant can be felt in Cranberry Wilderness. Nearly 60 miles of trails traverse the area's 35,864 acres. The bonds of civilization melt away as you step farther into the wilderness. The lush green of young red spruce seems to spring up through the ground and into the psyche. Clear streams wash away stresses and steep climbs build self-respect. The wilderness is a baptism of self-renewal.*

General description: Traveling from stream bank to ridge top, this hike delivers all of what is wonderful about Cranberry Wilderness, including spruce-covered ridge tops, hillsides carpeted in ferns, valleys alive with the chatter of streams, and solitude that only wilderness can provide.

General location: 17 miles west of Marlinton

Length: 16.25 miles

Difficulty: Difficult

Special attractions: Red spruce forests, moss- and fern-covered forest floors, cascading waterfalls, and seasonal solitude.

Maps: Recreation Guide for the Gauley District; USGS quads: Hillsboro, Lobelia, Webster Springs SE, Woodrow

Camping: Because this hike is in designated wilderness, backcountry camping is permitted throughout the area. There are no developed or designated campsites within the wilderness. In high-use areas, it is best to camp in sites that have been previously used; dispersed camping is recommended in low-use parts of the wilderness.

There are four developed campgrounds nearby in the area managed as Cranberry Backcountry. Summit Lake Campground has thirty-three campsites, Big Rock Campground has five units next to the Cranberry River, Cranberry Campground has twenty-eight single and two double campsites, and Bishop Knob Campground has forty-nine single and six double campsites. Please consult the Recreation Guide for the Gauley District for the locations of these campgrounds. Monongahela National Forest rules stipulate that, unless otherwise posted, campers can stay no longer than fourteen days in any campsite.

Seasons: Open year-round.

For information: Gauley Ranger Station, USDA Forest Service, HC 80 Box 117, Richwood, WV 26261; (304) 846–2695

Finding the trailhead: From US 219, turn west on WV 39 near Mill Point. Travel up the mountain to the intersection with WV 150, the Highland Scenic Highway. Turn right on WV 150. The trailhead is on the left 8.7 miles from the intersection of WV 39 and WV 150. A sign at the small parking area announces North-South Trail, Trail No. 688.

Traveling east on WV 39 from Summersville, follow WV 39 to the intersection with WV 150, the Highlands Scenic Highway. Turn left onto WV 150 and follow the road 8.7 miles to the trailhead and parking on the left.

The hike: At the trailhead, a sign marks the beginning of the North-South Trail, number 688. The trail leaves the parking area and passes a small meadow and an information stand. A wide trail that appears to be the remnants of an old logging road branches off to the right. North-South Trail enters the forest straight ahead and points the hiker west.

Immediately the hiker realizes that this forest is unique. The ground is dotted with ferns and moss-covered rocks. The dense canopy of red spruce and yellow birch filters out most of the sunlight and leaves the forest floor in cool shade. The combination of foliage and dark shade creates a scene of rich, saturated greens.

At 0.5 mile, North-South Trail continues straight ahead as the North Fork Trail moves off to the right and left. Turn right and follow North Fork Trail north. The wide and grassy trail sometimes becomes choked with young red spruce. This can be particularly bothersome on rainy days when the spruce create a "car wash" effect, drenching the hiker's legs. The trail travels lightly downhill and reaches another intersection at the 1.5-mile mark. Turn left and follow Middle Fork Trail downhill to the left.

The trail travels downhill at an easy angle to its namesake, the Middle Fork of the Williams River. Upon reaching the stream, turn right and follow it down the valley. There are numerous campsites on both sides of the creek along the Middle Fork Trail, which is wide and easy to follow. As the trail continues to lose elevation, maple begins appearing in the canopy.

At about 5.0 miles from the parking area, the trail crosses the Middle Fork. This first ford is not difficult and can often be accomplished without removing your boots. At 5.75 miles the stream is crossed again, this time requiring a barefoot approach. Several "stair step" waterfalls are passed on the Middle Fork Trail, but the most notable are those at Slick Rock Run, a small feeder stream that intersects Middle Fork from the right. Just past the confluence of these two streams, at about 6.25 miles, the Middle Fork slides and cascades down an inclined slab of sandstone. This is wonderful summer fun.

The trail continues on its way to Big Beechy Trail. At 7.75 miles, Hell for Certain Creek can be seen cascading into Middle Fork to the left. There are campsites in this area. The trail is as wide as a road here and is lined with hemlock and rhododendron. At 8.5 miles, Big Beechy Creek and the intersection with Big Beechy Trail are reached. A gorgeous 10-foot waterfall at Big Beechy Creek makes a pleasant backdrop for lunch.

Big Beechy Trail, number 207, begins at a sign on the southeast bank of Big Beechy Creek. Take a right off Middle Fork Trail and hike uphill to the east. This trail is blazed with double blue blazes, albeit infrequently. A double blaze on this trail does not indicate a trail junction as it normally would.

The trail wraps around the ridge and immediately starts to gain elevation

Middle Fork to Big Beechy Trail Loop, Middle Fork to North-South Trail Loop

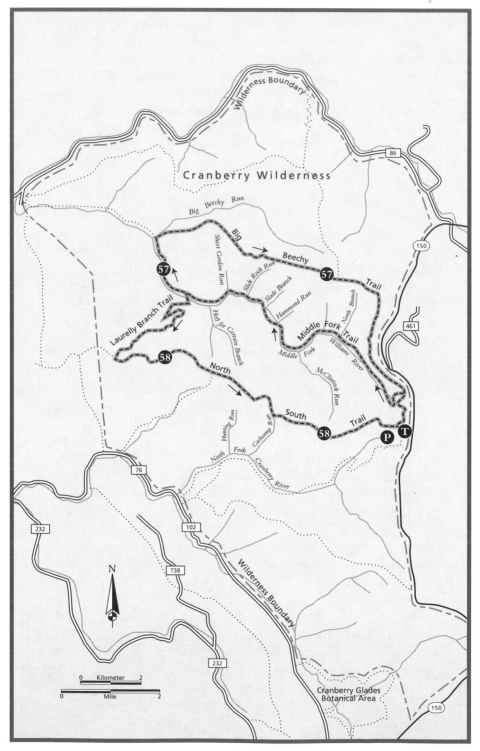

Wilderness Boundary

Cranberry Wilderness

86

150

461

Big Beechy Run

Big Beechy Trail

Sheet Gordon Run

57

57

Slick Rock Run

Slade Branch

Hammond Run

Laurelly Branch Trail

Hell for Certain Branch

Middle Fork Trail

North Branch

Williams River

Middle Fork

58

North

South Trail

McClintock Run

58

P T

Hunting Run

North Fork

Cashamp Run

Cranberry River

76

232

102

738

N

232

Kilometer

Mile

Cranberry Glades
Botanical Area

150

over the stream valley that lies to the left. The stream valley is wide and level, and there are many good places to set down a tent. Make sure water bottles are full before leaving the stream; the moderate incline will last for about 3 miles, turning a not-so-difficult hike into a burner. Some respite is felt along the way as short easy sections break up the climb. The forest in the section begins with hemlock, beech, and tulip poplar dominating, but as elevation is gained these species give way to ridge tops thickly covered with spruce.

As Big Beechy Trail nears the ridge top, a marvelous scene with a prehistoric aura greets the hiker. Tall sandstone pillars are surrounded by spruce, and the forest floor is covered with ferns. The trail bends around the ridge to the right and starts to travel in a southerly direction.

At about 1.5 miles from Middle Fork Trail, 10.25 miles overall, Big Beechy Trail reaches the crest of the shoulder. The trail then climbs and drops as it travels across the ridge crest. The forest varies from bright, open-canopied beech forest to dense, shady spruce forest where little light reaches the forest floor. At 10.5 miles, Big Beechy Trail weaves through a rhododendron jungle and passes through a thick stand of young spruce at 12.0 miles. Route finding can be difficult in this area as the spruce chokes out the path. At the 13.0-mile mark, another stand of rhododendron is encountered. The trail starts a final descent to North Fork Trail at 14.25 miles. The descent is moderate and lasts for about 0.5 mile. Big Beechy Trail reaches North Fork Trail by an open meadow.

At the junction a sign points left and reads HIGHLANDS SCENIC HIGHWAY. The highway is about 0.25 mile away and intersects WV 150 about 1 mile from the original parking area. To continue the hike on trails, turn right at this junction and follow North Fork Trail south. The trail is wide and flat, which is welcome this late in a long hike, but portions of the trail are choked with young spruce. At 15.25 miles, the North Fork Trail reaches the intersection with Middle Fork Trail. Take the left fork at this Y intersection and hike uphill. This portion of the hike backtracks the earlier part of the hike. At 16.25 miles, the junction with North-South Trail is reached. Turn left and hike the short distance to the information stand and the parking lot.

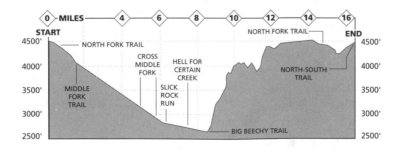

58 Middle Fork to North-South Trail Loop / *Cranberry Wilderness*

Overview: *With 35,864 acres, Cranberry Wilderness is one of the largest wilderness areas east of the Mississippi River. Owing to its beauty, Cranberry Wilderness is a favorite among hikers and backpackers. Do yourself and the wilderness a favor and disperse use.*

General description: This long loop descends along the Middle Fork of the Williams River, then makes a major climb to the North-South Trail and the high bogs on Little Levels.

General location: 12 miles northwest of Marlinton

Length: 19.7 miles

Difficulty: Difficult

Special attractions: A spruce bog near the summit of Green Mountain.

Maps: Monongahela National Forest Cranberry Wilderness map; USGS quads: Hillsboro, Lobelia, Webster Springs SE, Woodrow

Camping: Backpacking is permitted.

Seasons: The wilderness is open to the public year-round, but the Highlands Scenic Road can be closed due to snow.

For information: Gauley Ranger District, USDA Forest Service, HC 80 Box 117, Richwood, WV 26261; (304) 846–2695

See map on page 196.

Finding the trailhead: From the intersection of WV 39 and US 219 in Marlinton, travel southwest on US 219/WV 39. Proceed 8.4 miles and turn west on WV 39. Continue 6.5 miles to WV 150, the Highland Scenic Road. Turn right and proceed 8.7 miles to a parking area on the left.

The Hike: At the trailhead, a sign marks the beginning of the North-South Trail, number 688. The trail leaves the parking area and passes a small meadow and an information stand. A wide trail that appears to be the remnants of an old logging road branches off to the right. North-South Trail enters the forest straight ahead and points the hiker west.

Immediately the hiker realizes that this forest is unique. The ground is dotted with ferns and moss-covered rocks. The dense canopy of red spruce and yellow birch filters out most of the sunlight and leaves the forest floor in cool shade. The combination of foliage and dark shade creates a scene of rich, saturated greens.

At 0.5 mile, North-South Trail continues straight ahead as the North Fork Trail moves off to the right and left. Turn right and follow North Fork Trail north. The wide and grassy trail sometimes becomes choked with young red spruce. This can be particularly bothersome on rainy days when the spruce create a "car wash" effect, drenching the hiker's legs. The trail travels lightly downhill and reaches another intersection at the 1.5-mile mark. Turn left and follow Middle Fork Trail downhill to the left.

The trail travels downhill at an easy angle to its namesake, the Middle Fork of the Williams River. Upon reaching the stream, turn right and follow it down the valley. There are numerous campsites on both sides of the creek along the Middle Fork Trail, which is wide and easy to follow. As the trail continues to lose elevation, maple begins appearing in the canopy.

At about 5.0 miles from the parking area, the trail crosses the Middle Fork. This first ford is not difficult and can often be accomplished without removing your boots. At 5.75 miles the stream is crossed again, this time requiring a barefoot approach. Several "stairstep" waterfalls are passed on the Middle Fork Trail, but the most notable are those at Slick Rock Run, a small feeder stream that intersects Middle Fork from the right. Just past the confluence of these two streams, at about 6.25 miles. The Middle Fork slides and cascades down an inclined slab of sandstone. This is wonderful summer fun.

The trail continues on its way to Big Beechy Trail. At 7.75 miles, Hell for Certain Creek can be seen cascading into Middle Fork to the left. Just beyond the campsite at the confluence of North Fork Williams River and Hell for Certain Creek, there is a small sign for the Laurelly Branch Trail. Watch carefully for this junction. The trail exits back hard to the left and is easy to miss. If you reach an earthen barrier on the Middle Fork Trail, you've hiked past the trail junction. The elevation at this junction is 2,800 feet.

The trail follows an old road and descends to the river. It is impossible to cross the river without taking off your boots. After the crossing, the trail parallels the North Fork upstream a short distance, makes a right switchback, and begins to climb the ridge toward Little Levels. The grade is moderate at the beginning of the climb. About 0.4 mile from the Middle Fork Trail, the Laurelly Trail intersects a road on the left. Continue straight at this junction.

The trail bends left and enters a narrow, steep-walled hollow. This is the drainage of the Laurelly Branch. The grade is now easy. A right switchback

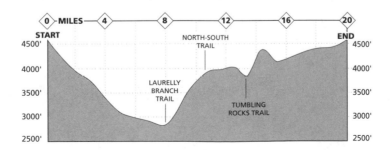

leads away from the hollow, but a left switchback brings it back, climbing steadily up the hollow. At approximately 2.0 miles, the trail crosses a small feeder stream. Hemlock and rhododendron thrive in this moist environment. The climb gradually changes from easy to moderate. After crossing the Laurelly Creek, there is some trail confusion, but the trail bends left back toward the creek. Cross the creek again and begin a moderate climb through a forest of red spruce to the junction with the North-South Trail near the western wilderness boundary.

Contrary to its name, the North-South Trail runs primarily from west to east along this section. The elevation at this junction is 3,925 feet. Turn left to continue the loop, beginning with a short, easy climb through a forest of red spruce. This is followed by a descent that leads out of the spruce and into a stand of upland hardwoods. The trail then begins a second easy climb to the narrow, rocky ridge crest. The crest climbs over the 4,000-foot level, then begins a series of easy climbs and descents that ascend gradually to about 4,350 feet. These easy ups and downs end abruptly approximately 1.75 miles from the junction.

A steep descent heads down to the junction with the Tumbling Rock Trail (TR 214), which exits to the right and begins a descent to FDR 76. The elevation here is 3,800 feet. A massive oak tree marks the junction, and there is a great log to sit on and ponder the upcoming climb. The steep ascent begins shortly after the junction, climbing back to almost 4,400 feet over the next 0.75 mile.

After a short descent through a forest of hardwoods, the trail begins a long gradual climb through a dense forest of red spruce. This area, known as Little Levels, is a high upland bog. The ground is soggy and the trail is often wet and muddy. At times small streams flow along and over the path. The forest floor is carpeted with dense layers of moss, and the area has the feeling of a jungle. Near the junction at the beginning of the loop, the trail is firmer and less waterlogged. At the trail junction, elevation 4,480 feet, continue straight. The distance to the road is about 0.4 mile.

Sods Circuit
Dolly Sods Wilderness

Overview: *Truly one of the most unique ecosystems in West Virginia is that contained in Dolly Sods. Today, northern hardwood forests characterize the lower elevations while open heath barrens and wide-open sods occupy higher elevations. The beauty of the area is stunning. Even though this wilderness is one of the most popular hiking destinations in West Virginia, the sense of solitude is strong. You can truly feel alone when standing in the open sods while the gentle breeze whispers the only audible sound.*

While the landscape may be beautiful to behold, it is the unnatural history of Dolly Sods that has created this ecosystem. When settlers arrived in the area, the red spruces averaged 4 feet in diameter and the forest floor consisted of a humus layer more than 5 feet thick. During the late nineteenth century, most of the eastern forests were cut; the Dolly Sods area was not spared. The years after the logging saw forest fires rage through the leftover slash timber, burning the humus layer to bedrock. The extreme environment that was left was barely hospitable for the red spruce to regenerate and was subsequently used for grazing livestock. It is a family of sheep farmers, the Dahle family, for which the area is named. As time progressed, nature and man have attempted to heal the area's wounds. The Civilian Conservation Corps reclaimed the area in the 1930s, but it was not until 1975 that Congress officially protected the 10,215-acre wilderness.

A quick note about the mortars: the U.S. military used the area for various exercises during WWII. Some remnants of these exercises still remain. Live mortars are sometimes found in the area, albeit infrequently. If you find a mortar, DO NOT TOUCH IT. Note the location and alert the Forest Service. Although the ordnance removal project has been completed and all trails should be open, some ordnance may still remain.

General description: This is a highly recommended hike encompassing the best of what this wilderness has to offer. The trail hikes along the cascading Red Creek and Stonecoal Run and travels through the wonderfully scenic and unique barrens of the Sods. A steep climb up the ridge keeps you honest, but a rocky ridge-top view of the Red Creek Valley adds icing to the cake.

General location: Less than 1 mile from the town of Laneville, approximately 22 miles west of Petersburg

Length: 15.4 miles, plus a 0.5-mile side trip on Rocky Point Trail

Difficulty: Difficult

Special attractions: Wide, windswept plains, heath barrens, mountain bogs, crystal clear streams, ridgetop vistas.

Maps: Dolly Sods and Roaring Plains hiking guide map from the Forest Service; USGS quads: Blackbird Knob, Blackwater Falls, Hopeville, Laneville

Camping: Dolly Sods is designated wilderness; backcountry camping is permitted throughout the area. There are no developed or designated campsites within the wilderness. As in all wilderness lands, in high-use areas it is best to camp in sites

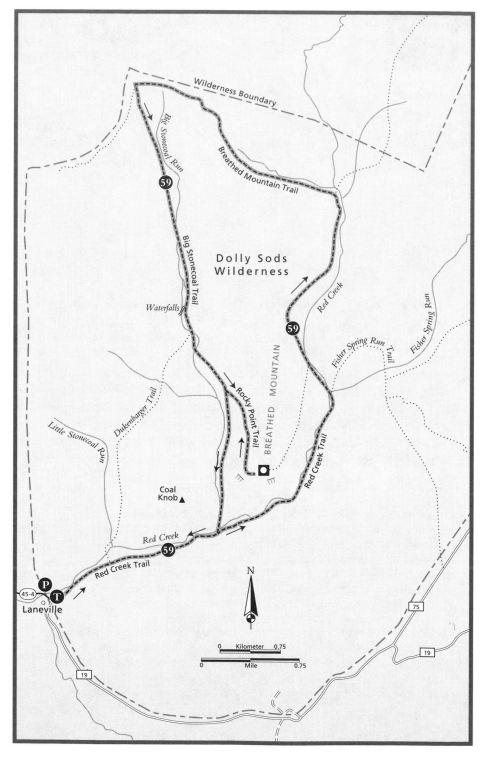

Wilderness Boundary

Big Stonecoal Run

59

Breathed Mountain Trail

Dolly Sods
Wilderness

Big Stonecoal Trail

Waterfalls

Red Creek

59

Fisher Spring Run

Fisher Spring Run Trail

Rocky Point Trail

BREATHED MOUNTAIN

Little Stonecoal Run

Dukenbarger Trail

Coal
Knob ▲

Red Creek Trail

Red Creek

59

Red Creek Trail

P

45-4

T

Laneville

19

N

19

75

0   Kilometer   0.75

0   Mile   0.75

that have been used before, while dispersed camping is recommended in low-use parts of the wilderness. If you prefer campground camping, Red Creek Campground is located on FR 75, just outside the boundary northeast of the wilderness. The campground has twelve fee campsites that are filled on a first-come, first-served basis.

Seasons: The wilderness is open year-round. In winter, high snows often close FR 19 and make hiking difficult. If any snow is forecast it is best to avoid FR 19 and FR 75, as windblown snow may block the road.

For information: Potomac Ranger District, HC 59, Box 240, Petersburg, WV 26847; (304) 257–4488

Finding the trailhead: Dolly Sods Wilderness is located west of Petersburg, northwest of Seneca Rocks, and east of the town of Dryfork. From Seneca Rocks, follow WV 55/28 north to CR 28-7 and turn left. If traveling from Petersburg, follow WV 55/28 south to this intersection and make a right. From the intersection of SR 55/28 to the trailhead is 11 miles. Follow CR 28-7 uphill to the intersection with FR 19 and turn left. Almost immediately, the pavement ends and the gravel begins. Travel 6 miles to the intersection with FR 75. Turn left at this intersection and continue to follow FR 19 past the picnic area. The road begins to travel downhill. Follow FR 19 to the trailhead at the bottom of the mountain on the right side of the road. There are several small wooden buildings, an information stand, and a small parking lot at the trailhead. If you reach the bridge over Red Creek and the paved CR 45-4, you have gone too far.

From the west, follow WV 32 in Dryfork to CR 45-4. Turn right on CR 45-4. If traveling south on WV 32, turn left onto CR 45-4. Follow this road past Laneville. The trailhead is located on the left just after the bridge over Red Creek. If you start uphill on the gravel FR 19, you have gone too far.

The hike: An information stand sits at the trailhead for Red Creek Trail. Take a few minutes to read the latest postings regarding rules and possible trail closings. Past the info stand, Red Creek Trail begins, following the stream through a forest of red spruce, sugar maple, yellow birch, and hemlock.

The hike follows Red Creek up the valley, sometimes near the creek bank, sometimes higher on the ridge. At under 0.5 mile, the trail reaches a feeder

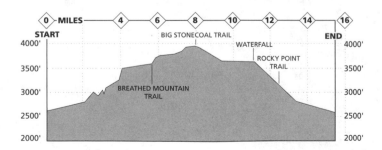

stream coming in from the right. To the left a wide, rocky path is cut by old stream flow. Take care to turn right at this intersection, and follow the feeder upstream. Following the rocky path will take the hiker to the main stream channel, and off Red Creek Trail.

At 0.75 mile, Red Creek Trail bends right and hikes moderately up the eastern ridge, moving out of the creek valley. The trail levels off and wraps across the ridge through a rhododendron tunnel. Red Creek Trail turns left and drops back to the valley floor at a point where an old trail travels up the ridge to the right. There is a rock cairn at this intersection. In the valley floor, Red Creek Trail moves over to the creek bank and intersects with Big Stonecoal Trail, which crosses Red Creek and hikes up the western ridge. Our hike will travel down this trail later in the day.

To continue Red Creek Trail, turn right and follow the narrow single-track north along the stream bank. The trail again climbs the eastern ridge, gaining considerable elevation over Red Creek, and snakes across shoulders of the ridge. Two hollows contain feeder streams that cascade over rocks and short falls. The falls feel hidden, like a secret only the hiker knows. Views to the west reveal the rocky peak along Rocky Point Trail. At 3.0 miles another trail junction is reached. A sign indicates that Red Creek Trail travels down and to the left, while Fisher Spring Trail travels right and farther out the ridge. Turn left and follow Red Creek Trail down to Red Creek.

The trail fords Red Creek and travels north along the creek bank. A highlight in the valley is a cascade in Red Creek over a large slab of sandstone. There are many campsites in this area. At 4.0 miles, the Red Creek Trail bends left and climbs steeply up the western ridge, leaving Red Creek for good. The trail climbs for about 0.5 mile before finally leveling off. The trail is wide, well traveled, and often muddy. Although several rock outcrops are passed along the way, there are few views from this ridge. At about 5.5 miles, Red Creek Trail reaches the 3-mile Breathed Mountain Trail.

Turn left on Breathed Mountain Trail, which climbs steeply out of the Red Creek valley. The difficult hike is made even harder by the rocky path. Get used to the rocks, there are millions more to come. After 0.25 mile, the angle levels off and the first of the sods is reached. The sods are large, grassy, windswept plains. The area is noticeably quiet; the wind is the loudest sound. Differing from the nearby Flatrock and Roaring Plains, the sods contain little groundcover other than grasses. Spruces are sporadic, and the rhododendron and mountain laurel that are impassable in Flatrock and Roaring Plains are unnoticed if not completely absent here. The open, whispering sods elicit quiet contentment.

Most trails in Dolly Sods Wilderness are very rocky.

Breathed Mountain Trail crosses stretches of open plains separated by stands of forest. The hike is predominantly level and the path is easy to follow. Forests of black cherry, beech, sugar maple, and pure, planted stands of red pine give way to wide open spaces. Often, acres of the forest floor are covered with running cedar; other sections are covered with ferns. Frequently, the rocky trail is an acrobatic exercise of rock hopping. The trail crosses a small stream and then exits the wilderness onto a gravel road. An information stand and the trailhead for Big Stonecoal Trail are to the left. Hike distance thus far is 8.0 miles.

Big Stonecoal Trail travels 3.25 miles across beautiful high plains before intersecting with Rocky Point Trail and dropping back to Red Creek. The trail is easy to follow and travels at an easy angle across rocky sods and through quiet forests. After about 2.5 miles, Big Stonecoal Trail intersects with Dunkenbarger Trail, which follows Dunkenbarger Run until it meets Little Stonecoal Run. Remain on Big Stonecoal Trail as it continues on the left branch and straight.

Nearly the entire hike of Big Stonecoal Trail parallels Big Stonecoal Run, crossing the creek several times. There is an impressive waterfall about 3.0 miles from the intersection with Breathed Mountain Trail.

Shortly after the falls, Big Stonecoal Trail intersects with Rocky Point Trail, which travels around the ridge to intersect with Red Creek Trail. As the name implies, Rocky Point Trail passes by large ridge-top outcrops that provide wonderful views of the Red Creek Valley. The hike to Rocky Point is highly recommended. Follow the trail across the ridge to the point where it begins to bend around the shoulder. Uphill to the left is a taluslike pile of boulders. With great care, scramble up the boulders for a vertigo-equipped view. The hike to Rocky Point is about 0.25 mile, making the round-trip 0.5 mile.

After returning to Big Stonecoal Trail, begin the steep descent off the mountain. At just under 1 mile from the intersection with Rocky Point Trail, the trail bottoms out at Big Stonecoal Run in the creek valley and follows the run to its terminus at Red Creek 13.9 miles into the hike. Cross the creek and follow Red Creek Trail up the opposite ridge and then south toward the trailhead. This section of the hike is a backtrack from earlier in the day. The distance from Big Stonecoal to the parking area is about 1.5 miles. Evening shadows grow large on the hike, and the wonders of civilization are realized at the trailhead parking lot. The day's effort, 15.4 miles, can be seen in the dust on your well-worn boots.

60

Plains Circuit
Flatrock and Roaring Plains Backcountry

Overview: *Just south of Dolly Sods Wilderness is the equally scenic Flatrock and Roaring Plains. The area is very similar to the Dolly Sods Wilderness. Northern hardwood forests at lower elevations give way to heath barrens and mountain plains at higher elevations. However, the Flatrock and Roaring Plains are more thickly vegetated than their counterparts in Dolly Sods. Most of the trail through the plains is so thickly bordered by rhododendron and laurel that bushwhacking is out of the question. The hike is noticeably quiet. Often the only audible sounds are your footsteps and the wind. The hike is also noticeably lonely. It seems that the droves of hikers that descend on Dolly Sods completely ignore Flatrock and Roaring Plains.*

General description: This hike climbs steeply up the side of Mt. Porte Crayon to Roaring Plains, with gorgeous views of the surrounding countryside and north into Dolly Sods Wilderness. The descent back to Red Creek is steeper than the climb up but a little shorter.

General location: Laneville, approximately 22 miles west of Petersburg

Length: 14.5 miles

Difficulty: Difficult

Special attractions: Cascading streams, spruce forests, rhododendron and laurel jungles on wonderfully quiet plains.

Maps: Dolly Sods and Roaring Plains hiking guide map from the Forest Service; USGS quads: Harman, Hopeville, Laneville, Onega

Camping: Camping is permitted, but suitable sites may be difficult to find.

Seasons: The Flatrock and Roaring Plains Backcountry is open year-round.

For information: Potomac Ranger District, HC 59, Box 240, Petersburg, WV 26847; (304) 257-4488

Finding the trailhead: The trailhead is located near Laneville and the Dolly Sods Wilderness, west of Petersburg, northwest of Seneca Rocks, and east of the town of Dryfork. From Seneca Rocks, follow WV 55/28 north to CR 28-7 and turn left. From Petersburg, follow WV 55/28 south to this intersection and turn right. The distance from the intersection of WV 55/28 to the trailhead is 11 miles. Follow CR 28-7 uphill to the intersection with FR 19 and turn left. Almost immediately the pavement ends and the gravel begins. Travel 6 miles on FR 19 to the intersection with FR 75. Turn left at this intersection and continue to follow FR 19 past the picnic area. The road begins to travel downhill. Follow FR 19 to the bottom of the mountain and cross Red Creek, where the road becomes CR 45-4. Follow CR 45-4 to CR 32-2 and turn left. The parking lot is on the right just before the bridge over Red Creek.

Plains Circuit

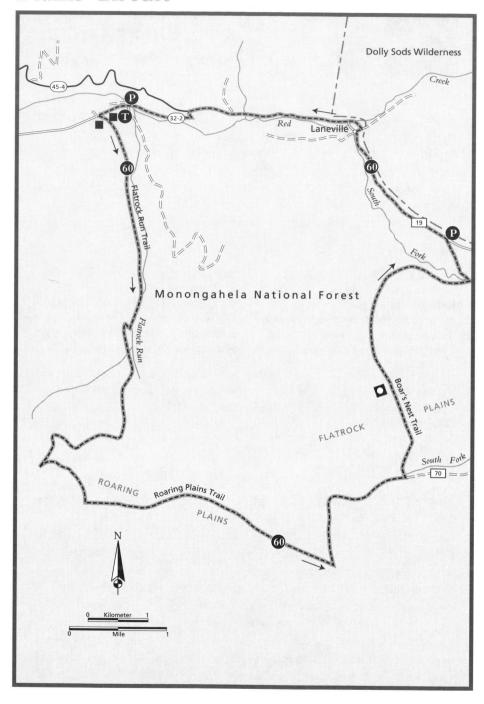

Dolly Sods Wilderness

Creek

45-4

P

T

32-2

Red

Laneville

60

60

South

19

P

Fork

Monongahela National Forest

Flatrock Run Trail

Flatrock Run

Boar's Nest Trail

PLAINS

FLATROCK

South   Fork

70

ROARING

Roaring Plains Trail

PLAINS

60

N

0   Kilometer   1

0   Mile   1

From the west, follow SR 32 in Dryfork to CR 45-4. Turn right on CR 45-4. If traveling south on SR 32, turn left onto CR 45-4. Follow this road to CR 32-2 and turn right. The parking lot is on the right just before the bridge over Red Creek.

The hike: The hike begins at the small parking area on the banks of Red Creek. Follow CR 32-2 across the bridge and continue hiking along the road until you see a driveway that leads between two horse barns. The driveway is less than 0.25 mile from the parking area. Turn left and follow the driveway between the barns to a fence line and a gate. A white diamond marks a post and a sign indicates that it is 5.0 miles to Roaring Plains Trail. These 5 miles are almost entirely uphill, as the trail will gain 2,200 feet on its way up to Roaring Plains.

Cross between two posts and follow the old road along a fence line and through the pastures. The angle is an easy ascent. The trail continues to rise up and away from the farms, and at 1.0 miles crosses onto National Forest property. The property line marks the transition from farmland to a forest made up of oak, sugar maple, yellow birch, beech, and occasional stands of hemlock.

Flatrock Run is down the ridge to the left. There are occasional cascades as the run tumbles off the mountain. A set of cascades can be viewed just before the trail reaches a small meadow. There are remnants of an old cabin to the left, and the trail bends right as it travels through the meadow. Just past the meadow there are more cascades in Flatrock Run. The trail makes an S curve and moves away from the stream as another fire road continues straight up the valley following Flatrock Run. Follow the blaze and the steeper trail to the right. Another cascade in the stream precedes another trail intersection. At about 2.25 miles, four old fire roads come together. Follow the blazes. Flatrock Run Trail turns right and hikes northwest at an easy angle away from the creek.

The next section of trail continues up the ridge at a moderate angle. The trail travels across the face of the ridge, moving away from the creek valley.

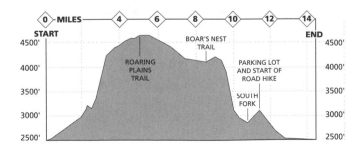

Finally, the trail switches back to the left (an old fire road continues straight and to the right) and begins hiking southeasterly. The ridge to the left drops off very steeply. The lack of a lower canopy allows for long views through the forest. Flatrock Run can be seen far down in the valley, but in a matter of steps the run rises quickly to trail level. The trail bends left and crosses the creek 2.5 miles from the trailhead. Stop at the creek and filter some water. The trail ahead will make a fit hiker sweat in the dead of winter.

Hiking east on the opposite ridge, Flatrock Run Trail crosses a small feeder stream that tumbles over sandstone on its way to the run. There are beautiful views to the left of the amphitheater-like valley carved out by Flatrock Run. Take in a few final views. The trail now leaves Flatrock Run for good.

At a double blue blaze, Flatrock Run Trail bends right, moves off the aged fire road, and becomes single-track. The tough fun now begins. For the next mile the trail is an aerobics exercise as it makes many turns, crosses many fire roads, and exposes many double blue blazes to the hiker. Make no mistake, though, the trail does not meander. It is now the dirt and rock equivalent of a white-water river; it may turn and dodge, but its one purpose is to change elevation quickly. Although difficult, the hike is magnificent. At one point the rocky ridge is covered with moss and ferns as the trail leads through a nearly pure stand of yellow birch. Finally, as the spruce begins to crowd the forest, the trail switches back onto an old, muddy fire road and the climb is over.

Flatrock Run Trail takes on yet another mood as the muddy trail travels south through a mossy forest of black cherry, spruce, and American mountain ash. The spruce is so thick to either side of the trail that losing the trail would be difficult even if you wanted to. At 4.5 miles, the trail turns 90 degrees to the left. There is a double blue blaze at this turn. Flatrock Run Trail passes by a sign indicating the trail name.

Shortly after the sign, the trail exits the forest onto Roaring Plains. The plains are gigantic grassy balds dotted with winterberry and an occasional spruce. The trail starts out across the plain and soon encounters another sign, indicating the end of Flatrock Run Trail and the beginning of Roaring Plains Trail. A side trail at this sign leads to a large pile of small boulders. From the boulders there are views of the windswept plains to the north and south.

The character of the hike changes again as Roaring Plains Trail begins. The path becomes very rocky for the next 3 miles. The trail angle is nearly flat across the plain, and the sides of the trail become choked with alternating stands of rhododendron and mountain laurel. The density of the laurel and rhododendron prevent any camping in this area. When a communications tower comes into view to the north, the trail is nearing its end. Roaring Plains Trail drops down to a stream and passes a campsite just before the trail ends at a gravel road, FR 70.

Boar's Nest Trail often travels a pathway of stone.

A short road hike connects Roaring Plains Trail with Boar's Nest Trail. At the gravel road, turn right and hike to the metal gate. Cross the gate and hike 0.5 mile to the trailhead for Boar's Nest Trail, which is on the left and marked by a sign. Reenter the forest at this sign and begin hiking the 3-mile Boar's Nest Trail.

This trail is also about 3.0 miles in length and is marked by three distinct sections The trail immediately crosses a small creek and then travels across

Flatrock Plains. Similar to Roaring Plains, Flatrock Plains are wide-open, windswept plains thickly vegetated with rhododendron and laurel. Several sections of the trail are cobblestone walkways built up about a foot above the surrounding ground level. The trail reaches magnificent vistas north into the Dolly Sods Wilderness. Large rock outcrops provide a place to drop the pack and sit down to soak in the view.

Past the viewpoint, Boar's Nest Trail begins its second phase: descent. The trail drops very steeply off the ridge to the South Fork in the valley below. Take care to hike slowly or your knees might never forgive you. The trail is easy to follow. It drops down to a feeder stream and follows it to the South Fork. From this point, the hike angle is easier. South Fork is reached at just less than 3.0 miles from FR 70, just under 11.0 miles from the beginning of the hike.

At South Fork, ford the creek and pick up the trail on the opposite creek bank. The trail now starts phase three and climbs the ridge to the parking lot. The moderate to difficult climb, although short, is unwelcome after the tough hike so far. In just over 0.25 mile, the trail reaches the Boar's Nest trailhead parking lot. The total hike thus far is about 11.5 miles.

To reach the parking area for Flatrock Run Trail, turn left out of the Boar's Nest parking area and hike downhill to Laneville. Travel the road around Laneville to CR 32-2. Follow CR 32-2 to the parking area at Red Creek. The road hike is approximately 3.0 miles.

61 Laurel River Trail North
Laurel Fork North Wilderness

Overview: *Congress designated the Laurel Fork Wilderness complex, containing almost 12,200 acres, in 1983. The wilderness area is a narrow valley through which the Laurel Fork flows. The crest of Rich Mountain serves as the eastern boundary of the wilderness, while the crest of Mill Mountain serves as the western boundary. The Laurel Fork is also home to native populations of brook and brown trout, making fly-fishing another popular pastime within the confines of the wilderness.*

General description: The Laurel River Trail North meanders along the pristine Laurel Fork beneath a canopy of tall cove hardwoods.

General location: 17 miles southeast of Elkins

Length: 4.3 miles one-way

Difficulty: Easy

Special attractions: A beautiful hike along the fast-flowing Laurel Fork River, beaver dams, and wide-open glades.

Maps: Monongahela National Forest Laurel Fork Wilderness brochure; USGS quads: Gladys, Sinks of Gandy

Camping: The Laurel Fork Campground has sixteen spaces filled on a first-come, first-served basis. Backcountry camping is permitted throughout the wilderness.

Seasons: The wilderness is open year-round, but the roads leading to the trailheads may be impassable during the winter.

For information: District Ranger, Greenbrier Ranger District, Monongahela National Forest, Bartow, WV 24920; (304) 456–3335

Finding the trailhead: Take US 33 to Alpena and turn south on CR 27. Travel 9.5 miles to Gladys and turn left onto CR 22. Continue 2.2 miles and take the left fork on FR 422. Travel 2.6 miles to the Y intersection and bear right on CR 10, Middle Mountain Road. At the next Y intersection take the left fork onto FR 423 and travel 1.5 miles to the Laurel Fork Campground. Parking is across the bridge on the left. This is the trailhead for the Laurel River Trail.

Trailheads for the trails that branch off of the Laurel River Trail can be reached by traveling north on Middle Mountain Road.

The hike: There is a Forest Service trail map at the end of the picnic area. The trail on the right is the Laurel River Trail, which begins by following an old railroad grade. The grade is wide and flat. At 0.1 mile cross a small meadow. At the end of the meadow, cross Five Lick Run and parallel the Laurel Fork. The trail is very close to the river. After a right bend, the trail enters the forest. At the next right bend, pass under a canopy of small hemlock. There is a small meadow on the left at approximately 1.5 miles.

Laurel River Trail North, Laurel River Trail South

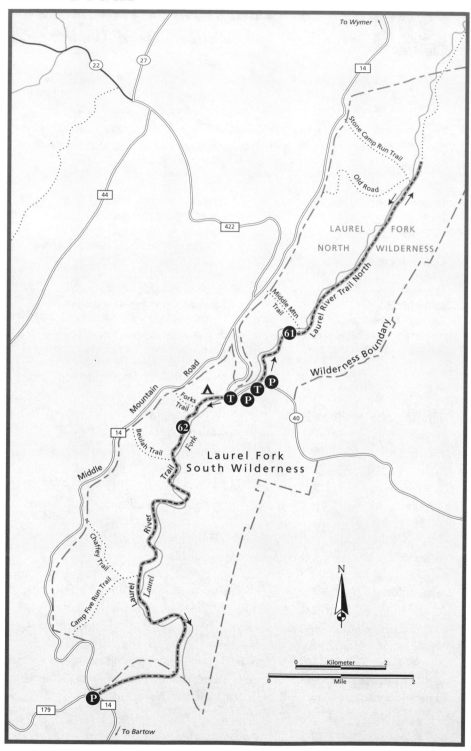

Looking east over Laurel Fork Wilderness.

At the meadow, an old road bears right and begins to climb. Bear left on the railroad grade, which stays close to the creek. It is overgrown in places and washed out in others. Watch closely for the unsigned junction with the Middle Mountain Trail (Trail 307), which exits to the left and enters a narrow hollow.

On the Laurel River Trail, the road climbs gradually for approximately 0.25 mile and then begins an easy descent back to the railroad grade.

When the old road and the railroad grade reconnect, the trail begins a long easy descent. At times the trail parallels the river and at other times the river is at the opposite end of the narrow valley. The woods begin to thin out and the trail enters an area of small glades, some of which are wet and soggy. The Laurel River Trail intersects the Stone Camp Run Trail in a large meadow at

4.3 miles. The Laurel River Trail continues straight on as the Stone Camp Run Trail exits left. Continuing north on the Laurel River Trail is not recommended because it comes to a dead end in the forest. It would be better to backtrack to the parking area or to explore one of the side trail options, looping back on the Middle Mountain Road.

Middle Mountain Trail Option: The 1.1-mile Middle Mountain Trail exits the Laurel River Trail to the left and descends sharply to the creek. The elevation is 3,000 feet. After crossing the old railroad grade, the trail crosses the river, which is wide and must be waded. The trail then begins a moderate climb up a narrow hollow, crosses a small stream, and parallels the right side of the creek. Climb up the hollow and make a right bend out of the creek bottom. After a left bend, the grade becomes a little easier. Tall cove hardwoods dominate the overstory. There is a right switchback just before reaching the road at an elevation of 3,620 feet.

Stone Camp Run Trail Option: The 1.5-mile Stone Camp Run Trail exits the Laurel River Trail to the left and passes through the meadow to the Laurel Fork. It is necessary to wade the river. The trail follows an old road into the woods. About 100 yards from the river, there is a junction with another old road. Continue straight on the Stone Camp Run Trail, which enters a narrow hollow and begins a moderate climb. After crisscrossing the run several times, the trail leaves the stream behind and climbs the left side of the hollow. The area is filled with tall yellow birch, maple, and black bark cherry. The grade becomes easy just before reaching the road at an elevation of 3,600 feet.

Old Road Option: The 2.1-mile Old Road exits the Stone Camp Run Trail to the left just after the river crossing. The road climbs gradually to the southwest up the right side of the narrow river valley. After 0.6 mile, the trail bends right and enters a narrow hollow. The easy climb continues up the hollow, then the trail crosses a small stream as it wraps left around the end of the hollow. At 1.4 miles, the road climbs over a finger ridge. The gradual climb continues to Middle Mountain Road.

Laurel River Trail South
Laurel Fork South Wilderness

Overview: *The Laurel Fork South is the southern half of the Laurel Fork Wilderness Complex. Middle Mountain forms the western boundary of the wilderness, while Rich Mountain forms the eastern boundary. Between these two high ridges runs the fast flowing Laurel Fork. This clear running river is the centerpiece of this masterpiece of nature. Hardworking beavers have altered the upper portion of the river basin significantly. Tall grasses thrive in the former backwaters of their old dams.*

General description: A prime backpack area with loops of any size when the trail system is combined with the Middle Mountain Road.

General location: 17 miles southeast of Elkins

Length: 7.5 miles one-way

Difficulty: Moderate

Special attractions: A beautiful hike along the fast-flowing Laurel Fork River, beaver dams, and wide-open glades.

Maps: Monongahela National Forest Laurel Fork Wilderness brochure; USGS quad: Sinks of Gandy

Camping: The Laurel Fork Campground has sixteen spaces filled on a first-come first-served basis. Backcountry camping is permitted throughout the wilderness.

Seasons: The wilderness is open year-round, but the roads leading to the trailheads may be impassable during the winter.

For information: District Ranger, Greenbrier Ranger District, Monongahela National Forest, Bartow, WV 24920; (304) 456–3335

See map on page 214.

Finding the trailhead: *Note:* This is a one-way hike; transportation is needed at both trailheads. Take US 33 to Alpena and turn south on CR 27. Travel 9.5 miles to Gladys and turn left onto CR 22. Continue 2.2 miles and take the left fork on FR 422. Travel 2.6 miles to the Y intersection and bear right on CR 10, Middle Mountain Road. At the next Y intersection, take the left fork onto FR 423 and travel 1.5 miles to the Laurel Fork Campground. Parking is across the bridge on the left. This is the trailhead for the Laurel River Trail.

To reach the southern trailhead, return to Middle Mountain Road and turn left. Travel 8.0 miles to FR 97 and the Laurel River trailhead. There is parking on the left. Do not block the gate.

Trailheads for the trails that branch off of the Laurel River Trail can also be found on Middle Mountain Road.

The hike: The trailhead for the Laurel River Trail is located behind the privies in the campground. After leaving the campground, the trail passes a bold spring on the right, with good, clear, cool water. The trail follows an old grade on the right side of the creek, climbing gradually through a forest dominated by black bark cherry and yellow birch

At 0.5 mile, the Laurel River Trail intersects the Forks Trail (Trail 323). A post marks the trail numbers at the junction. The Laurel River Trail continues straight and parallels the Laurel Fork River. After dropping into an open glade, the trail crosses a small feeder stream. Hemlock and spruce occupy the canopy of the forest. The trail hugs the river a short distance before crossing it. Within 150 yards, cross the river again. It can be possible to do both crossings without taking off your boots.

After the second crossing, the trail becomes a footpath. Running cedar covers the forest floor. The trail climbs the right side of the hollow, then drops to a large creek. Cross the creek to the junction with the Beulah Trail, which exits to the right at 1.5 miles

The Laurel River Trail continues straight, climbing gradually. After crossing a small feeder, the trail drops back to the creek and rejoins the old logging railroad grade. Cross tee markings are still visible. Climb away from the creek again to a junction; take the left fork and begin to descend. The trail is now a footpath that wraps around the end of a finger ridge then drops into a small glade. There is some trail confusion in this area; rock cairns mark the way. The trail crosses two small creeks and eventually drops to the river's edge and parallels the river a short distance.

Climb up away from the creek again and pass through a thicket of young red spruce. The trail drops back to the creek. There is a forest of tall pines on the right. Enter a wide boggy area and cross the Camp Five Run. Parallel the run upstream a short distance to the junction with the Camp Five Run Trail at 4.0 miles.

The Laurel River Trail bears to the left and drops down to the river. Cross the river, taking off your boots if necessary. An old logging road leads up into a stand of widely spaced red spruce. Follow the trail to a small clearing where a small stream comes down the mountain from the left. Follow the stream toward the Laurel River to an old road. Turn left on the road, which climbs

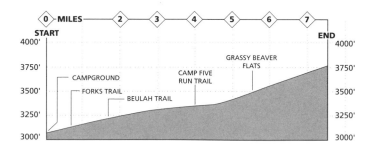

The Laurel Fork.

gradually through a stand of tall pine. There are several blue blazes as the road leads out of the woods and into a grassy beaver flat. Follow the trail to the river and cross. This crossing is too wide to jump and too deep to cross without taking off your boots.

The trail soon hits an old road and begins an easy climb away from the Laurel Fork River. The road parallels a small stream, climbing gradually to the crest of the ridge. As the trail bends right, there is a small sign for the Laurel River Trail and the Laurel Fork Campground at FR 97. Turn right on FR 97 and continue an easy walk to Middle Mountain Road. There is a locked gate at the road. Retrace your steps back to the Laurel Fork Campground and parking area or explore one of the side trail options, looping back on Middle Mountain Road.

Forks Trail Option: The 0.5-mile Forks Trail (Trail 323) exits Laurel River Trail to the right and begins an easy climb to Middle Mountain Road. The Forks Trail parallels a small creek, then breaks away from the creek and climbs through a narrow hollow. Just before reaching Middle Mountain Road, the hollow opens out into a broad expanse dominated by tall hardwoods. The elevation at the Middle Mountain Road is 3,200 feet.

Beulah Trail Option: The 1-mile Beulah Trail (Trail 310) parallels a small, fast-following feeder, passing through a narrow hollow as it climbs to Middle Mountain Road. Initially the grade is moderate, becoming easy after 0.25 mile. At 0.5 mile, the trail crosses a series of springs. The ground can be wet and muddy in this area. Soon the trail crosses the creek and continues its easy climb as the narrow hollow begins to open up. The stream becomes a small trickle. Just before Middle Mountain Road, the trail bends left and then right. A hiking sign marks the trailhead, at an elevation of 3,600 feet.

Camp Five Run Trail Option: The 1.5-mile Camp Five Run Trail (Trail 315) exits to the right and parallels the Camp Five Run. The trail meanders along the left bank of the creek just above an inviting open glade. The trail ties into an old railroad grade then enters a narrow hollow and leaves the glade behind. The Chaffey Trail exits to the right, and the Camp Five Run Trail begins an easy climb up the hollow. The trail crosses the run three times then enters a small meadow. Cross the creek again and follow the right creek branch up the old road. The trail passes a small pond just before reaching the cabins. There is a water pump at the cabins, and Middle Mountain Road is straight ahead.

Chaffey Trail Option: The 1.0-mile Chaffey Trail (Trail 309) begins where the Camp Five Trail leaves the glade. There is no trailhead marker. The trail drops down and crosses the Camp Five Run, passes through the glade, and enters a second small hollow. A wide and grassy old road climbs up this hollow. At the fork of the two roads, continue straight. Sections of the trail are lined with thick black bark cherry. The trail grade is easy as it climbs to the junction with Middle Mountain Road at an elevation of 3,750 feet.

East-West Loop
Otter Creek Wilderness

Overview: *At 20,000 acres, Otter Creek is the second largest wilderness area in West Virginia. Nearly 40 miles of trails travel this wilderness, making it possible to create day hikes and backpacking trips of various lengths. Campsites dot the main trail along Otter Creek. Otter Creek Wilderness is a favorite among West Virginia hikers. To disperse use, keep group size low and try to visit the area on a weekday, especially in the warmer months.*

General description: This is a long hike that traverses the wilderness from southeast to northwest and back. The trek is often wet and sometimes steep but never boring. The hike travels five separate trails and tops two separate ridge crests along the way.

General location: 13 miles east of Elkins

Length: 22.9 miles

Difficulty: Difficult

Special attractions: Red spruce forests, high plateau bogs, cascading mountain streams, laurel and rhododendron thickets, snowshoe hare.

Maps: Otter Creek Wilderness, Cheat Ranger District; USGS quads: Bath Alum, Green Valley, Montrose, Parsons

Camping: Because this hike is in designated wilderness, backcountry camping is permitted throughout the area. There are no developed campsites. As in all designated wilderness, camp in sites that have been used before in high-use areas, while dispersed camping is recommended in low-use parts of the wilderness.

Seasons: Open year-round.

For information: USDA Forest Service, Cheat Ranger District, P. O. Box 368, Parsons, WV 26287; (304) 478–3251

Finding the trailhead: This hike begins at the trailhead for Mylius Trail. From Elkins, follow US 33/WV 55 east. From Seneca Rocks, follow US 33/WV 55 west. Turn north onto CR-12 at Alpena, between Wymer and Bowden. Follow CR-12 to a Forest Road that branches left, just before CR-12 crosses Glady Creek. The parking area and trailhead are on the left on the forest road.

The hike: An information stand at the parking lot contains a trail register and rules regarding fires and camping. Mylius Trail (number 128) begins past a steel gate. The old fire road that is the trail leads west at a moderate climb, passing an old pasture dotted with autumn olive. The trail turns into single-track as it reenters the forest from the pasture. After a short steep climb, Mylius Trail bends to the right and the angle levels off.

The trail now travels across the ridge, crossing contour lines at a more acceptable pace. The path is shady, damp, and green. At just under 1.0 mile, the trail bends through a drainage area. The stinging nettle that lines the trail

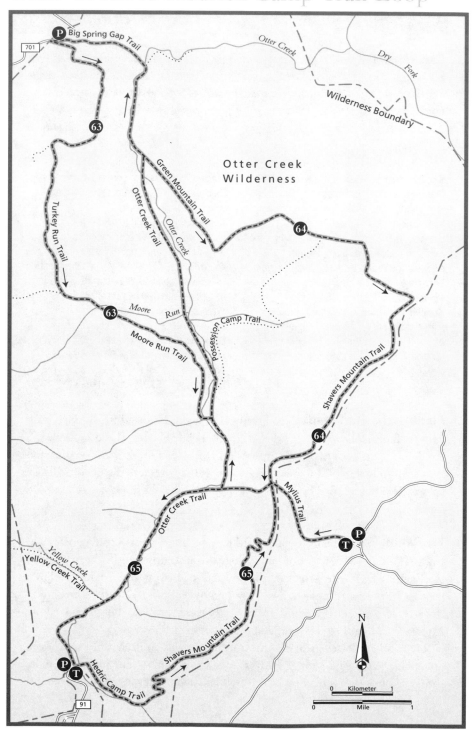

reminds you that you should put on your gaiters. The trail passes through another drainage area and then crosses an old fire road. The direction of the trail is emphasized by rock cairns placed before and after the fire road.

Mylius Trail tops Shavers Mountain and intersects Shavers Mountain Trail (number129) at a saddle in the ridge. Shavers Mountain Trail travels across the ridge top of the mountain. Continue straight as Mylius Trail crosses the saddle and begins to hike west down to the creek valley. The saddle has ample space for camping, and water can be found via a short hike down Mylius Trail on the Otter Creek side of the ridge.

From the ridge top, Mylius Trail eases its way to Otter Creek. Within 0.25 mile of the ridge crest, the trail crosses a small creek. The trail is wide enough for two people to hike abreast, but it is often muddy. The banks of Otter Creek are reached 2.5 miles from the trailhead. Water flows around large sandstone boulders dotted with dime-size pebbles, and the stream bottom is orange with tannins. Because there are no bridges over Otter Creek inside the wilderness, the stream must be forded. Chances are good that you can rock-hop across this particular crossing. Depending on water levels, though, many streams in the wilderness require barefoot crossings.

Across the creek, there is a campsite near the stream just before the junction of Mylius Trail and Otter Creek Trail (number 131). A left on Otter Creek Trail leads approximately 3 miles to FR 91. Turn right and hike Otter Creek Trail downstream. The trail initially travels in an easterly direction, but bends left and travels north. Otter Creek Trail is thickly lined with rhododendron, while yellow birch and hemlock dominate the canopy.

At about 3.0 miles, the trail crosses Otter Creek, which soon slides down a long slab of bedrock into a large and deep swimming hole. The trail continues along the banks of the picturesque stream. There are both spacious and intimate campsites throughout the area, perfect for setting up a "spike" camp for access to other trails in the wilderness. At approximately 3.6 miles, Otter Creek Trail reaches a junction with two other trails: Possession Camp and Moore Run Trails. Possession Camp Trail (number 158) heads off to the right and will reach Green Mountain Trail in about 3.1 miles. To the left, Moore

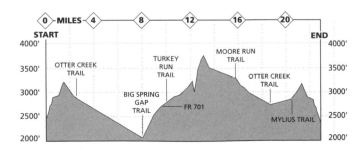

223

Perfect campsites abound along Otter Creek Trail.

Run Trail crosses the creek and heads up McGowan Mountain. Stay on Otter Creek Trail, the center trail, which sticks to the banks of its namesake and continues to follow the creek downstream 4.5 miles to the junction with Big Spring Gap Trail.

Just past the triple trail junction, Otter Creek Trail passes a trail shelter and a small meadow perfect for tent camping. Cross the creek again and shortly thereafter pass a small cascade. The trail is often made narrow by encroaching rhododendron, and campsites are frequent along the trail. Pass another meadow and continue to follow the western bank of the stream.

At 6.6 miles, Otter Creek Trail again crosses the stream. Green Mountain Trail (number 130) intersects Otter Creek Trail from the right at about 7.0 miles. Otter Creek Trail continues downstream and passes by several deep, blue water holes. At 8.1 miles, the junction with Big Spring Gap Trail is reached.

A rock cairn alerts the hiker to the junction with Big Spring Gap Trail (number 151). Otter Creek Trail continues straight along the stream. Follow Big Spring Gap Trail as it crosses Otter Creek and begins to hike out of the stream valley. Otter Creek is very wide at this part of the hike. If stream flow is high, great caution should be taken in crossing. Although not particularly deep, the water moves fast over the slippery rocks. Winter hikers need to be especially aware of the dangers a dip in the icy waters would pose. Wet clothes can quickly cause hypothermia, and the Mylius Trail parking lot is a long hike away.

Across the creek, Big Spring Gap Trail travels up a drainage area to FR

701, passing through a mixed stand of beech, birch, maple, and tulip poplar. An aggravating ground cover of stinging nettle will have you searching for your gaiters again. Big Spring Gap Trail travels 0.9 mile, making the tally 9.0 miles as it leaves the forest at FR 701. There is a gate at the road and a sign marking the trail.

Turn left on FR 701 and hike the road uphill to reach the junction with Turkey Run Trail (number 150). The road hike is just under 0.5 mile. There is a small parking area on the left, and a sign announces the trail. There is a register at this trailhead.

The first portion of Turkey Run Trail is wrought with nettle and mud, and you will wonder why anyone would hike it at all. The upper portion of the trail is so beautiful, however, that you will forget the first part ever existed. As the trail leaves FR 701, it begins a long uphill climb. The first portion of the climb is at an easy angle through a forest of maple, tulip poplar, and black cherry. The trail travels an old fire road, though, and the gap in the canopy, coupled with the dampness of runoff, gives rise to many weeds. The most numerous of these is the stinging nettle.

At approximately 11.75 miles, Turkey Run Trail passes an old fire road heading up the ridge to the right. Stay left as the trail travels down a small dip and then continues up. Just after this junction, the trail begins to get interesting. It crosses a feeder stream and then changes to single-track. Almost like magic, ferns appear and completely cover the forest floor. The easy uphill hike becomes moderate to difficult. Striped maple, hemlock, and rhododendron fill the middle and upper canopy, while ferns and moss cover the rocky forest floor. The trail moves over large rocks as an infant stream develops in the middle of the path. This portion of the hike is a unique experience with a strong feeling of primeval forest. When the trail levels off, spruce fills the canopy. A small footbridge crosses a boggy area thick with green moss and black soil. The trail finally starts to descend and rhododendron again chokes the understory. At 15.5 miles, Turkey Run Trail reaches Moore Run and McGowan Mountain Trails.

Turn left and follow Moore Run Trail, which travels 4.1 miles down the mountain to the triple junction with Otter Creek and Possession Camp Trails. The forest near the beginning of Moore Run Trail is thick with a jungle of rhododendron. The sound of a stream can be heard mere feet away from the trail, while a vision of the trail remains hidden behind a wall of vegetation. Soon enough, however, the trail crosses the stream and then continues to follow closely to its bank. The streambed is made up of countless small pebbles that remain after the less resistant portions of the bedrock have eroded away. The hike near the stream is made difficult by mud and exposed roots. After the trail crosses a small feeder stream it begins to move away from the main stream. The rhododendrons are replaced by an open forest understory and a canopy of large hemlock. Moore Run Trail travels downhill at a light angle. The stream, however, drops off of the mountain very quickly and the trail has substantial elevation over the valley to the left. Finally, views of Otter Creek can be seen down to the left. As Moore Run Trail passes on the left of a campsite it reaches the banks of Otter Creek. The trail crosses the creek and meets the junction of Otter Creek Trail and Possession Camp Trail at approximately 19 total hiking miles.

The rest of the hike backtracks along earlier portions of the hike. At the triple junction, turn right and follow Otter Creek Trail south 1.1 miles to the intersection with Mylius Trail. Turn left onto Mylius trail and hike 2.5 miles over Shavers Mountain and down to the trailhead parking lot.

Mylius to Shavers Mountain Trail Loop / *Otter Creek Wilderness*

Overview: *Hikes from the stream valley to the ridge-tops of Otter Creek Wilderness display ever changing ecosystems as the elevation changes. Birch and cherry hardwood forests dominate the creek valley and the slopes, while red spruce and the imported Norway spruce occupy the higher elevations. Otter Creek Wilderness has 40 miles of trails on its 20,000 acres. Its popularity makes it especially busy on summer weekends.*

General description: This loop meanders along the beautiful Otter Creek before making a big climb to the summit of Green Mountain. After the summit, the trail descends gradually down Shaver Mountain back to the junction with the Mylius Trail.
General location: 13 miles east of Elkins
Length: 15.2 miles
Difficulty: Difficult
Special attractions: The wonderful sounds of fast-flowing Otter Creek and the quiet solitude of a high mountain spruce bog.
Maps: Otter Creek Wilderness, Cheat Ranger District; USGS quads: Bath Alum, Green Valley, Montrose, Parsons

Camping: Because this hike is in designated wilderness backcountry, camping is permitted throughout the area. There are no developed campsites. As in all designated wildernesses, camp in sites that have been used before in high-use areas, while dispersed camping is recommended in low-use parts of the wilderness.
Seasons: Open year-round
For information: USDA Forest Service, Cheat Ranger District, P.O. Box 368, Parsons, WV 26287; (304) 478–3251

See map on page 222.

Finding the trailhead: This hike begins at the trailhead for Mylius Trail. From Elkins, follow US 33/WV 55 east. From Seneca Rocks, follow US 33/WV 55 west. Turn north onto CR 12 at Alpena, between Wymer and Bowden. Follow CR 12 about 4.5 miles to FDR 162 and turn left, just before CR 12 crosses Glady Creek. Proceed 0.1 mile to the parking area and trailhead on the left.

The hike: An information stand at the parking lot contains a trail register and rules regarding fires and camping. Mylius Trail (number 128) begins past a steel gate. The old fire road that is the trail leads west at a moderate climb, passing an old pasture dotted with autumn olive. The trail turns into single-track as it reenters the forest from the pasture. After a short steep climb, Mylius Trail bends to the right and the angle levels off.

The trail travels across the ridge, crossing contour lines at a more acceptable pace. The path is shady, damp, and green. At just under 1.0 mile, the trail bends through a drainage area. The stinging nettle that lines the trail reminds you that you should put on your gaiters. The trail passes through another drainage area and then crosses an old fire road. The direction of the trail is emphasized by rock cairns placed before and after the fire road.

Mylius Trail tops Shavers Mountain and intersects Shavers Mountain Trail (number 129) at a saddle in the ridge. Shavers Mountain Trail travels across the ridge top of the mountain. Continue straight as Mylius Trail crosses the saddle and begins to hike west down to the creek valley. The saddle has ample space for camping, and water can be found via a short hike down Mylius Trail on the Otter Creek side of the ridge.

From the ridge top, Mylius Trail eases its way to Otter Creek. Within 0.25 mile of the ridge crest, the trail crosses a small creek. The trail is wide enough for two people to hike abreast, but it is often muddy. The banks of Otter Creek are reached 2.5 miles from the trailhead. Water flows around large sandstone boulders dotted with dime-sized pebbles, and the stream bottom is orange with tannins. Because there are no bridges over Otter Creek inside the

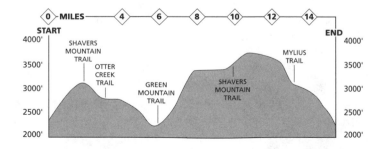

A log serves as a bridge over a boggy section of trail.

wilderness, the stream must be forded. Chances are good that you can rock-hop across this particular crossing. Depending on water levels, though, many streams in the wilderness require barefoot crossings.

Across the creek there is a campsite near the stream just before the junction of Mylius Trail and Otter Creek Trail (number 131). A left on Otter Creek Trail leads approximately 3 miles to FR 91. Turn right and hike Otter Creek Trail downstream. The trail initially travels in an easterly direction, but bends left and travels north. Otter Creek Trail is thickly lined with rhododendron, while yellow birch and hemlock dominate the canopy.

At about 3.0 miles, the trail crosses Otter Creek, which soon slides down a long slab of bedrock into a large and deep swimming hole. The trail continues along the banks of the picturesque stream. There are both spacious and intimate campsites throughout the area, perfect for setting up a "spike" camp for access to other trails in the wilderness. At approximately 3.6 miles, Otter Creek Trail reaches a junction with two other trails: Possession Camp and Moore Run Trails. Possession Camp Trail (number 158) heads off to the right and will reach Green Mountain Trail in about 3.1 miles. To the left, Moore Run Trail crosses the creek and heads up McGowan Mountain. Stay on Otter Creek Trail, the center trail, which sticks to the banks of its namesake and continues to follow the creek downstream.

Just past the triple trail junction, Otter Creek Trail passes a trail shelter and a small meadow perfect for tent camping. Cross the creek again and shortly thereafter pass a small cascade. The trail is often made narrow by encroaching rhododendrons, and campsites are frequent along the trail. Pass another meadow and continue to follow the western bank of the stream.

At 6.6 miles, Otter Creek Trail again crosses the stream. At about 7.0 miles, the Green Mountain Trail (number 130) intersects Otter Creek Trail; turn right on the Green Mountain Trail as it heads southeast. The elevation at the junction is 2,200 feet. The trail begins with an easy climb, angling up the mountain and away from the creek. The forest floor is covered with ferns, and tall straight hardwoods dominate the canopy. The easy grade is short-lived, becoming moderate as the trail quickly begins to climb Green Mountain. At 0.5 mile, the trail crosses a small feeder stream then reaches a short level area. There is a small campsite on the right. Enjoy the flat spot because the grade soon becomes steep and the trail rocky.

At 3,300 feet, a rock cairn marks the end of the steep climb at a small clearing. The climb from the Otter River to the crest is approximately 1.0 mile. The trail turns left and begins to meander along the crest of the mountain on an easy grade. Vigilance is necessary at times because the trail is not well marked. Fortunately, the length of this confusing section is short. The forest understory is covered with moss, ferns, and rhododendron. The rhododendron is usually in full bloom in late June and early July.

After an abrupt right turn, the trail begins to follow a wide, level path south. Pass through a small meadow on the left and cross the upper reaches of Possession Camp Run. There are several campsites in this region, and water is available. The junction with the Possession Camp Trail is in a second small meadow. This trail exits to the right and begins to descend 3.1 miles to the Otter River Trail.

Remain on the Green Mountain Trail as it begins an easy climb to a small clearing. The trail skirts the edge of a bog and enters a stand of red spruce at the upper end of the Shavers Lick Run. The elevation in this area is almost 3,600 feet, the highest point of the Green Mountain Trail. After a short descent, turn right at a T intersection onto the Shavers Mountain Trail. A sign at the left fork indicates that the trail has been abandoned.

Shavers Mountain Trail begins with a gradual climb out of the bog into a spruce forest. There is an area of significant downfall on the left. Blue blazes mark the trail, but they are spotty at best. Top the crest of a rounded knoll and begin an easy descent to a trail crossing. A right leads down into small meadows and secluded campsites. There is also water in this area. A left leads 100 yards to an old Adirondack shelter, providing a good view to the east. The distance from the junction with the Green Mountain Trail is about 0.5 mile.

Shavers Mountain Trail continues straight and begins an easy climb into a dense stand of red spruce. The top of this climb is the highest point on the loop (3,760 feet), which is followed by a long moderate descent. The spruce gives way to tall hemlock, which eventually gives way to tall straight hardwoods. When the trail drops to the east side of the ridge, the grade becomes steep, but only for about 0.25 mile.

At the end of this long descent, the trail enters a narrow gap and reaches the junction with the Mylius Trail. The distance from the Green Mountain Trail to this junction is 2.7 miles. Turn left to return to the Mylius Trailhead.

65 Otter Creek to Hedrick Camp Trail Loop / *Otter Creek Wilderness*

Overview: *Shavers Mountain and Green Mountain form the eastern boundary of the Otter Creek Wilderness. These two mountains rise from the banks of the Otter Creek to almost 4,000 feet. Tall stands of cove hardwoods thrive in the sheltered bottom land of Otter Creek, while the high ridge crests support dense stands of spruce and hemlock. The creek itself tumbles over huge rock boulders and passes through narrow crevices. Quiet pools form below many of the small falls, creating delightfully cool swimming holes.*

General description: This loop follows the fast-flowing Otter Creek to the Mylius Trail, then makes a long climb to the summit of Shavers Mountain. A quick drop off the mountain leads to the very upper reaches of the rhododendron-covered Otter Creek.

General location: 13 miles east of Elkins

Length: 9.0 miles

Difficulty: Moderate

Special attractions: A high mountain summit, a great view to the east, and a wonderful hike along a free, fast-flowing river.

Maps: Otter Creek Wilderness, Cheat Ranger District; USGS quads: Bath Alum, Green Valley, Montrose, Parsons

Camping: Because this hike is in designated wilderness, backcountry camping is permitted throughout the area. There are no developed campsites. As in all designated wildernesses, camp in sites that have been used before in high-use areas, while dispersed camping is recommended in low-use parts of the wilderness.

Seasons: Open year-round.

For information: USDA Forest Service, Cheat Ranger District, P.O. Box 368, Parsons, WV 26287; (304) 478–3251

See map on page 222.

Finding the trailhead: Take US 33 east out of Elkins about 12 miles to Alpena Gap and turn north on FR 91. Travel 1.2 miles to a Y intersection, take the right fork on FR 303, and continue 0.5 mile to the parking area.

The hike: From the parking area, cross the Otter Creek on a wooden bridge and follow FR 303 about 0.25 mile to a trail sign. The trail exits the road to the left and begins to climb gradually, following an old road. After a short climb, there is a spillway visible to the right, and the trail begins an easy descent to the creek bottom. The trail parallels the Otter Creek, passing a campsite in a grassy meadow. After crossing Yellow Creek, the Yellow Creek Trail exits to the left at 1.2 miles. It heads in a northwesterly direction, eventually connecting with the McGowan Mountain Trail.

Continue on the Otter Creek Trail, which follows an old railroad grade along the left bank of the Otter Creek. There are several campsites on the left side of the trail. A massive boulder is the major landmark of this section. After crossing over two small feeder streams and passing through some small meadows, the trail intersects the Mylius Trail 1.8 miles from the Yellow Creek Trail junction.

Turn right on the Mylius Trail and drop down to the Otter Creek. Ford the creek, then begin an easy 0.5-mile climb to a saddle on Shavers Mountain. The ridge is moist, and rhododendron crowds the trail.

From the saddle, the Shavers Mountain Trail turns south and begins an easy climb up the crest. Rhododendrons are plentiful, and hardwoods tower overhead. The trail climbs steadily to the 3,800-foot summit of Shavers Mountain. Two switchbacks just before the summit mark the end of the climb. After topping the summit, the grade becomes easy, and a hemlock thicket shadows the ground. The trail travels along the long summit ridge for 1.7 miles. There is a pleasant campsite on the left about midway along the summit. Ferns dominate the understory in several places.

A steady descent begins when the trail drops off the southeast side of the ridge. Two switchbacks are followed by a moderate descent. The descent continues with two more switchbacks. Thick, knurled old-growth hardwoods dominate this finger ridge. At the bottom of the descent, the trail begins to follow an old road, which heads in a southwesterly direction alongside a stream.

The junction with the Hedrick Camp Trail is about 0.25 mile from the bottom of the descent. The Shavers Mountain Trail exits to the left and continues another 3.0 miles to US 33. Take the right fork onto the Hedrick Camp Trail, which follows an old road that descends gradually along the very upper reaches of the Otter Creek. The creek is on the left, lined with rhododendron and hemlock. At times this section of the trail can be wet and mucky. Moss and mushrooms thrive here.

The trail exits the road to the left, drops into a lush green forest, and parallels the creek bank. There are many signs of beaver activity in this vicinity. Cross the creek on a two-log bridge and enter a clear area under a stand of tall hemlocks. There are several campsites here. Follow the stream through a boggy area before crossing a bridge and exiting the woods. The loop is completed at FR 303.

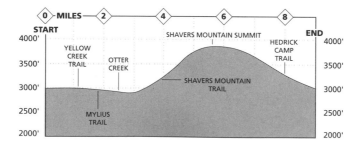

North Fork Mountain Trail

Spruce Knob–Seneca Rocks National Recreation Area

66

Overview: *Encompassing more than 100,000 acres, the Spruce Knob-Seneca Rocks National Recreation Area contains two of the most popular outdoor attractions in West Virginia. Seneca Creek Backcountry has the highest point in West Virginia, and Seneca Rocks has some of the best rock climbing on the east coast. The area of high ridges and steep cliffs was established in 1965 to protect the natural beauty of the region. North Fork Mountain forms the eastern boundary of the recreation area.*

General description: The North Fork Mountain Trail is an excellent two- to three-day backpack, offering some of the most scenic vistas in the entire state. The major drawback to this trail is a lack of water along the crest.

General location: 6 miles northwest of Franklin

Length: 23.8 miles one-way

Difficulty: Difficult

Special attractions: The trail offers many tremendous views from the sandstone cliffs that line North Fork Mountain.

Maps: USGS quads: Circleville, Franklin, Upper Tract, Hopeville, Petersburg West

Camping: Backpacking is permitted along the North Fork Mountain Trail.

Seasons: The trail is open to hikers year-round.

For information: District Ranger, Potomac Ranger District, Monongahela National Forest, HC 59 Box 240, Petersburg, WV 26847; (304) 257–4488

Finding the trailhead: To reach the southern trailhead, at the intersection of US 220 and US 33 in Franklin, take US 220 north/US 33 west 0.5 mile and turn left on US 33 west. Travel 8.3 miles to the summit of North Fork Mountain. Parking is on the right. There is a small metal building and a gate across the road. This is private land. *Do not block the gate.*

To reach the northern trailhead, at the intersection of WV 28, WV 55, and US 33 in Seneca Rocks, take WV 28 north/WV 55 east toward Petersburg. Proceed 15.7 miles to CR 28/11 (Smoke Hole Road) and turn right. There is a sign for Big Bend at the intersection. Cross the bridge and travel 0.4 mile to the parking area on the right.

To reach the middle parking areas from the northern trailhead, turn right on CR 28/11 and proceed 2.2 miles to the Landis trailhead or 7.5 miles to the Redman Run trailhead. To reach the middle parking area for the North Fork Mountain Trail, proceed 12.1 miles from the northern trailhead to a T intersection. Turn right and travel 3.9 miles on FR 79 to a left bend. The parking area is on the right.

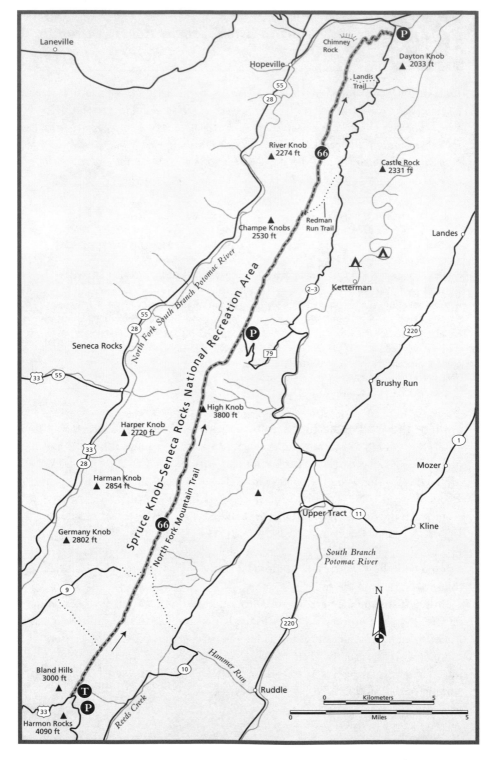

The hike: This trail description begins at the southern trailhead and proceeds north. It is highly recommended to hike the North Fork Mountain Trail (Trail 501) in this direction, especially if the hike is tackled as a day hike, because the elevation gain is minimal. The elevation at this trailhead is 3,592 feet. The elevation at the northern end of the trail is 1,300 feet.

From the road, hike past the gate and into the woods. There are NO TRESPASSING signs posted at the beginning of the hike; remember to stay on the trail, which is marked with blue blazes. The trail is wide and easy to follow as it travels an old road grade along the ridge crest. The forest is composed primarily of second-growth hardwoods. The hike begins with a series of easy climbs and descents, gradually increasing in elevation. After topping out (elevation 3,752 feet) about 2.0 miles from the trailhead, there is a moderate descent to a power line crossing. A large rock outcropping at the power line provides an exceptional view of Germany Valley and Spruce Knob.

The trail continues following an old road with easy climbs and descents. At 3.25 miles the trail crosses an old logging road. Germany Valley is 2.0 miles to the west and Reeds Creek is 2.0 miles to the east. Just past a short climb to a wooden platform used for launching hang gliders, the road ends and the trail becomes a footpath.

The path is narrow but easy to follow. The North Fork Mountain Trail hugs the eastern slope of the mountain just below the ridge crest. Even on very windy days, there is little wind on the trail, which contours the eastern slope. The ridge is steep along this section. After contouring for approximately 0.75 mile, the trail descends to a narrow saddle and again contours on the leeward side of the mountain. This is followed by a short, steep climb and then another drop to another narrow saddle. The trail climbs again, reaching a wide level region known as High Knob. Pines dominate the canopy and mountain laurel crowds the trail. Many short side trails lead to the western ridge. There is an excellent view of Seneca Rocks, and several flat campsites, but there is no water.

Not far beyond this area, the trail drops over to the western side of the mountain. It can be very windy along this short section of the hike. There is another descent followed by a long moderate climb along an old road. At 10.1

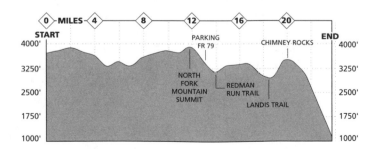

235

Tuscarora sandstone cliffs are frequent in the valley.

miles, the trail reaches a gas pipeline. There is a sign for US 33 to the south and Chimney Rock to the north. The road climbs at an easy grade to the highest point of the hike (elevation 3,895 feet). There is a metal building located on this high point and one of the few clear views to the east.

After the summit, the trail descends 1.4 miles following FR 79, a gravel road. The middle parking area is at a sharp right bend for the North Fork Mountain Trail. The distance is 11.9 miles, the halfway point of the trail.

The trail reenters the forest and leaves the road behind, again becoming a narrow path. There is an easy climb to a pleasant campsite, then the trail begins a series of easy climbs and descents, staying near the 3,100-foot level. About 2.5 miles from FR 79, a sloping stone slab lies west of the trail. At the top of this slab is a view of Champe Rocks, the Dolly Sods region, and the South Branch of the Potomac River. The trail continues the long gradual climbs and descents to Redman Run Trail (Trail 507, which exits right and drops 1.6 miles to CR 28/11. This distance from the middle parking area to the trail junction is 3.8 miles; the elevation is 3,000 feet. There are several campsites at the trail junction and a good view to the west.

After the trail junction, the North Fork Mountain Trail begins a long gradual descent, followed by a moderate climb to almost 3,400 feet. Small red spruce and big slabs of rock dot the landscape. Near the top of this climb, there are large rock cliffs to the left and a small campsite near the cliffs. The North Fork Mountain Trail descends to the junction with the Landis Trail (Trail 502). A sign for Chimney Rock marks the junction. The Landis Trail, also marked with blue blazes, exits right and descends 1.4 miles to CR 28/11. Combining the Landis Trail with the northern end of the North Fork Mountain Trail and CR 28/11 makes a loop trail of 7.2 miles.

The North Fork Mountain Trail bears left, then makes a short climb to a level area with several campsites. Another short climb leads to a set of massive cliffs known as Chimney Rock. There are several great views to the north and west from the cliff face. Occasionally, the trail is rerouted away from the cliffs to protect wildlife in the area.

The rocky trail drops to the right away from the cliffs and begins a steep descent, dropping 1,750 feet over 2.5 miles to CR 28/11. At the beginning of the descent, the canopy is dominated by small scrubby pine. Near the end of the descent, tall second-growth hardwoods reign supreme. There are several switchbacks during this descent. A sign marks the trailhead at an elevation of 1,300 feet.

Seneca Rocks Trail
Spruce Knob–Seneca Rocks National Recreation Area

67

Overview: *The sandstone "fin" of Seneca Rocks soars high above the clear, fast flowing South Fork Branch of the Potomac River in the Spruce Knob–Seneca Rocks National Recreation Area. The river is a favorite for both anglers and paddlers.*

General description: Seneca Rocks Trail leads to a massive rock face rising almost a thousand feet above the Potomac River.
General location: 0.25 mile east of Seneca Rocks
Length: 1.3 miles one-way
Difficulty: Moderate
Special attractions: This short trail climbs to a high observation deck on Seneca Rocks.

Maps: USGS quad: Upper Tract
Camping: Camping is available at nearby Seneca Shadows Campground.
Seasons: The trail is open year-round.
For information: District Ranger, Potomac Ranger District, Monongahela National Forest, HC 59 Box 240, Petersburg, WV 26847; (304) 257–4488

Finding the trailhead: At the intersection of US 33 and WV 28-55, go north on WV 28-55 about 0.2 mile and turn right into the Seneca Rocks picnic area parking lot.

The hike: The trail to the observation deck exits the parking lot and descends slightly to the North Fork of the South Branch of the Potomac River. The trail

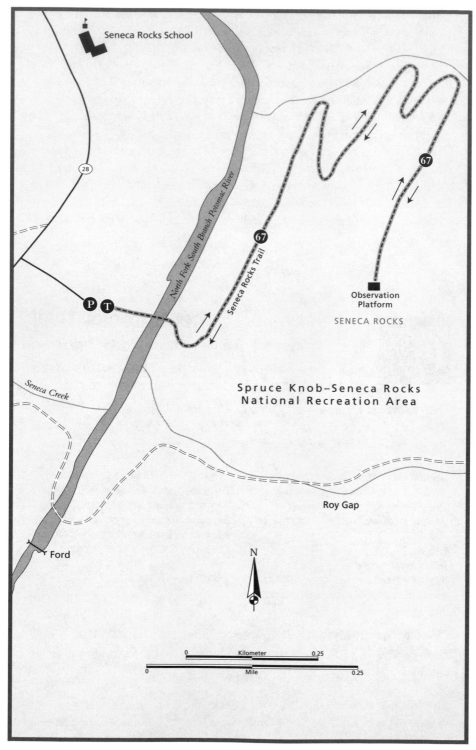

Seneca Rocks School

28

North Fork South Branch Potomac River

Seneca Rocks Trail

67

67

P T

Observation
Platform

SENECA ROCKS

Seneca Creek

Spruce Knob–Seneca Rocks
National Recreation Area

Roy Gap

Ford

N

| 0 | Kilometer | 0.25 |
| 0 | Mile | 0.25 |

Seneca Rocks.

crosses the river via a beautifully designed bridge. On the opposite shore, the trail turns right and briefly parallels the river upstream, then bends left at the creek that runs through Roy Gap. At the T intersection, climbers take the right fork and hikers take the left fork.

The wide gravel trail climbs gradually for about 0.25 mile. Stairs assist with the steeper sections of the trail. After the first set of stairs, there is a sign, ¼ WAY. The trail is now flat. This flat section quickly ends and the grade becomes more moderate. Another set of wooden steps leads to a right switchback and the halfway point of the trail. This is followed by another easy stretch and a third set of steps.

The trail makes a left and right switchback under a stand of towering hardwoods. After another set of switchbacks, the trail climbs to a small saddle. A short set of stairs leads to the observation platform. The view to the west is absolutely worth the climb. The Potomac River far below leads the eyes to the Dolly Sods region farther north. Retrace your route along the trail to the parking lot.

68

Spruce Knob Summit
Spruce Knob–Seneca Rocks National Recreation Area

Overview: *With more than 60 miles of trails through beautiful northern hardwood forests, it's easy to understand why Seneca Creek Backcountry is a favorite among West Virginia backpackers. Trails dance across the cold, clear water of Seneca Creek, muscle their way up steep ridges and rest in mountain meadows, and travel through spruce forests near the summit of Spruce Knob, the highest point in West Virginia at 4,863 feet. The thick forests of birch, beech, maple, and cherry offer cool shade in the summer. Deep snows blanket the area in winter, and often in the fall and spring! Give yourself extra time when visiting the backcountry. This beautiful area should not be rushed through.*

General description: A "must hike" trail! The summit ridge of Spruce Mountain is a hiker's delight.

General location: 17 miles south of Harman

Length: 11.0 miles one-way

Difficulty: Difficult

Special attractions: Ridge-crest meadows containing blueberries, azaleas, and wildflowers; thick spruce forests; crystal-clear mountain streams.

Maps: Seneca Creek Backcountry, US Forest Service; USGS quads: Circleville, Onega, Spruce Knob, Whitmer

Camping: Camping is allowed in the backcountry. Seneca Creek Backcountry should be treated in a manner similar to wilderness. There are no developed or designated campsites. In high-use areas it is best to camp in sites that have been used before, while dispersed camping is recommended in low-use parts of the wilderness. If backcountry camping is not your cup of tea, the Gatewood campground has six sites, and the campground at Spruce Knob Lake has more than forty.

Seasons: Seneca Creek Backcountry is open year-round. Back roads are not maintained during the winter, so call ahead for local conditions.

For information: US Forest Service, Monongahela National Forest, HC 59 Box 240, Petersburg, WV 26847; (304) 257–4488

Finding the trailhead: The hike requires two vehicles, one at each trailhead. From Seneca Rocks follow US 33/WV 28 south to CR 33-4 near a small car dealership. Turn right, heading up the mountain to the intersection with FR 112 at a fork in the road. Take a left at the fork, and follow FR 112 to the intersection with FR 104. Turn right onto FR 104 and travel along the ridge crest of Spruce Mountain to the summit parking lot.

From the summit parking lot take the second car to the starting trailhead. Follow FR 104 back to FR 112 and turn right. Travel down the western side of the mountain, passing by the Gatewood Campground. Turn right onto FR 1 at a Y intersection. Follow FR 1 past Spruce Knob Lake to CR 29. Turn right onto CR 29 and follow it north along Ganby Creek past many parking areas and

Spruce Knob Summit

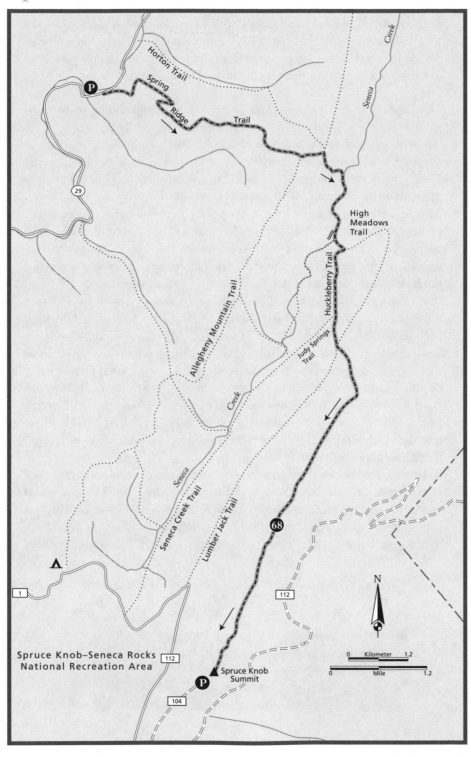

Horton Trail

P

Spring

Ridge

Trail

Seneca Creek

29

High
Meadows
Trail

Allegheny Mountain Trail

Huckleberry Trail

Judy Springs Trail

Creek

Seneca

Seneca Creek Trail

Lumber Jack Trail

68

1

N

112

Spruce Knob–Seneca Rocks
National Recreation Area

112

P

Spruce Knob
Summit

104

0   Kilometer   1.2

0   Mile   1.2

trailheads. There are several pull-off spots along this road suitable for car camping. After CR 29 crosses Ganby Creek, keep a lookout on the right for the trailhead for Spring Ridge Trail. A large information sign marks the trailhead. An old fire road climbs steeply away from the road. Although other trailhead parking lots are spacious, there is only limited parking at this trailhead.

The hike: The first leg of this hike follows Spring Ridge Trail (number 561) to the crest of Allegheny Mountain. Spring Ridge Trail begins at an information stand on the east side of CR 29. The trail is blazed with a blue diamond. Lined with striped maple, yellow birch, and rhododendron, Spring Ridge Trail travels 3 miles before reaching the ridge crest. The trail angle is predominantly moderate, with a few difficult sections to keep you honest. After the initial hike out of the creek valley, water is scarce. Small feeder streams on the east side of Allegheny Mountain will be the next filterable water source. The hike to the ridge crest passes several small meadows that provide star-filled night skies. These meadows are a picturesque place to put down if the hike is begun late in the day.

At the crest of Allegheny Mountain, there are several turns and trail intersections to negotiate. First, Spring Ridge Trail intersects Allegheny Mountain Trail. Turn left at this intersection and hike downhill through a small meadow, another wonderful area in which to camp. As the trail reaches the tree line it splits: One trail enters the forest, one travels more steeply downhill to the right, staying just on the meadow side of the forest. Follow this right-hand split. The trail enters the forest and begins a steep downhill on the first section of bona fide single-track of the hike. As the trail levels off, it intersects with Horton Trail. Turn right at this intersection and follow Horton Trail downhill to the south.

Horton Trail travels through a forest of sugar maple and black cherry until it intersects with Seneca Creek and Seneca Creek Trail. The descent is predominantly at a moderate angle. At the 4-mile mark, Horton Trail crosses over a small feeder stream, the first watering hole since the hike began. Drink if you wish, but a nicer break will come at the waterfall that waits at Seneca

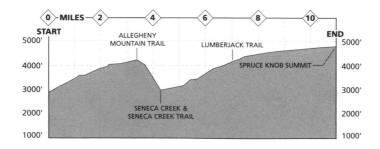

Hikers on the ridge crest of Spruce Mountain.

Creek. Shortly after the stream is crossed, rhododendron and mountain laurel begin to fill the forest understory. There are limited views of Spruce Mountain to the left. Horton Trail crosses another small stream that cascades down the mountain and then descends to the banks of Seneca Creek. Seneca Creek is reached at just over 4.5 miles.

The next part of the hike is a short but wonderful walk along Seneca Creek. Cross the creek via a small wooden footbridge and climb the opposite creek bank to reach Seneca Creek Trail, a remnant of an old logging road. Horton Trail marks the northern end of the maintained portion of Seneca Creek Trail. The trail can be followed farther downstream, but the bushwhacking becomes difficult very soon. Seneca Creek also crosses private property before it reaches a road, so any hike north of this point is an out-and-back.

Turn right on Seneca Creek Trail and follow it south. Within minutes the trail passes a cascading waterfall dropping into a clear, cold pool. Take some time to take in the view and soak in the water. The long hike to the summit of Spruce Knob begins here.

Seneca Creek Trail reaches Huckleberry Trail just after the falls. The rest of the hike is almost entirely uphill. You are, after all, hiking to the high point of West Virginia. A sign marks the intersection just before Seneca Creek Trail crosses the creek. Turn left and follow Huckleberry Trail up a short, steep embankment. The bank tops out at an old fire road; turn right and follow Huckleberry Trail uphill. The trail crosses a small feeder stream, turns right, and then travels lightly downhill. Follow the blue blazes as the trail wraps around a ridge and then bends left to follow a stream uphill and away from Seneca Creek.

As Huckleberry Trail travels up the ridge of Spruce Mountain, several landmarks are passed. First, a small, steep meadow is reached at about 5.0 miles. A sign at a trail junction in this meadow points directions to Huckleberry Trail, High Meadows Trail, and Huckleberry Trail/Seneca Creek. Turn right and follow Huckleberry Trail to another expansive, scenic pasture. There are plenty of places suitable for camping in this area. The trail hikes up a forested ridge at a moderate to difficult angle. At about 6.5 miles, another trail junction is reached at the edge of yet another meadow. Huckleberry Trail continues straight as Judy Springs Trail heads down and to the right. Spruce begins to spring up in the understory.

As Huckleberry Trail begins to near the ridge crest, the angle becomes steeper. Huckleberry Trail crosses over Lumberjack Trail (right) and High Meadows Trail (left). Pass straight through this intersection and continue up. A difficult ascent leads Huckleberry Trail through a thick, almost pure stand of striped maple, and the trail opens up onto the first summit bald.

The ridge crest of Spruce Mountain is invigorating. The climb becomes a mere predecessor to reaching this picture-postcard landscape. The ridge crest is open to the sky and covered with grasses, wildflowers, blueberry, huckleberry, azalea, and spruce. The trail passes from open sky to deeply shaded spruce forest in a matter of steps. Often rocky, the trail is nevertheless a delight to hike. Views are primarily to the west. On its way to the summit parking lot, the trail bounces across the ridge top at an easy up angle for about 4.5 miles. The trail is easy to follow and passes by two trail signs along the way.

Huckleberry Trail widens and the path becomes covered in gravel just before it reaches the civilization of the summit parking lot. Follow the paved road to the paved trail that leads to the lookout tower at the 4,863-foot summit of Spruce Knob. The 360-degree views from the summit tower are stunning.

George Washington and Jefferson NATIONAL FORESTS

The George Washington and Jefferson National Forests tip just slightly into West Virginia from Virginia. Management of the two separate national forests was combined into one administrative unit in 1995. The former Jefferson National Forest dips into West Virginia along Peters Mountain in Monroe County. The former George Washington National Forest occupies two landmasses in West Virginia: one just east of the towns of Mathias, Lost River, and Baker in Hardy County, and the other east of the towns of Sugar Grove, Brandywine, and Fort Seybert in Pendleton County. The forests occupy more than 123,000 acres in West Virginia, approximately 7 percent of the forest's 1.7 million acres.

The trails described here are rugged and can be unforgiving. Don't underestimate the difficulty of even a short trail. The surrounding area is very rural, so make sure you are well supplied before you begin your trip. Finding supplies near the trailhead may be difficult if not impossible. Camping is available in campgrounds and by dispersed camping in the forest.

As with all national forests, hunting is allowed in the George Washington and Jefferson National Forests. Although hunting seasons tend to be in the fall and early winter, check local hunting calendars any time a hike is planned in the forest. If planning a hike during a hunting season, wear blaze orange and stick to well-marked trails.

69

Tuscarora Trail (Southwest)
George Washington National Forest

Overview: *The George Washington National Forest lies on the West Virginia/ Virginia border, and encompasses more than 100,000 acres of forested land in West Virginia. From an easy walk around Rockcliff Lake to multiday backpacks, the National Forest offers hiking opportunities for any ability. The trails of the National Forest meander along the banks of slow moving streams and under canopies of dense rhododendron. They offer magnificent vistas from rock outcrops. In addition to hiking, the George Washington National Forest offers a host of other recreational activities, including camping, canoeing, mountain biking, hunting, and fishing.*

General description: Hawk is a small campground on the western slope of Great North Mountain.

General location: 7.5 miles northeast of Wardensville

Length: 1.5 miles one-way

Difficulty: Easy

Special attractions: A quiet, remote place, perfect for a peaceful retreat.

Maps: Lee Ranger District map; USGS quads: Capon Springs, Mountain Falls, Wardensville

Camping: Camping is available year-round. There are thirteen sites available on a first-come, first-served basis. There is no charge for camping.

Seasons: The area is open year-round, but access can be difficult in the winter.

For information: Lee Ranger District, 109 Molineu Road, Edinburg, VA 22824; (540) 984–4101

Finding the trailhead: At the intersection of WV 55 and WV 259 just north of Wardensville, proceed north on WV 259 about 8.0 miles to the intersection of WV 259 and CR 16 (Capon Springs Road). Turn right on CR 16 and continue 4.2 miles to FR 502. Turn right, travel 1.3 miles, and turn right on FR 347. The campground entrance is on the right about 0.7 mile down the mountain.

The hike: Two sets of blue blazes leave the picnic area. Follow the blazes that head away from the picnic area entrance in a westerly direction along an old road that crosses FR 347. There is a gradual descent for about 0.25 mile, then the trail crosses FR 347 again. Continue following the old logging road. The trail makes an easy climb to a game clearing on the right.

A right turn marked by a double blue blaze is followed by an easy climb to a small knoll. Young hardwoods dominate the canopy, and deer are represented in large numbers. A short descent is followed by another easy climb to the crest of a small ridge. The trail is now flat. At the fork, go right

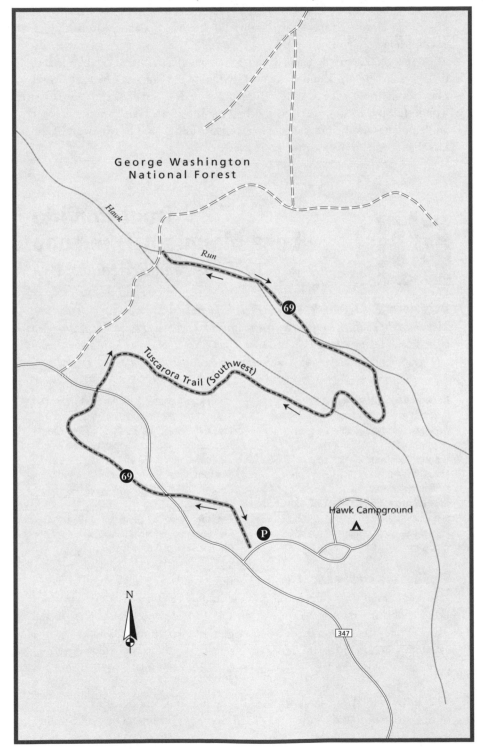

George Washington
National Forest

Hawk

Run

69

Tuscarora Trail (Southwest)

69

P

Hawk Campground

N

347

to follow the trail as it makes another easy descent, crosses a small feeder creek, and climbs again. After a right and left bend, a sharp drop leads to Hawk Run at approximately 1.25 miles.

At the creek, turn left and begin following the fast flowing Hawk Run downstream. Hemlock and white pine dominate the canopy. The trail crosses Hawk Run three times. At the third crossing is a small shelf waterfall, a wonderful spot to stop and have lunch. The Tuscarora Trail crosses the creek and continues up the hill, but the roads that it follows are heavily scarred and less than scenic. Return by the same route.

70 Trout Pond to Long Mountain Trail Loop
Trout Pond Recreation Area

Overview: *Trout Pond Recreation Area is located on the western slope of Long Mountain. In addition to the trail system around Trout Pond Lake, the local region offers several hiking adventures. The Trout Pond Recreation Area also includes a small lake for fishing and swimming, plus a relaxing picnic facility and a campground.*

General description: A long strenuous hike with great views from Lina Constable Overlook and long sections on wide grassy trails.
General location: 7 miles south of Baker
Length: 8.4 miles
Difficulty: Difficult
Special attractions: Great rock formations and quiet solitude.
Maps: Lee Ranger District map; USGS quad: Wolf Gap

Camping: Available from the fourth Tuesday in April until the close of hunting season; fees for camping are $13 and $16 before May 22 and after September 12, $17 and $20 between May 22 and September 12.
Seasons: The recreation area is closed from December to April. The trail system is open year-round.
For information: Lee Ranger District, 109 Molineu Road, Edinburg, VA 22824; (540) 984–4101

Finding the trailhead: At the intersection of WV 55 and WV 259 in Baker, turn south on WV 259 and travel 7.1 miles to CR 12. There is a sign for Trout Pond at this intersection. Turn east on CR 12 and proceed 4.7 miles to the Trout Pond Recreation Area. Turn right and continue 2.0 miles to the swimming area. During the off-season, travel 0.4 mile to the ridge crest and park in the lot on the left. This is the trailhead for the Fishermen's Trail.

The hike: The Trout Pond to Long Mountain Trail Loop begins at the end of the parking lot and climbs a small hill to the power line. The trail parallels

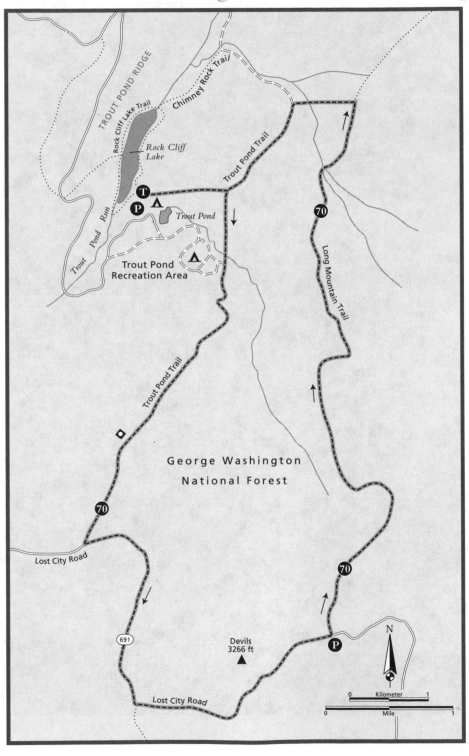

TROUT POND RIDGE

Rock Cliff Lake Trail

Chimney Rock Trail/

Rock Cliff
Lake

Trout Pond Trail

Trout Pond Run

T

P

Trout Pond

70

Long Mountain Trail

Trout Pond
Recreation Area

Trout Pond Trail

◇

George Washington

National Forest

70

Lost City Road

691

70

70

P

Devils
3266 ft
▲

N

Lost City Road

0   Kilometer   1

0   Mile   1

Chimney Rock.

the power line a short distance down to the maintenance road; turn right. After about 0.25 mile, the trail exits the road to the left. There is a purple blaze at this junction.

Following a wide grassy road, the trail crosses a small creek and enters the campground at site 31. Turn left on the campground loop and walk to campsite 27. A sign for the Junior Poe Trail notes LIFE'S ALWAYS AN UPHILL CLIMB. This is an accurate description of the next mile as the Trout Pond Trail climbs from about 2,000 feet to 2,800 feet.

The Trout Pond Trail exits left and follows an old road 2.0 miles to Lost City Road. The hike begins with a steep climb to a small building on the left. Past the building, the road is grassy and less traveled and the climb moderates somewhat. Near the halfway point of the climb, the Lina Constable Overlook is on the right. There is a great view from the overlook, with a sign pointing out all the high landmarks on the horizon. There is even a bench where you can sit and rest.

The climbs mellow to an easy grade as the trail passes through two wildlife clearings and then begins a short descent to Lost City Road. At the beginning of the descent, another road exits to the left; continue straight. At the gravel road, turn left and begin an easy climb on the Lost City Road. After 1.0 mile on Lost City Road, the loop passes the North Mountain Trail. Continue the easy climb into Virginia. The elevation here is 3,005 feet. At the border, the road begins a gradual descent.

The Long Mountain Trail exits to the left 0.9 mile from the North Mountain Trail. The trail follows a grassy old road. There is a gradual descent through a forest of small pine and oak, and mountain laurel and blueberry crowd the understory. The trail descends to a small clearing and a junction. The Long Mountain Trail takes the left fork and becomes a narrow footpath.

Following the west side of the ridge, there is a gradual descent to a narrow rock spine. The trail passes through the spine and begins a moderate descent on the dry western slope. Cross over one finger ridge and through a narrow hollow. After crossing over a second finger ridge, the trail passes through another narrow spine. The trail parallels the spine a short distance before turning north away from it. A short moderate descent leads to a wide area and a magnificent stand of hardwoods. The knurled old oaks are a wonderful sight. After a left switchback, the trail passes to the left of a small clearing.

Just beyond the clearing is the junction with the purple blazed Trout Pond Trail. The elevation at this junction is 2,040 feet. The Long Mountain Trail turns right. Turn left on the Trout Pond Trail to continue the loop.

The Trout Pond Trail is a grassy, wide old road lined with mature hardwoods. Following a wide left bend, the trail intersects the orange blazed Chimney Rock Trail. Continue straight, following the gravel road to a path that exits the road on the right. This path leads up to the power line and back to the parking area.

Rockcliff Lake to Trout Pond Loop Option: The white-blazed Rockcliff Lake Trail exits to the right of the parking area, climbs a small hill, and drops back down to the lake. The trail hugs the lakeshore to an earthen dam at 0.4 mile. After crossing the dam, the trail passes through a gap in a small rock cliff. On the opposite side of this cliff, the trail intersects with the orange blazed Chimney Rock Trail.

Turn right on the Chimney Rock Trail as the white–blazed Rockcliff Lake Trail turns left and heads back to the parking area. *Note*: About 0.2 mile from this intersection, the Rockcliff Lake Trail intersects the blue blazed Fishermen's Trail, which exits left. This trail is the access trail to the recreation area during the off-season.

Follow the overflow spillway on the Chimney Rock Trail. The trail bends right and drops to the creek, then bends left and parallels it a short distance. Large cove hardwoods thrive in this sheltered creek bottom. At 0.7 mile the trail crosses the creek and passes through another gap in the rocks. The pinnacle on the left is Chimney Rock. On the opposite side of the gap, the trail becomes a wide grassy road. At the purple blazed Trout Pond Trail, turn right and follow the gravel road to a path that exits the road to the right. This path leads up to a power line and follows it back to the parking area.

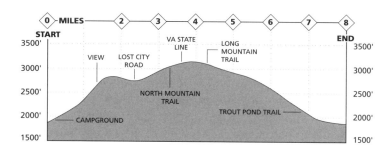

Appendix A:
USGS 1:24,000 Quad Map List

Northern Panhandle
Grand Vue Park—Moundsville
Oglebay Park—Wheeling
Tomlinson Run State Park—East
   Liverpool South
Wheeling Heritage Trails—Wheeling
   and Tiltonsville

Mountaineer Country
Cathedral State Park—Aurora
Coopers Rock State Forest—Bruceton
   Mills, Masontown, and Lake Lynn
Valley Falls State Park—Fairmont East
Watters Smith Memorial State Park—
   West Milford

Eastern Gateway
Cacapon Resort State Park—Great
   Cacapon and Ridge
*Harpers Ferry National Historical
   Park*—Harpers Ferry
Tuscarora Trail (Northeast)—Glengary
   and Stotlers Crossroads

Potomac Highlands
Beartown State Park—Droop
Blackwater Falls State Park—
   Blackwater Falls
Droop Mountain Battlefield State Park—
   Droop
Jennings Randolph Lake Project—
   Kitzmiller and Westernport
Kumbrabow State Forest—Adolph,
   Pickens, Samp, and Valley Head
Lost River State Park—Lost River State
   Park

Seneca State Forest—Clover Lick and
   Paddy Knob
Watoga State Park—Denmar,
   Hillsboro, Lake Sherwood, and
   Marlinton

Mountain Lakes
Audra State Park—Audra
Cedar Creek State Park—Cedarville,
   Glenville, Normantown, and Tanner
Holly River State Park—Goshen and
   Hacker Valley

New River/Greenbrier Valley
Babcock State Park—Danese,
   Fayetteville, Thurmond, and
   Winona
Bluestone National Scenic River—Flat
   Top and Pipestem
Camp Creek State Park—Odd
Greenbrier River Trail—Cass,
   Cloverlick, Edray, Marlinton,
   Hillsboro, Denmar, Droop,
   Anthony, White Sulphur Springs,
   and Lewisburg
Greenbrier State Forest—Glace and
   White Sulphur Springs
New River Gorge National River—
   Meadow Creek and Prince
Pipestem Resort State Park—Flat Top
   and Pipestem

Metro Valley
Beech Fork State Park—Winslow
Cabwaylingo State Forest—Kiahsville,
   Radnor, Webb, and Wilsondale

Huntington Museum of Art National Recreation Trail—Huntington
Kanawha State Forest—Belle, Charleston East, Charleston West, and Racine
Kanawha Trace Trail—Barboursville, Glenwood, Mount Olive, Milton, and Winfield

Mid-Ohio Valley

Blennerhassett Island Historical Park—Parkersburg
McDonough Wildlife Refuge—Parkersburg
North Bend Rail Trail—(west to east) South Parkersburg, Kanawha, Petroleum, Cairo, Harrisville, Ellenboro, Pennsboro, West Union, Smithburg, Salem, Wolf Summit
North Bend State Park—Cairo and Harrisville

Monongahela National Forest

Cranberry Glades Botanical Area—Lobelia
Cranberry Wilderness—Webster Springs SE and Woodrow

Dolly Sods Wilderness—Blackbird Knob, Blackwater Falls, Hopeville, and Laneville
Flatrock and Roaring Plains Backcountry—Harman, Hopeville, Laneville, and Onega
Laurel Fork North Wilderness—Gladys and Sinks of Gandy
Laurel Fork South Wilderness—Sinks of Gandy
Otter Creek Wilderness—Bath Alum, Green Valley, Montrose, and Parsons
Spruce Knob–Seneca Creek National Recreation Area—Circleville, Franklin, Upper Tract, Hopeville, Petersburg West, Circleville, Onega, Spruce Knob, and Whitmer

George Washington National Forest

Tuscarora Trail (Southwest)—Capon Springs, Mountain Falls, and Wardensville
Trout Pond Recreation Area—Wolf Gap

Appendix B:
For More Information

Audra State Park
Route 4, Box 564
Buckhannon, WV 26201
(304) 457–1162
www.wvparks.com/audra

Appalachian Trail Conference
P.O. Box 807
Harpers Ferry, WV 25425-0807
(304) 535–6331
www.atconf.org

Babcock State Park
HC 35, Box 150
Clifftop, WV 25831-9801
(304) 438–3004 or (800) CALL–WVA
www.babcocksp.com

Beartown State Park
HC 64, Box 189
Hillsboro, WV 24946
(304) 653–4254
www.wvparks.com/beartown

Beech Fork State Park
5601 Long Branch Road
Barboursville, WV 25504
(304) 522–0303 or (800) CALL–WVA
www.beechfork.com

Blackwater Falls State Park
Drawer 490
Davis, WV 26260
(304) 259–5216 or (800) CALL–WVA
www.blackwaterfalls.com

Blennerhassett Island Historical State Park
137 Juliana Street
Parkersburg, WV 26101
(304) 420–4800 or (800) CALL–WVA
www.wvparks.com/blennerhassett

Bluestone State Park
HC 78, Box 3
Hinton, WV 25951
(304) 466–2805 or (800) CALL–WVA
www.bluestonesp.com

Cabwaylingo State Forest
Route 1, Box 85
Dunlow, WV 25511
(304) 385–4255
www.cabwaylingo.com

Cacapon Resort State Park
Route 1, Box 230
Berkeley Springs, WV 25411
(304) 258–6691 or (800) CALL–WVA
www.cacaponresort.com

Camp Creek State Park
P.O. Box 119
Camp Creek, WV 25820
(304) 425–9481
www.wvparks.com/campcreek

Cass Scenic Railroad State Park
Route 66, Box 107
Cass, WV 24927
(304) 456–4300 or (800) CALL–WVA
www.neumedia.net/~cassrr

Cathedral State Park
Route 1, Box 370
Aurora, WV 26705
(304) 735–3771
www.wvparks.com/cathedral

Cedar Creek State Park
Route 1, Box 9
Glenville, WV 26351
(304) 462–8517 or (800) CALL–WVA
www.wvparks.com/cedarcreek

Coopers Rock State Forest
Route 1, Box 270
Bruceton Mills, WV 26525
(304) 594–1561
www.wvparks.com/coopersrock

Droop Mountain Battlefield State Park
HC 64, Box 189
Hillsboro, WV 24946
(304) 653–4254
www.wvparks.com/droopmountainbattle
  field

George Washington National Forest
Lee Ranger District
109 Molineu Road
Edinburg, VA 22824
(540) 984–4101

Grand Vue Park
Road 4 Box 16A
Moundsville, WV 26041
(304) 845–9810

Greenbrier River Trail
Watoga State Park
HC-82, Box 252
Marlinton, WV 24954-9550
(304) 799–4087 or (800) CALL–WVA
www.wvparks.com/greenbrierrivertrail

Greenbrier State Forest
HC-30, Box 154
Caldwell, WV 24925-9709
(304) 536–1944
www.greenbriersf.com

Hawks Nest State Park
P.O. Box 857
Ansted, WV 25812
(304) 658–5196 or (800) CALL–WVA
www.hawksnestsp.com

Harpers National Historical Park
P.O. Box 65
Harpers Ferry, WV 25425
(304) 535–6223
www.nps.gov/hafe/home

Holly River State Park
P.O. Box 70
Hacker Valley, WV 26222
(304) 493–6353 or
(800) CALL–WVA
www.hollyriver.com

Kanawha State Forest
Route 2, Box 285
Charleston, WV 25314
(304) 558–3500
www.wvparks.com/kanawha

Kumbrabow State Forest
Box 65
Huttonsville, WV 26273
(304) 335–2219
www.kumbrabow.com

Lost River State Park
HC 67, Box 24
Mathias, WV 26812
(304) 897–5372 or (800) CALL–WVA
www.lostriversp.com

McDonough Wildlife Refuge
Director of Parks, City of Vienna
609 29th Street, P.O. Box 5097
Vienna, WV 26105
(304) 295–4473

Monongahela National Forest
Supervisor's Office, Forest
Headquarters
200 Sycamore Street
Elkins, WV 26241
(304) 636–1800

Monongahela National Forest
Cheat Ranger District Office
P.O. Box 368
Parsons, WV 26287
(304) 478–3251

Monongahela National Forest
Cranberry Mountain Nature Center
HC 80, Box 117
Richwood, WV 26261
(304) 653–4826

Monongahela National Forest
Gauley Ranger District Office
HC 80, Box 117
Richwood, WV 26261
(304) 846–2695

Monongahela National Forest
Greenbrier Ranger District Office
Box 67
Bartow, WV 24920
(304) 456–3335

Monongahela National Forest
Marlinton Ranger District Office
P.O. Box 210
Marlinton, WV 24954-0210
(304) 799–4334

Monongahela National Forest
Potomac Ranger District Office
HC 59, Box 240
Petersburg, WV 26847
(304) 257–4488

Monongahela National Forest
Seneca Rocks Discovery Center
Box 13, Seneca Rocks, WV 26884
(304) 567–2827

Monongahela National Forest
White Sulphur Springs District Office
410 East Main Street
White Sulphur Springs, WV 24986
(304) 536–2144

North Bend State Park
Route 1, Box 221
Cairo, WV 26337
(304) 643–2931 or (800) CALL–WVA
www.northbendsp.com

North Bend Rail Trail
North Bend State Park
Route 1, Box 221
Cairo, WV 26337
(304) 643–2931 or (800) CALL–WVA
www.wvparks.com/northbendtrail/index.
    htm

Pipestem Resort State Park
Route 20, Box 150
Pipestem, WV 25979
(304) 466–2804 or (800) CALL–WVA
www.pipestemresort.com

Randolf Jennings Lake Project
Reservoir Manager
P.O. Box 247
Elk Garden, WV 26717
(304) 355–2346

Seneca State Forest
Route 1, Box 140
Dunmore, WV 24934
(304) 799–6213
www.wvparks.com/seneca

Tomlinson Run State Park
P.O. Box 97
New Manchester, WV 26056
(304) 564–3651 or (800) CALL–WVA
www.tomlinsonrunsp.com

Twin Falls Resort State Park
P.O. Box 1023
Mullens, WV 25882
(304) 294–6000 or (800) CALL–WVA
www.twinfallsresort.com

Valley Falls State Park
Route 6, Box 244
Fairmont, WV 26554
(304) 367–2719
www.wvparks.com/valleyfalls

Watoga State Park
HC-82, Box 252
Marlinton, WV 24954-9550
(304) 799–4087 or (800) CALL–WVA
www.watoga.com

Watters Smith State Park
P.O. Box 296
Lost Creek, WV 26385
(304) 745–3081
www.wvparks.com/watterssmith
    memorial

About the Authors

Mark Miller is a business owner, writer, and outdoor enthusiast. He and his wife, Cindy, live in Lexington, Virginia, with their three daughters. Mark began hiking in northern Minnesota at a young age. He has hiked extensively in Montana, North Carolina, and Virginia. In addition to hiking, other interests include bicycling and gardening. Mark is employed by the Southern Appalachian Forest Coalition and works on forest and land management issues on the George Washington and Jefferson National Forests.

Steven Carroll grew up hiking in Virginia. Aside from hiking, Steven enjoys fly-fishing, mountain biking, and photography. A University of Virginia graduate, Steven works as a field geologist for an environmental consultant.

Mark and Steven have collaborated on two previous hiking guides: *Wild Virginia* and *Fine Trails of Rockbridge*.